THE FOREVER WAR

THE FOREVER WAR

America's Unending Conflict With Itself

NICK BRYANT

BLOOMSBURY CONTINUUM
LONDON · OXFORD · NEW YORK · NEW DELHI · SYDNEY

BLOOMSBURY CONTINUUM
Bloomsbury Publishing Plc
50 Bedford Square, London, WC1B 3DP, UK
29 Earlsfort Terrace, Dublin 2, Ireland

BLOOMSBURY, BLOOMSBURY CONTINUUM and the Diana logo are trademarks of
Bloomsbury Publishing Plc

First published in Great Britain 2024

A catalogue record for this book is available from the British Library

Library of Congress Cataloguing-in-Publication data has been applied for

ISBN: HB: 978-1-3994-0930-8; eBook: 978-1-3994-0932-2; ePDF: 978-1-3994-0927-8

2 4 6 8 10 9 7 5 3

Typeset by Deanta Global Publishing Services, Chennai, India
Printed and bound in the U.S.A. by Berryville Graphics Inc., Berryville, Virginia

To find out more about our authors and books visit www.bloomsbury.com
and sign up for our newsletters

To the people I love the most: Fleur, Bill, Wren and Honor

CONTENTS

PROLOGUE
'Democracy has prevailed'

It is two o'clock in the morning, and in ten hours' time we will be able to speak of the presidency of Donald Trump, for the next four years at least, in the past tense. Lying in my Washington hotel room, just a few blocks from the White House, I am finding it impossible to fall asleep, partly because what should be a peaceful transfer of power comes with the menace of political violence: American fighting American. Never before have we watched the clock so intensely in the concluding hours and minutes of a presidency. But if the Trump years have taught us anything, it is that nothing can be taken for granted.

Outside of my hotel, troops are dressed in full combat fatigues, with M16s, the military version of the AR-15, strapped diagonally across their flak jackets. Concrete crash barriers block the avenues. Army trucks and Humvees rumble up and down the empty streets – cold steel which makes the capital feel even more like a garrison town. To fortify the city limits, bridges have been closed and multi-lane highways barricaded by heavy trucks. In a perverse twist, Customs and Border Protection aircraft usually on the lookout for unauthorised immigrants now patrol the skies to surveil for insurgents. Group protest is being allowed, but only in designated 'First Amendment Zones'.

Shop windows are boarded up with plywood, as if a hurricane is about to rip through. An ugly seven-foot fence, topped with coils of razor wire, encloses an area called the 'Green Zone' – terminology last used following the invasion of Iraq. So vast is the military mobilisation that Washington is being likened to Baghdad. Some 25,000 troops have been placed on high alert, ten times more than the present deployment in Afghanistan.

National Guardsmen are spending the night billeted inside the halls of Congress, some stretching out their sleeping bags underneath a bust of Abraham Lincoln, who also had to be protected by troops during his inauguration in 1861, little more than a month before the first shots were fired in the American Civil War. They have made their beds on marble floors that in the hours after the January 6th insurrection had to be scrubbed clean of excrement.

Fearing that troops themselves might be seditious, the Pentagon has issued a statement to all military personnel reminding them that Joe Biden will soon be their commander-in-chief and that they have a duty to uphold the Constitution. Already, a dozen soldiers have been stood down from inauguration duties because of their far-right leanings.

Knowing that I had to get up at some ungodly hour to make it onto the press stand at the US Capitol, I went to bed earlier than normal. Yet as is so often the case during the Trump presidency, the likelihood of late-breaking news makes it difficult to switch off. True to form, just after midnight the White House announces that Donald Trump has pardoned his former campaign chief Steve Bannon, the guerrilla-like provocateur who had called for America's Covid tsar, Dr Anthony Fauci, to be beheaded, and manned a 'war room' command centre at a downtown hotel in Washington on January 6th.

The more newsworthy disclosure, however, is that Trump has decided against granting himself clemency as a safeguard against future prosecution, or to cloak members of his family with the same legal protection. In these final hours comes a rare act of presidential self-restraint. Perhaps he thinks he is beyond the reach of the law.

Now wide awake, I doom-scroll through Twitter, the social media platform that has consumed far too much of our professional lives over the past 1461 days, and from which Trump is now banned. Sleeplessness seems a fitting coda for a presidency during which the news cycles were incessant. Not so much 24/7 as 25/8.

After dressing for the Washington cold, I head down to the hotel lobby, where there is a life-sized cardboard cutout of the 78-year-old incoming president on display. This Joe Biden has been made to look about 25 years younger, and has the twinkling smile of a Florida realtor selling timeshares in West Palm Beach. Accurately it portrays his amiability. But there is no hint of how doddery he appeared during the 2020 campaign, when speeches often turned into wandering soliloquies and his taut complexion made it look like he had already been embalmed. Just as this representation of Biden does not convey his true age, nor does it reflect the mood of the hour. Perhaps those smiling Irish-American eyes are a nod to the notion that inaugurations should be a celebration of rejuvenation and renewal. Alas, this transition of power feels more like an exercise in urgent resuscitation.

Already the breakfast bar is crowded with people, most of them middle-aged white men wearing hoodies, sagging jeans and faded baseball caps. Such is the mood of suspicion and hypervigilance that, on first glance, these satellite engineers and camera operators from the television networks look like mutineers. It reminds me of the racial profiling so widespread after the attacks of September 11th, when a young Muslim boarding a crowded subway train wearing a backpack would be eyed with such wariness. Twenty years on, however, the threat comes from domestic terrorists born in the USA.

The drive to Capitol Hill involves presenting our credentials at a series of checkpoints and slaloming around various concrete barricades, but eventually we reach our camera position on the inaugural platform. Now the west terrace of the Capitol is festooned with red, white and blue bunting, but it feels still like it should be sequestered with yellow tape. For this is where walls were scaled, in the manner of a marauding medieval army; where windows were shattered and thresholds breached; where police officers were forced to fight for their lives in hand-to-hand combat; where a gallows was erected, with a dangling noose ready to be tightened around the neck of Vice-President Mike Pence.

As I follow the same path up to the viewing stand that insurrectionists only two weeks before had used as a bridgehead, I notice some familiar words on a giant teleprompter positioned in front of the presidential podium.

Four score and seven years ago our fathers brought forth on this continent a new nation, conceived in liberty, and dedicated to the proposition that all men are created equal. Now we are engaged in a great civil war, testing whether that nation, or any nation so conceived and so dedicated, can long endure.

To test that the screen is working properly, the teleprompter has been loaded with the 272 words of Lincoln's Gettysburg address. Maybe this is some kind of sick joke. A rogue technician, perhaps, with a dark sense of humour. But these passages from America's most celebrated sermon – a speech that took just two minutes to deliver – could hardly be described as out of place. In the latter stages of the 2020 campaign, Biden had even travelled to Gettysburg, a battlefield where more than 40,000 Americans had lain dead, dying or wounded, in the hope this epic backdrop would concentrate minds as he issued his plea for national unity.

Before the new president takes centre stage, we have to see the departing president off the premises. Rather than observing the traditional rites of passage, Trump is boycotting the inaugural ceremony. Instead of meeting the First Couple at the front entrance of the White House, he is sloping out the back. For this twice-impeached president, however, this will be no walk of shame. A ceremonial red carpet has been laid out before him, and he receives the usual rigid salutes from the military honour guard stationed at the door.

Marine One takes off from the South Lawn, and barrels towards us on the inaugural stand, a flight path that will take him to Andrews Air Force Base, where Air Force One is standing by for the journey to Florida. Just before the helicopter reaches the dome of the Capitol, though, it banks sharply to the left, performs a 180-degree turn, and heads back in the direction of the White House. Perhaps the president has left something behind. Perhaps, more ominously, he is not yet ready to relinquish power.

Perhaps the conspiracy theorists of QAnon believe they are watching a prophecy unfold before their eyes. 'Q' has foretold that 20 January will be the date of 'the Storm': 'a Great Reawakening' when Donald Trump will declare martial law, order the mass arrest of his political enemies – including the president-elect and House Speaker

Nancy Pelosi – and cart them off to Guantánamo Bay. There, they will be executed for running an international Satanic child sex-trafficking network, which is harvesting the blood of the young in order to prolong their own lives.

Now, though, Marine One is altering course once more. Rather than heading in to land at the White House, it swoops left in a giant arc and completes a lap around the Washington Monument. Then, without further drama, it returns to its original flight path, and belatedly heads towards Andrews.

Even as his power slips away, Trump is our mesmerising focus. We cannot avert our gaze. We cannot kick the habit. The New York property tycoon who had always understood the art of the attention economy better than the art of the deal continues to command our attentiveness. And, ever the executive producer of his own presidency, he has choreographed one final scene: counter-programming to divert from Biden's swearing-in.

Waiting for him on the tarmac at Andrews as he emerges from the helicopter is a military band that strikes up 'Hail to the Chief'. There is another honour guard and a second red carpet. The departing commander-in-chief has also insisted upon an additional martial trapping, a 21-gun salute fired from a row of army cannons. This is the kind of self-indulgence that all of his predecessors eschewed. This is the kind of authoritarian flourish that has become his signature.

On a flag-dressed stage, Trump delivers valedictory remarks, a boastful summation of his accomplishments in office – which adds to the tally of falsehoods and blatant lies that finally rests, according to fact-checkers at the *Washington Post*, at 30,573 during his time in office.[1] Then he makes his exit to the pulsing beat of Village People's 'Y.M.C.A.', the camp 1970s disco hit that has become something of a personal anthem.

There is one last Trumpian grace note to come. As Air Force One taxies along the runway, speakers blare out Frank Sinatra's 'My Way', the musical bed for the closing credits of his presidency. 'Yes, it was my way,' crones Sinatra, as the presidential jumbo noses into the sky.

At that very moment, the TV feed we are watching cuts abruptly to pictures of the Biden family at prayer. They are attending mass at the Catholic cathedral where the requiem for John F. Kennedy was held. Watching this tableau of conventionality, it is tempting to think that normal programming has been resumed, but that will take more than the flick of a switch in a television control room. Split-screen America – the good, the bad, the ugly and the unhinged – feels like it is on a never-ending loop.

The Biden team, in keeping with the subdued national mood and the ongoing threat from Covid, has organised a scaled-down inaugural. There will be no parade along Pennsylvania Avenue, nor any black-tie balls. Because of the ongoing pandemic, a field of some 200,000 US flags occupies the turf on the National Mall where spectators normally gather to represent those unable to attend.

Nonetheless, there are still shades of the spectacular, with the incoming president able to draw once more from the country's A-list of celebrities. Whereas Trump had to rely on a runner-up in *America's Got Talent* to perform the national anthem four years ago, Biden has enlisted Lady Gaga, who appears on stage clutching a golden microphone and wearing a giant brooch depicting a dove carrying an olive branch. Jennifer Lopez, wearing suffragette white, performs a patriotic mash-up of 'America the Beautiful' and the Woody Guthrie classic 'This Land Is Your Land'.

As Kamala Harris takes her oath of office, we also witness a ceremonial first. Never before have the words 'Madam Vice-President' been uttered during an inauguration. What gives this moment an added frisson is the simple fact that Biden is about to become the oldest-ever occupant of the White House. Though we are here to witness the ascent to power of America's 46th president, it asks of us the question: are we also in the presence of the 47th?

Following Biden's swearing-in, there is an unexpected lull in the proceedings. The new president retakes his seat. A functionary wipes down the presidential podium with disinfectant. But what begins as a nervous pause starts to feel like an unnerving hiatus. Why isn't anything happening? Why isn't anyone speaking? Why isn't anyone moving? For

90 long seconds America seems to be in a state of suspended animation. 'Q' must be getting his hopes up. Then, finally, the new president is introduced and launches into his inaugural address.

If Trump's first speech as president was defined by two words, 'American carnage,' Biden's will be remembered for three, 'Democracy has prevailed' – a statement uttered not out of triumph but with a sense of profound relief, since presently the country is in survival mode. Then he outlines his presidential mission in a triplet of staccato sentences: 'Bringing America together. Uniting our people. Uniting our nation.' Maybe they will become the holy trinity of his presidency, but they feel more like a holy grail.

After Biden has finished speaking, the race is on to complete our television report in time for the evening news in Britain. There are script lines to write. There is my commentary to record. And time is running out. Inauguration Day always imposes the most nerve-racking deadline of the four-year presidential cycle, not least because the ceremony invariably runs late.

Yet as I punch the final words into my laptop, and hurriedly try to deliver them into my microphone, I can't help but notice a striking young woman wearing a canary yellow coat and a satin scarlet headband walking, hesitantly, to front of stage. At first she doesn't seem quite sure what route to take. Then she pauses, while an official gives the podium another deep cleanse. Even though my deadline is fast approaching, she already has us in her thrall. We sense that this young woman has something important to say, and that every word should be heeded.

Amanda Gorman, America's first national youth poet laureate, has composed a new work, 'The Hill We Climb'. The title is a play on John Winthrop's famed sermon, delivered on the deck of the *Arbella* in 1630 as the Pilgrim Fathers headed for a new world, in which he spoke of a 'city upon a hill', a phrase central to the creed of American exceptionalism. 'Where can we find light in this never-ending shade?' she begins by asking, a question she answers at the end of her spellbinding poem. 'For there is always light, if only we're brave enough to see it, if only we're brave enough to be it.'

This 22-year-old African-American is a virtual unknown, but instantly becomes the lode star of the ceremony: outshining Lady Gaga; eclipsing Jennifer Lopez; offering a more brightly lit path than the elderly new president. Yet even though her poetry is so transcendent, she will instantly become a polarising figure. Such is the asymmetry of this chronically divided nation that conservative America will seek to topple her precisely because liberal America has placed her on a pedestal.

What we are witnessing is America in full. From the grubbiness of Steve Bannon's midnight pardon to the grandeur of its national rituals. From the gracelessness of Trump's back-door exit to the dignity of his deputy Mike Pence, who refused to boycott the inaugural ceremony, just as he refused to support the coup attempt on January 6th.

On display are so many things that I love about America. In this polyglot nation, it is stirring to see a Latino Supreme Court justice, Sonia Sotomayor, swear in as vice-president a woman with an Indian-born mother, a Jamaican-born father and a Jewish husband, the country's first 'Second Gentleman'. Watching a Black female fire-department captain recite the Pledge of Allegiance reminds me of the summer camps I attended as a teenager in the redwood forests of northern California, where the daily spectacle of my new friends affirming their fidelity 'to the flag of the United States of America, and for the Republic for which it stands, one nation under God, indivisible, with liberty and justice for all' was always an inspiration. There is something uniquely American about Stefani Joanne Angelina Germanotta – aka Lady Gaga – a brash New Yorker who is always reimagining and reinventing herself. Amanda Gorman reminds me of a younger version of Maya Angelou, that queen of letters who I watched in my student days deliver another transfixing poem, 'On the Pulse of Morning', at Bill Clinton's first inaugural in 1993.

Yet also evident are many of the things I have come to loathe. Lady Gaga stepped onto the inaugural platform with a bulletproof vest woven into her gown. In the lead-up to the ceremony, Amanda Gorman had considered backing out, because of the threat to her personal safety. Before travelling to Washington, her mother made her crouch on the floor of their living-room to rehearse shielding her body from gunfire.

Though I have always enjoyed a rousing American pageant, and the thumping beat of a John Philip Sousa march, the militaristic machismo that marked Trump's departure is disquieting. Prior to January 6th, it could have been written off as the comic opera of a dollar-shop authoritarian. Post-January 6th, it looks more sinister and fascistic.

Because we now live in a perpetual state of unpredictability, the sight of his helicopter veering off course, along with the silent strangeness of that unexplained 90-second stoppage during the ceremony, was also disconcerting. Deviations from the norm are taking us to dangerous places. Constantly, we are being forced to imagine the previously unimaginable.

So once my report is filed – we just made our deadline – I hurry to Union Station to catch the first train out of town. I want to get out. Rather than stick around with my colleagues to reflect over a drink on the weirdness of what we have witnessed, I want to be with my family in New York.

Inauguration Day has not felt like a new beginning but rather a continuation of a tragic storyline. The question posed by Lincoln that appeared on the teleprompter prior to the ceremony feels almost as pertinent now as it did in 1863: can this nation long endure?

INTRODUCTION
Escaping Camelot

My love of America has been such a continual thread in my life that I have rarely examined where, or how, the original stitch was sewn. I suspect it was early in my childhood, peering up at a beautiful mosaic in the middle of an ugly traffic roundabout in Birmingham, Britain's second city. Admittedly, this was not the most stirring of settings. Close to the inner-city church that I attended as a child, it was reached through a warren of dank pedestrian tunnels that almost always reeked of urine. Perhaps, though, the squalid location made the mural all the more startling and transcendent.

It depicted a handsome, youthful-looking man, who was standing in front of a golden insignia that looked like the Ark of the Covenant, addressing a richly multiethnic audience. That luminous emblem was the US presidential seal. That adoring crowd included the Reverend Dr Martin Luther King Jr. That 40-something politician, with chestnut hair and red-carpet good looks, was John Fitzgerald Kennedy.

Erected within the shadow of the city's Roman Catholic cathedral, the mural had been commissioned by Birmingham's Irish community to memorialise a president whose ancestors had set sail for America in the mid-19th century to escape the potato famine. Its appeal, though, was universal. JFK seemed to embody America's best self: its dynamism, glamour, modernity, promise of immigrant success and exceptionalism. His speeches, with their clever rhetorical inversions, were elegant and inspirational. His family was staggeringly telegenic. His administration, staffed by thrusting aides dubbed New Frontiersmen with sharp minds and sleek suits, seemed brave and adventurous. His White House, a salon where the arts and sciences both found a home, was a place of rationality and refinement.

No wonder my parents could tell me precisely where they were when the news came through at teatime on a Friday in Britain that the 46-year-old president had been gunned down in Dallas. Almost every adult who was alive that day would come to have the same instant recall. November 22nd, 1963, the day of his murder, became one of the first historical dates that I committed to memory. Even as a child I had a vague sense it was a major turning point of the 20th century, a world-altering event that deserved to be memorialised with a giant mosaic.

For years I subscribed to the widely held view that the United States lost its innocence the instant that its boyish young president was slain. Prior to Dallas, it seemed, Americans had faith in their national institutions, looked upon politics, by and large, as a noble undertaking, and broadly supported the kind of interventionist foreign policy that made the United States the unquestioned leader of the free world – a standing Jack Kennedy revelled in when he declared 'Ich bin ein Berliner' on a visit to West Berlin in June 1963, just months before his death.

Kennedy encouraged the idea that the United States could conquer new frontiers in space and defeat any earthly foe. Its people believed that the post-war economy would deliver continual improvements in their family's quality of life, the essence of the American dream. The suburbs were growing. Consumerism was rampant. Almost every household now owned a television – a modern medium employed by Kennedy in the same way that Franklin Delano Roosevelt harnessed the power of radio. No other country came close to rivalling its standard of living or can-do spirit.

Back then, US politics was also more respectful and productive. Democrats and Republicans, acting out of a sense of patriotic bipartisanship forged during the Cold War by the ideological challenge posed by the Soviet Union, regularly worked together in pursuit of the national good. The political game in Washington, though adversarial and occasionally aggressive, was not a battle to the death.

The 1960 presidential election offered a case in point. Though Kennedy won with a wafer-thin plurality of 112,827 votes – and amidst believable allegations of voter fraud in Chicago, where mayor Richard J. Daley had conjured up enough phantom votes for him to take Illinois – his opponent, the then vice president Richard Nixon, conceded by lunchtime the next day. 'I want to say that one of the great features of America is that we have political contests,' he told a crowd of supporters, 'and once the decision is made we unite behind the man who is elected.'[1]

For much of my early adulthood, then, I embraced what might be called the lone gunman theory of post-war US history: that Lee Harvey Oswald had robbed the country of a brighter future, just as John Wilkes Booth, who shot dead Abraham Lincoln only five days after the Confederate surrender at Appomattox, put to death the possibility of a more equitable postbellum peace.

Kennedy's murder was followed by the humiliation of Vietnam, the inner-city race riots of the late 1960s, and the assassinations, within five weeks of each other, of Martin Luther King and Robert Kennedy. Then, in the early 1970s, came Watergate. Polls suggest that public trust in the US government began its steady 50-year decline in the month after the Warren Commission published its finding in 1964 that Lee Harvey Oswald acted alone.

The assassination of JFK, and the murder of his alleged killer two days later live on television, understandably made the country more prone to conspiracy theories. The war in Vietnam, a humbling conflict which undercut America's claim of military pre-eminence, created a wariness about interfering in foreign conflicts that lasted decades. Dallas, Vietnam and Watergate had a cumulative impact. They suggested that Americans were being institutionally deceived, that their political and military leaders were not telling the truth.

Fear rather than hope became the driver of politics, as Richard Nixon demonstrated during the 1968 presidential election. With Roger Ailes, the future head of Fox News, advising him, the Republican nominee stoked white racial anxieties about Black lawlessness and Black economic advance, a brand of grievance politics labelled the 'southern strategy', which over the decades came to be nationalised. Nixon cast himself as the authentic voice of the 'silent majority', protecting the country against Black agitators in the civil rights movement, feminists in the women's movement, and long-haired hippies in the anti-war movement. The death of a president had dramatically altered the trajectory of politics and history.

Yet was America really that different the day after Kennedy's slaying than it had been when he stepped off the plane in Texas? Did it truly mark a definitive break from a more innocent past? Many Americans, after all, had rejoiced in the young president's assassination, as the author William Manchester observed in his landmark study *The Death of a President*. In Mississippi, when the news came over the intercom at a high school in Columbus, children in an American history class erupted into applause. A physician in Oklahoma City told his patient, 'Good, I hope they got Jackie.' In Dallas, Manchester reported, 'a man whooped and tossed his expensive Stetson in the air'.[2]

Long before anyone had heard of the Texas School Book Depository or the grassy knoll, Dallas had earned the moniker 'City of Hate', largely because it was the home to so many right-wing fanatics. Ahead of Kennedy's visit, supporters of the ultra-conservative John Birch Society, which believed that every president since Franklin Delano Roosevelt had been part of an international communist conspiracy, distributed a flyer entitled 'WANTED FOR TREASON', featuring pictures of the young president, head-on and in profile, which looked like a relic of the Wild West. In a litany of falsehoods, it accused JFK of giving 'support and encouragement to the Communist-inspired racial riots', of appointing 'Anti-Christians to Federal office' and of being 'caught in fantastic LIES to the American people (including personal ones like his previous marriage and divorce)'. An irony of the Kennedy assassination was that a communist sympathiser was blamed for pulling the trigger, rather than a 'radical rightist', as conservative extremists were then labelled.

Jack Kennedy had been advised against going to Dallas by his UN ambassador, Adlai Stevenson, who only weeks beforehand had been jostled, spat upon and struck on the head with a placard by demonstrators protesting outside the hotel where he was speaking. 'Are these human beings or animals?' asked Stevenson of his fellow Americans, as his car accelerated away and he reflected on the deplorability of the mob.[3]

What made this extremist show of force all the more noteworthy was that it was organised by a leading light in the John Birch Society, Edwin A. Walker, a former US Army Major General with a Strangelovian streak who had already become a poster boy of the American far right. In January 1961, *Newsweek* had featured him on their cover, alongside the headline 'Thunder on the RIGHT'. The following year, Walker amplified his fame by helping to orchestrate the 'Battle of Ole Miss', an armed insurrection mounted by white supremacists aimed at blocking James Meredith, its first Black enrolee, from attending the University of Mississippi, a bastion of segregation. 'Rally to the cause of freedom!' Walker had proclaimed as insurrectionists besieged the pillared registration building on campus and fired at US marshals: 'It's now or never!' Not since the Civil War era had there been such a brazen challenge to federal authority. Some insurgents even came dressed in the battle grey uniforms of the Confederate army.

Though seen as a fringe figure, this rogue general had become a central combatant in a battle of extremes. In April 1963, Lee Harvey Oswald had even tried to kill him, using the same mail-order rifle fitted with the same telescopic sight that he allegedly used seven months later to shoot the commander-in-chief.

Though we tend to think of the America of the '50s and early '60s as a haven of suburban tranquillity, even then it was awash with guns. Between 1959 and 1963, it was estimated that up to seven million firearms had been imported from foreign countries, which were readily available and ridiculously cheap. The Italian infantry rifle used to kill Kennedy cost just $12.78.[4] So prevalent was gun violence and crime that in 1960 the Los Angeles Police Chief William H. Parker opined, 'The United States has the dubious distinction of being the most lawless of the world's nations.'[5]

Kennedy's assassination did not come out of nowhere. 1963, the centenary of Abraham Lincoln's Emancipation Proclamation, had started with the racist howl of George Wallace's inaugural address as governor of Alabama. Speaking from the very spot in Montgomery where Jefferson Davis had been sworn in as the president of the Confederate States of America – what he called 'the Cradle of the Confederacy, this very Heart of the Great Anglo-Saxon Southland' – Wallace chanted, 'Segregation now, segregation tomorrow, segregation forever.'

Spring brought one of the most climactic struggles of the civil rights era, the demonstrations in Birmingham, Alabama, the so-called 'Johannesburg of America', where Bull Connor, the city's public safety commissioner, deployed ferocious police dogs and ordered firemen to train on young protesters high-velocity hoses that could strip the bark off trees.

This clash between white supremacist America and Black America brought the country to a state of near rebellion. The spring and summer of 1963 became seasons of fury, with some 1,340 demonstrations in more than 200 cities, many of which had never before been touched by racial turbulence. Martin Luther King warned that America had reached an 'explosion point' and that the struggle for Black equality had moved from being a 'Negro protest' to being a 'Negro revolution'.

On the very night in June that President Kennedy belatedly responded to the crisis, by delivering a televised address from the Oval Office promising sweeping civil rights legislation, Medgar Evers, a World War II veteran and the first field secretary in Mississippi of the National Association for the Advancement of Colored People (NAACP), was gunned down in the driveway of his home. In his hands, the moment he was killed, was a stack of t-shirts reading 'Jim Crow Must Go'.

Rather than murder and disorderliness, 1963 is often remembered for King's great paean to non-violence, the 'I Have a Dream' speech delivered on the steps of the Lincoln Memorial. However, the fear of a massive race riot in the heart of the nation's capital, and the besiegement of Capitol Hill, prompted the Kennedy brothers to pressure King and his fellow organisers to cancel their plan for a March on

Washington. When that failed, the White House ordered the biggest military build-up on American soil in peacetime history. At the military bases that ringed Washington, a heavily armed 4,000-strong taskforce was placed on stand-by for deployment. At Fort Bragg in North Carolina, 15,000 special forces were ready to be airlifted to the capital, in a mission that went by the forbidding codename 'Operation Washington'.[6]

On that sweltering August afternoon, King hoped he had subpoenaed the conscience of white America. However, the homicidal backlash was swift in coming. Little more than two weeks later, members of the Ku Klux Klan planted 19 sticks of dynamite in the back stairwell of the 16th Street Baptist Church in Birmingham, the headquarters of the city's Black protest movement. When the dynamite detonated, the basement of the church was crowded with children attending Sunday school. Four schoolgirls were killed, the latest victims of an American Civil War that had never truly come to an end.

A sickness infected the country that public intellectuals had already diagnosed. The day before Air Force One touched down at Love Field in Dallas, the historian Richard Hofstadter delivered a bleak lecture at Oxford University, which became the basis for his seminal essay, *The Paranoid Style in American Politics*. Political life back at home, Hofstadter argued, had 'served again and again as an arena for uncommonly angry minds'. The paranoid style, he called it, 'because no other word adequately evokes the qualities of heated exaggeration, suspiciousness and conspiratorial fantasy'. When he published his essay in 1964, he identified a style of politics that was 'overheated, oversuspicious, overaggressive, grandiose and apocalyptic'.[7]

On the day of his own death, Kennedy intended to explore some of these same themes during a speech at the Dallas Trade Mart, where his motorcade was heading. Railing against 'ignorance and misinformation', his prepared text warned of 'voices preaching doctrines wholly unrelated to reality', and of a worrying rise in anti-government sentiment amongst conspiracy theorists. 'They fear [the] supposed hordes of civil servants far more than the actual hordes of opposing armies.

We cannot expect that everyone … will "talk sense to the American people". But we can hope that fewer people will listen to nonsense.' Again, words that in subsequent decades would find an echo.

When placed in its rightful context, then, November 22nd seems more like a continuum than a watershed. Not a wild deviation, or a loss of American innocence, but rather a murder that fitted and continued a historical pattern. Indeed, were one to select virtually any date in US history, it would be possible to find the same poisonous ingredients that produced such a pestilential brew on November 22nd, 1963. They percolated violently to the surface on January 6th, 2021.

In the telling of the American story, acts like Kennedy's assassination have been treated as abnormalities, a tendency that obscures the reality that they are more reflective of normalcy. And that speaks of a broader analytical failing. So much of our understanding of America is based on false narratives and self-validating folklore. In pausing to consider how millions of Americans have come to embrace an alternative reality about the here and now, we need also to reflect on the effect of manufacturing such a mythic past.

The valorisation of John F. Kennedy in the aftermath of his death exemplifies that habit. 'Camelot', a term never attached to his presidency during his thousand days in the White House, was the invention of his widow, Jackie, who, less than a week after her husband's murder, summoned the country's foremost political chronicler, Theodore H. White of *Life* magazine, in the hope of controlling history. The late president, she told White, had loved the hit Broadway musical based on the legend of King Arthur, and, in particular, the lyrics of its signature song that there would always be 'one brief shining moment' that would be remembered as Camelot.

Up against deadline, White phoned in his 1000-word essay from the servant quarters of the Kennedy compound, Hyannis Port – an inadvertently apt setting – to editors in New York who thought this first draft sounded too florid. At Jackie Kennedy's insistence, however, the numerous references to 'Camelot' survived, including her most pointed quote: 'There'll never be another Camelot again.'[8]

As well as posthumously crowning Kennedy, the myth of Camelot served as a form of American absolution. An assassin, or conspiracy, could be blamed for the problems which became ever more apparent in the years after Dallas, rather than the country as a whole. Under this mental schema, America had felt the full impact of the bullets, not just its Arthurian young president.

So often we have preferred to think of America as a 'Camelot' or a 'city upon a hill'. So often we fall back on the comforting idea, derived from Enlightenment thinking, about the inevitability of progress, that America is moving, albeit haphazardly at times, towards becoming a 'more perfect union' – the phrase from the preamble to the Constitution which became a staple of Barack Obama's most poetic speeches. So often we have wanted to focus on the best of America and push its more unsightly characteristics to the periphery. So often we have accepted the notion articulated by Abraham Lincoln that America represents 'the last best hope', without fully understanding, or even excavating, the history that contradicts it. So often we have engaged in reverse-engineering to make sure the arc of history bends towards justice.

Confessedly, there have been times in my life when I have been seduced by this kind of sentimentalism. Inspired by that hometown mosaic, one of the things that attracted me to the country in the first place was the myth of Camelot. I was fixated by the Kennedys. It was only in my late teens, through studying his presidency more closely at university, that I realised there was a contradictory story to tell. Far from being a liberal champion of the struggle for Black equality, the supposed hallmark of his liberalism, JFK for much of his presidency was a non-participant in the great social revolution of his age. Civil rights he regarded as a political irritation to manage and finesse, rather than a moral issue to champion.

A final year undergraduate dissertation on his inadequate response became the basis for my doctoral thesis, and ultimately a revisionist book with a title that encapsulated its thesis: *The Bystander*. What this exercise taught me was that my entire historical belief system was flawed, and that even the American history that I knew off by heart was often inexact.

Myths, I came also to realise, were closely guarded and fiercely protected. As part of my research, I spent a year at the John F. Kennedy Presidential Library and Museum in Boston, where yellow busloads of children would be deposited each day to be schooled in the Camelot fable. There I got to meet the keepers of the late president's flame, the celebrated scholar Arthur M. Schlesinger Jr, who had served as JFK's historian-in-residence at the White House, and Ted Sorensen, his brilliant speechwriter. Both had written hagiographic participant histories of their years with Kennedy. Both seemed perplexed that a young student who had started out as a fellow admirer now had the impudence to question Kennedy's liberal credentials. Yet delving into the archive, and sifting through box after box of declassified documents, gave me a fuller and more deprecatory account of his presidency. Episodes and chapters emerged that had not been included in their books.

Again, the experience underlined that there was so much American history that I had either misremembered, been mistaught or never been exposed to. It also demonstrated what historians are often up against. To describe the presidential libraries run by the National Archives, and the museums attached to them, as a network of state-sponsored mythmaking runs the risk of conspiratorialism. Unquestionably, however, they contribute to the misty-eyed view of the past.

To cover the Trump presidency, and to interrogate the historical forces which contributed to his rise, was to be reminded of these lessons anew. Part of the reason his victory was so shocking was because it exposed the frailty of so many national myths. The American dream had become a chimera to millions of people who no longer believed that their children would enjoy a higher standard of living than they did.

The great American melting pot could so easily become a toxic stew, poisoned by the hatred of nativism. American democracy was more vulnerable to demagoguery than we assumed, and demagogues had periodically raised their heads. The election of Barack Obama had not produced the great racial leap forward that many hoped for.

Instead, his presidency revealed the impossibility of bridging the country's racial breach. Rather than being an aberration, Trump's shock victory in 2016 was the culmination of political, sociological, economic, technological and cultural shifts that went back decades. His presidency had almost become historically inescapable.

This 50-year pre-history of Donald Trump I wrote about in *When America Stopped Being Great: A History of the Present*. It told of how, as a result of the great reforms of the civil rights era, divisions between the parties became more pronounced than divisions within the parties, as had previously been the case, an important milestone along the pathway of polarisation. Of how the end of the Cold War eroded the patriotic bipartisanship which had prevailed on Capitol Hill for much of the post-war years, and how the fall of the Berlin Wall coincided with a generational shift which meant that lawmakers from the Greatest Generation, who had been brothers and sisters in arms during World War II, were superseded by Baby Boomers whose formative political years came during the culture wars of the '60s. Of how growing income polarisation contributed to political polarisation. Of how a missing middle in the economy was mirrored by a missing middle in politics. Of how government came to be demonised by right-wing leaders such as Ronald Reagan and Newt Gingrich. Of how every president from Bill Clinton onwards came to be regarded as illegitimate by his partisan opponents, and how Washington increasingly became the stage for performative political histrionics.

The book seemed to hit a chord. To my surprise and delight, a copy ended up on Joe Biden's bookshelf in the Oval Office. Yet the only way to make sense of post-January 6th America is to delve back further, because every one of America's contemporary problems has such long-established roots. Some have been 250 years in the making, from the moment that the 13 rebel colonies signed the Declaration of Independence. Some predate the country's founding. Even seemingly modern-day problems, such as the spread of misinformation and conspiracy theories, form part of America's origin story.

So, tempting though it was to view Trump's victory as a radical departure from the American story, a case of the scriptwriters losing the plot, he was just as much a product of the country's past as Barack Obama, George W. Bush, or any of the other men who have taken the presidential oath of office.

Here, it is inviting to bastardise the mantra posted on the wall of Bill Clinton's war room in Little Rock, Arkansas during his success-ful 1992 campaign; an election, incidentally, which often felt like a referendum on the '60s: 'It's the history, stupid.' But a reworking of another famous political maxim works better. All politics is history. All history is politics.

Little, if any, of the American story is safely in the past. Indeed, the present-day United States is confronting a problem of historical overload. It is buckling under the weight of problems from yesteryear which have never been resolved. To use an idiom from these troubled times, it is not the American deep state that is the problem, but rather America's deep history.

1

The strange career of American democracy

American democracy has become so diseased because for most of the country's history it has never been that healthy. 'We the people', the rousing words that opened the preamble to the Constitution, were not conceived of as a catch-all for mass democracy or an inclusive statement of participatory intent. Rather, this nebulous term referred to what in modern parlance would be called the body politic. Much of the deliberations of the 55 male delegates at the constitutional convention in Philadelphia during the long hot summer of 1787 focused on how that body politic should be restrained in an intricately designed straitjacket.

To describe the outcome as an experiment in democracy is misleading, because the Founding Fathers did not care for the word, which is nowhere to be found either in the Declaration of Independence or the US Constitution. When the country's second president, John Adams, used the term 'democratical', it had a negative connotation. 'Throughout the founding era,' the historian Joseph Ellis has noted, 'the term "democracy" remained an epithet, used to tar an opponent with the charge of demagoguery or popular pandering.'[1]

The right to vote was never enshrined in the original Constitution, an omission which continues to astound many Americans. Likewise, the Bill of Rights, the bundle of ten amendments designed to rectify the shortcomings of the original text, says nothing about voting. Slave owners were granted more protections than would-be voters.

To this day, it is the dirty little secret of the US Constitution. Despite being amended 27 times, the country's operating manual still includes no positive assertion of the right to vote. The 15th Amendment, ratified after the Civil War, frames it only in a negative manner:

> The right of citizens of the United States to vote shall not be denied or abridged by the United States or by any state on account of race, color or previous condition of servitude.

Justifiably, then, voting has been described as the missing right. The wealthy elite, which gathered in their frock coats and silk stockings in Philadelphia, regarded government as a closed shop. Alexander Hamilton was keen for the new republic to retain hierarchical trappings, even going as far as to suggest that senators should serve for life and that the presidency should be akin to an elected monarchy. James Madison, its foremost framer, spoke unashamedly of how the Constitution had 'to protect the minority of the opulent against the majority'. Watching from Paris, where he was serving as America's ambassador at the time, Thomas Jefferson spoke of the Founding Fathers as an 'assembly of demigods'.[2] Later, he referred to America's rulers as 'a natural aristocracy'.[3]

It was not just a sense of blue-blooded entitlement that guided the Founding Fathers' thinking. In the period immediately after the final defeat of the British at the Battle of Yorktown in 1781, they had been alarmed by how newly independent Americans were exercising too much say in the running of the country. In some states, assemblies were elected on an annual basis. State assemblymen, who did not always come from the ruling class, displayed dangerously populist tendencies. The framers looked fretfully at former colonies, like Pennsylvania, which had been positively promiscuous when it came to deciding who could vote. Anyone who had paid taxes and been resident for a year was eligible – almost 90 per cent of white men.[4] In Virginia, Jefferson bemoaned the concentration of so much power in a popularly elected legislature, describing it as an 'elective despotism'.[5]

These fears came to a head during the Shays' Rebellion of 1786, an armed uprising of debt-ridden farmers in western Massachusetts protesting the excessive taxation imposed by the state legislature in Boston. Led by Daniel Shays, a former captain in the Continental Army who had fought at Lexington, Bunker Hill and Saratoga, this pitchfork army demonstrated how a grassroots movement could imperil the fledgling nation. Though recent historical accounts have emphasised how the revolt was overwhelmingly nonviolent – an 'honorable rebellion' – it terrified much of the ruling elite.[6] On hearing the 'melancholy information' coming out of Massachusetts, George Washington warned Madison the country was 'fast verging to anarchy and confusion!' and believed the passions of the populace had to be tamed.[7] Consequently, 1786, the year of the Shays' Rebellion, loomed even larger in the minds of many of the framers than 1776, the year of the Declaration of Independence.

The fear of the unruly mob explains the thinking behind an oft-cited quote from John Adams, which he penned in 1814: 'Remember, democracy never lasts long. It soon wastes, exhausts and murders itself. There never was a democracy yet, that did not commit suicide.' His fear was not of unchecked presidential power, the meaning projected onto the quote during the Trump years. More worrying was unchecked people power, which had been demonstrated so murderously during the French Revolution: 'This democratical Hurricane, Inundation, Earthquake, Pestilence call it which you will,' as Adams described it.[8] Such was his fear of the popular will that in 1787 he wrote to Jefferson, noting: 'Elections, my dear sir ... I look at with terror.'[9]

The framers therefore designed a system of government to guard against 'the tyranny of the majority', a phrase thought to have been first used by Adams in 1788, the year before the storming of the Bastille. The Massachusetts delegate Elbridge Gerry – whose name, fittingly, would inspire the term 'gerrymander', a form of electoral manipulation – put it best. 'Our chief danger arises from the democratic parts of our constitutions,' he said. 'The evils we experience flow from the excess of democracy.'[10]

Voters would get to directly elect just one branch of government, the House of Representatives. Yet the House could hardly be described as representative. Under the notorious three-fifths compromise agreed in Philadelphia, which allowed states to include three out of every five enslaved persons in their population tally, the south received a disproportionately high number of seats.

The make-up of the Senate was also grossly undemocratic. Each state was represented by two senators, even though there were large discrepancies between the populations of the 13 former colonies. The most populous state, Virginia, which harboured some 447,000 people, of whom more than 40 per cent were enslaved, was almost 20 times bigger than lowly Georgia. The malapportionment of the present-day system – where Wyoming's 576,851 citizens wield the same clout in the Senate as California's 39 million, and where South and North Dakota's combined population (1.6 million) gets four seats compared to Texas's two (29 million) – was baked in from the start. US senators were also appointed by state legislatures rather than elected by the people, a practice that continued until the ratification of the 17th Amendment in 1913.

Folklore has it that over breakfast one morning, Washington pointed to the saucer which Jefferson had just used to cool his coffee, and suggested an analogy with the Senate. But, as with many supposed quotes from the early years of the republic, scholars can find no documentary evidence that Washington ever referred to 'a senatorial saucer'. Nonetheless, that was the intention. As James Madison explained in *Federalist No. 62*, one of the essays penned to persuade Americans to adopt the new constitution, the make-up of the Senate would guard against the kind of 'sudden and violent passions' that could produce 'intemperate and pernicious resolutions'.[11]

The Electoral College, the mechanism for electing the president, also served as a firewall against the popular will. Initially, in a majority of states, state legislatures rather than voters picked the electors who selected the president. There was also a supplementary safeguard. The founders assumed that no presidential candidate besides Washington would secure a majority in the Electoral College, in which case the election would be decided in the House of Representatives. As Hamilton wrote in *Federalist No. 68*, the Electoral College would therefore 'afford as little opportunity as possible to tumult and disorder'. Thus the Founding Fathers produced a democratic anomaly: the only elected office in the land where the winning candidate did not necessarily have to win the most votes.[12]

In the early years of the new republic, the states decided who was eligible for the franchise, and most limited that right to white men of property – often landowners with holdings of at least 50 acres. For sure, the franchise was expansive compared to other countries. Europe at this time was dominated still by the great royal houses. Banishing hereditary succession was rightly considered radical. So, too, the notion that governments should be subject to the consent of the governed. Yet voting rights were heavily restricted.

Blacks were mostly excluded. States such as New Jersey, Maryland, Connecticut and Pennsylvania, where Black men born free were initially able to vote, soon withdrew this right.[13] The vote was also denied to Native Americans, who were not even all granted citizenship until 1924 and had to wait until the late 1950s before Utah and North Dakota became the last states to allow them to vote.

New Jersey was the only state in which white women were given the suffrage, although this right was wrenched away in 1807. Abigail Adams, who later served as the country's second First Lady, urged her husband to push for the enfranchisement of women, but he told her, dismissively, that the power women wielded in the home should not be transferred to the political arena. The tyranny of George III should not be replaced with what he called 'the despotism of the petticoat'.[14]

This was very much a partial democracy, rather than a mass democracy. Self-government was left to a self-selecting few. 'When the Founders spoke of "the People" they did not entertain notions of democracy – indeed they abhorred the idea,' writes David Reynolds in *America: Empire of Liberty*. 'In their republic they assumed that only whites, males and property owners would vote.'[15]

In post-Colonial America, then, only around 20 per cent of the adult population were eligible to vote. By the 1800 presidential election, when John Adams and Thomas Jefferson squared off against each other for the second time – and when voting lasted from April to October because states could decide their own election days – the population was more than five million people, but the electoral roll included the names of just 600,000 citizens.[16]

Overall, the fear of designing a democratic model that was excessively majoritarian produced a democratic model that was excessively minoritarian. Presidents could be elected despite losing the popular vote. The make-up of the Senate, as Alexis de Tocqueville observed in the 1830s, meant that 'a minority of the nation, dominating the Senate, entirely paralyses the will of the majority represented in the other house'.[17] The House of Representatives was notoriously unrepresentative because of the Faustian bargain which had produced the three-fifths compromise.

So while the Declaration of Independence was radical in intent, the Constitution was conservative by comparison. Revisionist historians have come to regard it as a counter-revolutionary text: a national rule book that conceived of democracy in a restrictive, sometimes even anti-democratic, form. 'The Constitution drafted in Philadelphia acted as a check on the Revolution,' the historian Jill Lepore has observed, 'a halt to its radicalism.'[18] The widely held notion, then, that America's founding document, which has since come to enjoy a near Biblical status, marked the culmination of the Revolution is a myth. The cold calculus, caution and compromise displayed at Philadelphia in 1787 was in many ways the antithesis of the spirit of 1776.

As the country expanded, so too did the franchise, with the main impetus coming from new frontier states that joined the Union, such as Vermont in 1791 and Kentucky the following year. In the early decades of the 19th century, most eastern states followed suit in eliminating property ownership and taxpaying as a prerequisite to vote. In an ever-more-urbanised country, it was unrealistic to expect citizens to meet property requirements based on acreage.

The country's third president, Thomas Jefferson, now enthusiastically backed this democratisation. Yeoman farmers and 'plain folk', he believed, would be a countervailing force to the oppressive Federalist Party aristocracy that wielded so much power during the presidency of John Adams, which he likened to the British monarchy. Jefferson also had a romanticised view of the French Revolution, and was nowhere near as fearful of the popular will as the Founding Fathers who had gathered in Philadelphia. Jefferson even characterised his election victory over John Adams at the turn of the century as 'the revolution of 1800'. Rather than the sword or musket, he later reflected, it had been brought about 'by the rational and peaceable instrument of reform, the suffrage of the people'.[19]

Jeffersonian democracy paved the way for Jacksonian democracy, which took its name from the country's first populist president, Andrew Jackson. At the 1824 election, when the House of Representatives made John Quincy Adams president even though more Americans backed Jackson, just 355,000 people cast votes. Four years later, when Jackson exacted his revenge, turnout had more than tripled to more than 1.1 million. By 1832, when Jackson won a second term in office, most white men in most states could vote. By then, in another democratic advance, all states, with the exception of South Carolina, chose their electors in the Electoral College through the popular vote.

Despite the advent of what David Reynolds has called 'a new style of mass politics', America remained a white male electorate.[20] Most Blacks continued to be denied access to the ballot. By the middle of the 19th century, they could vote in just five states – Maine, Massachusetts, New Hampshire, Rhode Island and Vermont.

It took the Civil War to turn America into a genuinely multiracial democracy, as well as the trifecta of constitutional amendments that came in its aftermath, which are sometimes referred to as the country's second founding. The 13th Amendment abolished enslavement, the 14th Amendment established birthright citizenship, and the 15th Amendment finally prohibited Black men from being denied the vote. The Reconstruction Acts enacted between 1867 and 1868, which set out the terms under which Confederate states would be readmitted to the union, also mandated that new state governments in the south had to be based on universal male suffrage. More than 700,000 Black men came to be enfranchised, in what the Black intellectual W. E. B. Du Bois later described as 'the finest effort to achieve democracy ... this world had ever seen'. Women, though, continued to be excluded. Indeed, the 14th Amendment inserted the word 'male' into the Constitution for the first time to reaffirm the point that only 'male citizens' could vote.

The era of Reconstruction, which stretched from 1863 to 1877, brought a flowering of Black politics, especially in southern states which then harboured 90 per cent of the country's African-American population. By 1872, there were about 2,000 Black lawmakers at the local, state and federal level, the vast majority of whom were Republicans, the party of Abraham Lincoln. Startlingly, as the historian Eric Foner has found, in South Carolina more than 200 African-Americans served in the lower house of state legislature and 29 in the state senate.[21] There were breakthroughs on Capitol Hill as well. The first Black US senator, Hiram Rhodes Revels, was appointed to represent the Deep South state of Mississippi. The second Black senator, Blanche Kelso Bruce, also hailed from the Magnolia State. Between 1870 and 1901, 20 African-Americans served in the House of Representatives. To put that in context, by 1945 there were just two.

These democratic advances were met with a violent backlash. In the forefront was a group founded in 1865 by ex-Confederate soldiers from Pulaski, Tennessee, which called itself the Ku Klux Klan. With its ghost-like regalia (an homage to the Confederate dead) and mysterious-sounding titles (its leader was called 'Grand Cyclops'), the KKK first seemed comical. Some of its early night-time rides even ended with practical jokes, rather than violence. Quickly, though, its membership swelled – those initials, KKK, were part of its mystique – and its mission became more murderous. By the end of the decade it had grown into a region-wide terrorist organisation waging a guerrilla campaign that included shootings, lynchings, mutilations and floggings. New Black office-holders, many of whom were killed or beaten, became its prime targets.

To counteract this violence, Congress passed the Enforcement Acts of 1870 and 1871, which placed the administration of federal elections under the purview of the government in Washington and empowered the president to use the army to enforce the 14th Amendment. Dubbed the Ku Klux Klan Acts, they succeeded in disrupting its activities. By the middle of the 1870s, however, the era of Reconstruction had come to an end. Its death knell came with the contested presidential election of 1876, and the grubby back-room deal that made the Republican candidate and former Union soldier Rutherford B. Hayes president in return for the withdrawal of federal troops stationed in the south. Without the protection either of US troops or a federal government willing to safeguard the rights of former slaves, white supremacy returned to the south with a vengeance. Jim Crow, the deceptively friendly name used to describe the system of racial apartheid, was in the chair.

Thereafter, southern states came up with a panoply of measures to prevent Blacks from voting. Literacy tests were applied, in which whites registering to vote would be asked simple questions, while Blacks would be required to read sections of the state constitution and were then told to decipher them. Sometimes they would even be asked how many jellybeans were in a jar, or how many bubbles were in a bar of soap. Poll taxes were levied, a voting fee in effect, which were prohibitively expensive for most freed Blacks. So-called 'grandfather clauses', which tied the voting rights of the current generation to those of their ancestors, also effectively nullified the 15th Amendment.

White primaries, which were introduced by the Democratic Party in most southern states around the turn of the century, blocked Blacks from taking part at all. Because the Democratic Party once again monopolised political power across the region after the end of Reconstruction, excluding non-whites from the primary process to pick candidates for elections where Democrats were guaranteed victory was tantamount to disenfranchising them.

The combined effect of literacy tests, poll taxes, character tests, white primaries and grandfather clauses killed off the multiracial democracy which had been the central promise of America's second founding. 'The slave went free; stood for a brief moment in the sun; then moved back again toward slavery,' sighed Du Bois. By the time of the New Deal at the beginning of the 1930s, less than four per cent of Black Americans were registered to vote.[22]

The one democratic bright spot in the early 20th century came from the enfranchisement of women, which remedied the most glaring deficiency of the 15th Amendment: the fact that it applied only to men. In 1920, almost 70 years after women's rights groups had met at Seneca Falls in New York and adopted a Declaration of Sentiment – which included the all-important corrective, 'We hold these truths to be self-evident: that all men and women are created equal' – the long-overdue 19th Amendment finally came into effect. Overnight, the electorate doubled in size (prior to this change, women had only been allowed to vote in nine states, starting with Wyoming in 1890). But once again the franchise was framed in a negative manner. The right to vote 'shall not be denied or abridged'.

Just as the First World War acted as a spur for female enfranchisement because of the role played by women on the home front, the Second World War lent the campaign for Black enfranchisement urgent momentum because of the role played by African-Americans in combat. Fighting fascism abroad underscored the moral incongruity of maintaining a system of racial apartheid at home. Black veterans demanded a full menu of rights. The Double V campaign, of victory at home as well as abroad, helped launch the civil rights movement of the post-war years.

Even before the guns of war had fallen silent, Blacks campaigners scored a milestone legal victory when the Supreme Court, in its 1944 *Smith v. Allwright* decision, ruled that white primaries were unconstitutional. Segregationists once again mounted a violent campaign to bar non-whites from voting. Across the south, there was a spate of church bombings and cross burnings. In July 1946, Maceo Snipes, a US army veteran who had fought in World War II, was fatally shot in

the back after becoming the only Black voter in his county to partic-
ipate in the Georgia Democratic primary. Just five days later, in an
attack that came to be known as the Moore's Ford lynchings, a white
mob executed two Black married couples who tried to vote, tying
them up and shooting them 60 times at close range. Leading southern politicians, such as Theodore Bilbo, the governor of Mississippi,
encouraged this kind of vigilantism: 'The best time to keep a n***er
away from a white primary in Mississippi,' he advised, 'was to see him
the night before.'[23]

The post-war south was witnessing an early form of 'massive
resistance', the term describing the white backlash to the Supreme
Court's 1954 *Brown* decision, which started the slow desegregation
of southern schools. But historians of the region, such as Professor
Tony Badger, have argued that the response to the *Smith v. Allwright*
decision was every bit as vociferous. Little wonder. Segregation could
not survive without the disenfranchisement of Blacks.

The 1950s saw piecemeal gains on voting rights. In 1957, at the
urging of the Eisenhower Justice Department, Congress passed its
first Civil Rights Act of the 20th century, which sought to ban voter
intimidation. But the measure was heavily watered down, in order to
break a filibuster mounted by southern Democrats. The inadequa-
cies of the 1957 reform served only to galvanise a newly invigorated
civil rights movement, headed by charismatic young leaders such as
Martin Luther King, which had become more insistent in its demand
for 'freedom now'.

At the start of the 1960s, vanquishing Jim Crow was the focus,
with the sit-in movement, freedom riders and Birmingham campaign
agitating for the desegregation of lunch counters, interstate buses,
restaurants and hotels. After the passage of the 1964 Civil Rights Act,
which outlawed segregation and finally granted African-Americans
access to restaurants, transportation and other public facilities, the
struggle for Black equality concentrated more on voting rights.
Selma, Alabama became the great battlefield, 'Bloody Sunday' its
most climactic fight. The sight that day of protesters, such as the
courageous young student leader John Lewis, being bludgeoned by

Alabama state troopers on the Edmund Pettus Bridge – a crossing named in honour of a Confederate brigadier who went on to become a US senator and a Grand Dragon of the KKK – shocked the nation, and prompted Lyndon Johnson to act. Addressing a joint session of Congress eight days later, the president called for lawmakers to pass an expansive voting rights act, ending his speech with words from the great anthem of the civil rights movement, 'We Shall Overcome', which he ventriloquised with a Texan hill-country drawl.

After its passage, Johnson justifiably described the 1965 Voting Rights Act as 'one of the most monumental laws in the entire history of the United States'. Literacy tests were outlawed and seven southern states with a history of discrimination were ordered to submit even the smallest changes to their voting laws for approval by the Justice Department – a process called pre-clearance. Almost instantly, this landmark act produced a democratic dividend. In Mississippi alone, black registration jumped from less than 7 per cent in 1965 to almost 60 per cent just two years later.[24]

After almost two centuries, the United States finally had universal suffrage, which is why the story of voting rights often stops in 1965. That, however, is a premature place to end.

———

No sooner had the Voting Rights Act become law than efforts to subvert it began – what has turned out to be a decades-long campaign of de-democratisation. This time there was no holler of massive resistance. Instead, segregationists conducted a quieter campaign of nullification. The first legal challenge came from the Deep South, when a voting registrar in New Orleans filed a lawsuit claiming the Act was unconstitutional. In short order, Governor George Wallace tried to thwart the work of examiners who had descended upon Alabama to make sure that African-Americans were included on the electoral roll.[25]

Segregationist senators, most of them still southern Democrats who had failed to block the bill's passage through Congress, pinned their hopes on the Voting Rights Act being overturned in the federal courts. However, in those early years the reform-minded Supreme Court resolutely defended voting rights. In a landslide 8–1 ruling handed down on the first anniversary of Bloody Sunday, it affirmed its constitutionality. That same month, the court scored another victory for democracy by ruling that the poll tax in Virginia was unconstitutional, which sounded its death knell throughout the south.[26]

To slow the pace of Black enfranchisement, white supremacists looked to the new president Richard Nixon, whose southern strategy had been rewarded with victories in Florida, Tennessee, Virginia and the Carolinas. Segregationist backers of Nixon, such as Strom Thurmond, the one-time 'Dixiecrat' presidential candidate who in 1964 had defected from the Democratic to the Republican Party, now demanded payback. So when the Voting Rights Act came up for renewal in 1970, as its five-year sunset clause was due to expire, Thurmond and his allies called on Nixon to invalidate it.

In the new attorney general, John Mitchell – who later gained notoriety as an arch-villain of the Watergate scandal – the south had an ally. As the chairman of Nixon's 1968 campaign, Mitchell had earned the moniker 'Mr Southern Strategy', because of his enthusiasm for pursuing redneck votes. Now he came up with an ingenious plan to thwart Black voting rights in the south. Under the guise of expanding the Voting Rights Act, and widening its implementation beyond the states of the old confederacy, he aimed to make it inoperable. As Mitchell well knew, the Justice Department did not have the resources to scrutinise every change to every voting law in every jurisdiction.

Mitchell's strategy boomeranged. For, as the bill made its way through Congress, the bipartisan coalition of Republicans and northern Democrats, who had secured the Voting Rights Act in the first place, joined forces to expand the franchise still further by lowering the voting age to 18, rather than 21. Indeed, moderate Republicans continually proved themselves throughout this period to be doughty defenders of democracy. As the historian Ari Berman notes in his landmark study, *Give Us the Ballot: The Modern Struggle for Voting*

Rights in America, 'The party of Lincoln had defeated the party of Thurmond – for now.'[27]

When in 1975 the Voting Rights Act came up for renewal again, the bipartisan coalition prevailed once more. And, as before, the legislation ended up being strengthened. Now it was expanded to protect 'language minorities' from discrimination, which helped Hispanics, Asian-Americans, Native Americans, indigenous Alaskans and Hawaiians. What made the 1975 renewal all the more significant was the support it received from southern lawmakers. Never before in the 20th century had a majority of southern congressmen voted in favour of a civil rights law. But since many now had to appeal to Black constituents, they had little choice. Even Strom Thurmond warned his fellow southerners, 'We can't win elections any more by cussin' Nigras.'[28]

The first significant weakening of the Voting Rights Act came from the Supreme Court, a more conservative body after Richard Nixon's four appointees had shifted its politics markedly to the right. In 1969, Chief Justice Earl Warren, the architect of the *Brown* ruling, had been replaced by Chief Justice Warren Burger, a critic of his predecessor's judicial activism. Nixon's appointees also included the ultra-conservative William Rehnquist, who as a high court clerk in the 1950s had defended school segregation and expressed support for the much-hated *Plessy v. Ferguson* ruling from the late-19th century, which enshrined the idea that 'separate was equal', a monumental victory for Jim Crow. On voting rights, Rehnquist had an especially egregious record. Early in his career, he had supported the all-white primary, while at the start of the 1960s he had participated in what was called Operation Eagle Eye, a Republican voter-suppression campaign in Arizona, which targeted minority voters in Democratic districts.

So in 1980, when the court took up a case in Mobile, Alabama, *Mobile v. Bolden*, Rehnquist and his fellow conservatives eyed an opportunity to slow the pace of Black representation. In this port city on Alabama's Gulf Coast, the City Commission continued to be a whites-only governing body, even though Blacks made up a third of the population. Elections were conducted on a citywide rather than district basis, a system deliberately designed during the Jim Crow era to make sure white voters would always outnumber Blacks. The lower federal courts had deemed that Mobile's form of municipal government was clearly discriminatory. Yet in a shock 6–3 ruling, the Supreme Court ruled against the Black plaintiff in the case, a World War I army veteran and NAACP activist, Wiley Bolden, and sided instead with the white supremacist status quo.

Democrats in Congress sought to invalidate the Supreme Court's *Mobile* ruling when in 1982 the Voting Rights Act came up for its third reauthorisation. Under their proposed changes, the burden of proof would no longer fall upon African-Americans to demonstrate they were being intentionally discriminated against. The Reagan Justice Department, however, was determined to uphold the *Mobile* decision, and complained that Democrats were trying to bring affirmative action into the polling booth. 'Racial quotas' became the outraged cry.

Among the most aggressive combatants in this legislative battle was a 26-year-old Harvard Law School graduate, who had joined the Justice Department after clerking for Rehnquist. Twenty years later, John Roberts would succeed his former boss to become the Chief Justice of the Supreme Court, but for now he sought to make a name for himself by circulating talking points to right-wing Republican senators, laying out the case against 'quotas' and ghostwriting opinion pieces on their behalf.

His arguments were fallacious. Blacks did not have an unfair advantage. In states covered by the Voting Rights Act, they made up only five per cent of elected representatives despite accounting for a quarter of the population. The aim of the Voting Rights Act, rather than to impose racial quotas, was merely to increase the number of Black elected officials from none to some. Despite Roberts's best efforts, then, the bipartisan coalition on voting rights held firm.[29]

In an East Room ceremony, President Reagan, who in the 1960s had described the Voting Rights Act as 'humiliating to the south', signed a 25-year extension into law. However, Black leaders present at the signing ceremony doubted whether the Civil Rights Division of the Reagan Justice Department would enforce it.[30] As Lyndon Johnson's attorney general, Nicholas Katzenbach, put it, 'The civil rights division changed sides.'[31] The bipartisan consensus on voting rights was fraying.

Certainly, the Republican Party was no longer so strongly wedded to the idea that everyone should be allowed to vote unfettered. By the late 1980s, Grand Old Party (GOP) strategists also realised how they could turn the enforcement of voting rights to their political advantage. Here, they latched onto a provision of the 1982 renewal legislation which encouraged the creation of majority-minority congressional districts, in which a high concentration of Black voters would lead to the election of more Black lawmakers.

Since the early days of the new republic, when the governor of Massachusetts, Elbridge Gerry, signed into law a redrawing of the political map that turned one of the senate districts into a shape that looked like a giant salamander – hence the portmanteau – gerrymandering had always been part of the country's political culture. But the new chairman of the Republican National Committee, Lee Atwater, a partisan strategist with rat-like cunning and pitbull-like aggression, seized upon the potential of racial gerrymandering and the shoehorning of African-American voters into the same congressional districts. If the Democratic Party in the south became more overtly African-American, Atwater gleefully told his staff, then white southerners would desert them and seek refuge with the Republicans. In a region where southern Democrat lawmakers still outnumbered southern Republican lawmakers, Atwater believed the creation of more minority-Black congressional seats could turn the once-solid Democratic south into a Republican stronghold. 'Project Ratfuck', as it was later dubbed, was up and running.[32]

What made the scheme even more Machiavellian was the GOP's success in enlisting the support of the Congressional Black Caucus, which at that time was exclusively Democratic. Here was a chance for them to boost minority representation in Washington. Through this unholy alliance, the number of Black members of Congress increased. Simultaneously, the number of white southern Democrats declined. Prior to the 1994 election, for example, Georgia was represented in Congress by nine Democrats, eight of whom were white – Congressman John Lewis, the hero of Selma, being the sole African-American. After 1994, it sent three Black members to Congress but just one white Democrat. For the first time since Reconstruction, Republicans outnumbered Democrats by 73 to 64.[33] The states of the Old Confederacy became the new spiritual home of the party of Abraham Lincoln, an extraordinary historical inversion.

In a decade of heightened partisanship and accelerating polarisation, the idea became more firmly embedded that the manipulation of voting rights, and the gerrymandering of Congress, was central to the electoral game. Politics trumped democracy.

Growing up during this period, I was aware of the struggle for voting rights, and the heroism of civil rights activists in attaining them, but I had not given much thought to the mechanics of US democracy. Always it was the spectacle that provided its lure. Those grand inaugurals, with their fanfares and flowery speeches. The majesty of the presidency, with its supersized motorcades and liveried aircraft. Those nominating conventions, with their folksy rollcalls and balloon drops.

It was the same when I became a Washington correspondent for the BBC in the late 1990s. Who could fail to be charmed by the idiosyncrasies of the Iowa caucus, where voters convene in school gymnasiums, grain elevators and even people's front rooms to take part in a political version of musical chairs, literally changing seats to indicate their voting intentions? For reporters making the quadrennial pilgrimage, New Hampshire's traditional first-in-the nation primary was like a Rockwellian winter wonderland, a theme park for political nerds. From Iowa to New Hampshire to South Carolina to the supernova of Super Tuesday, few things were more journalistically thrilling than journeying the road to the White House, my favourite ribbon of highway.

Outside of Faneuil Hall in Boston in the summer of 1988, on the day that the Democratic presidential nominee Mike Dukakis unveiled as his running mate the Texan senator Lloyd Bentsen, was the first time I experienced this carnival – red, white and blue bunting, TV satellite trucks, reporters rehearsing their stand-ups, and pot-bellied police officers leaning insouciantly on wooden security barriers. A student at the time, I did not have the press credentials to claim a seat inside this 'cradle of liberty', but later, on the evening news, I watched Dukakis talk of how his choice to put Bentsen on the Democratic ticket mirrored the Kennedy/Johnson axis of 1960; at which point his running mate might have been tempted to deliver a version of what became the most memorable line of the entire campaign, when he faced off against Senator Dan Quayle in the vice-presidential televised debate: 'I served with Jack Kennedy. I knew Jack Kennedy. Governor, you're no Jack Kennedy.'

That 1988 election, the last before the fall of the Berlin Wall, ended up being a sorry affair. From the racist stereotyping of the Willie Horton ad, which assailed Dukakis for sponsoring a week-end furlough program under which a convicted Black murderer had raped a white woman while on release, to the insinuation that a Greek-American was not sufficiently patriotic to serve as commander-in-chief (the Massachusetts governor was opposed to the mandatory recitation of the Pledge of Allegiance in schools), George Herbert Walker Bush wrapped himself in the Stars and Stripes and played the race card from the bottom of the pack. After a demoralising campaign, barely 50 per cent of eligible Americans even bothered to vote.

The 1992 campaign, the first that I got to report on, was not much better. Early in the race, the supermarket tabloids seemed to set the agenda, as the Democratic frontrunner, Bill Clinton, was hit with a slew of allegations about his extramarital affairs and draft-dodging. That year we also witnessed the emergence of not one but two proto-Trumps. First, the nativist Republican Pat Buchanan, with his calls to build a wall along the Mexican border and to 'Make America Great Again'. Then, Ross Perot, a billionaire businessman with disturbingly authoritarian tendencies, which extended to running his own private army and issuing decrees compelling female employees to wear skirts that covered their knees.

That very year Francis Fukuyama published *The End of History and the Last Man*, which trumpeted 'the universalisation of western liberal democracy as the final form of human government'. But the first election held after the fall of the Soviet empire, much like the 1988 contest beforehand, undermined his thesis about the ascendancy of the western model. Clinton won with just a 43 per cent share, which led Republicans to tag him a 'minority president', the start of their eight-year campaign to delegitimise his presidency (here, they overlooked that Nixon won in 1968 with a 43 per cent share and that Lincoln in 1860 received only 39 per cent). Bush also got the smallest percentage of any incumbent since William Howard Taft in 1912. Almost a fifth of voters rejected both the major parties, and opted instead for the anti-politician Perot, even though his campaign was so shambolic that at one point he dropped out of the race and declared himself a non-candidate.

Over the course of the decade in which the United States became the undisputed hyperpower in a unipolar world, its democracy slumped deeper into recession. At the 1996 presidential election, a lifeless contest in which Clinton easily saw off the challenge from the septuagenarian Senator Bob Dole, turn-out was pitiful. For the first time, it dropped below 50 per cent.

As the American century drew to an end, US democracy could hardly be described as enjoying a heyday, although most of us had drunk too much of Fukuyama's Kool-Aid to acknowledge its myriad flaws. The first presidential election of the new millennium, however, made its deficiencies impossible to ignore. The campaign itself, which pitted an overqualified vice president, Al Gore, against an under-qualified Texan governor, George W. Bush, was standard fare. The problem centred not on the proficiencies of the candidates but on the peculiarities of the electoral system. That became the story.

Perhaps for the first time, the watching world discovered that America did not have a standardised form of voting even in nation-wide elections – more than 8,000 separate jurisdictions administer the ballot. Perhaps for the first time, we were introduced to the anomalies of the Electoral College. Not since 1888 had the candidate who won the popular vote failed to win the presidency.

Well I remember the opening image of an early television report on the mayhem that unfolded in Florida – Ground Zero in the disputed election – which showed a polling station guarded by law enforcement officials, with yellow police tape stretched across the entrance. Then, in Palm Beach County, came the absurdities of the so-called 'butterfly ballot', whose complicated design – the work of a Democratic election official, who probably cost her party the presidency – explained why so many elderly Jewish retirees mistakenly voted for the third-party candidate, Pat Buchanan, a notorious anti-Semite.

The Florida recount debacle, a bleak comedy of errors, became the natural sequel to Bill Clinton's impeachment and the O. J. Simpson trial: a national melodrama with neatly episodic cliff-hangers – to count or not to count – and a colourful dramatis personae. The cast included Bush's younger sibling, the Florida governor, Jeb Bush, and his Republican ally, Florida's Secretary of State, Katherine Harris, who was likened to Cruella de Vil from *101 Dalmatians*. The vote-counters themselves also became unlikely stars. Footage of them peering through magnifying glasses at pregnant and hanging chads on the ballot papers, their eyes bulbous and distended, also looked like a Disney animation.

Operating behind the scenes were supporting characters who largely escaped attention: the legal eagles who parachuted into Florida to litigate the election. Not only did their number include an ambitious young conservative named Ted Cruz, but also three future Supreme Court justices, Brett Kavanaugh, Amy Coney Barrett and John Roberts, who became one of the Bush team's prime legal strategists.

Much of what happened in Florida was pure farce. But much of what happened bordered on the criminal. Quickly it emerged, for instance, that hundreds of African-Americans had been barred from voting by zealous state officials who, in purging ex-felons from the electoral rolls, had disqualified lawful voters. African-Americans who succeeded in voting often had their ballots rejected. As a report from the US Commission on Civil Rights later found, Black voters were nearly ten times more likely than non-Black voters to have their ballots deemed null and void. In a state where George W. Bush's winning margin turned out to be just 537 votes, that undercount alone was enough to swing him the election.

As the recount continued, Miami-Dade County witnessed a more flagrant attack on democracy, a forerunner in some ways of January 6th. Here the militia came dressed in shirts and blazers, a band of determined young conservatives who tried to storm an election office where officials were scrutinising ballots. The Brooks Brothers Riot, it came to be called, a tagline which made light of this ominous episode by focusing on what the mob was wearing rather than what it was trying to achieve. The aim was to block the electoral process from lawfully playing out, and its mastermind was Roger Stone, a dandyish right-wing provocateur and Nixonian dirty trickster, who served as an unofficial adviser to Donald Trump.

Soon after the Brooks Brothers Riot came a follow-up attack, this time from five right-wing jurists dressed in flowing black judicial robes. After the Florida Supreme Court ordered a statewide manual recount, a ruling thought to favour Gore, the conservative justices on the Supreme Court in Washington staged an intervention. First, they halted the recount. Then they heard oral arguments in a case famously docketed *Bush v. Gore*, which would essentially decide the winner. In a 5–4 decision split along ideological lines, the justices ruled that using different counting criteria in different counties violated the Equal Protection Clause of the 14th Amendment, thus handing victory to their fellow conservative, George W. Bush.

Because of the unique circumstances, the conservative justices warned against their ruling ever becoming binding precedent. They also declined to attach their names to the ruling, as was the

custom, because its legal basis was so shaky. One of its conservative authors, Antonin Scalia, privately described *Bush v. Gore* as 'a
piece of shit'.[34] Yet *Bush v. Gore* has since been cited in hundreds
of federal and state cases, most commonly to suppress the vote.
The majority opinion also included this shocking statement: 'The
individual citizen has no federal constitutional right to vote for
electors for the president of the United States.' Yet, undemocratic
and unAmerican though it sounded, it was also an incontrovertible statement of fact.

In the years after the Florida debacle, election skulduggery became
the norm. Republicans, especially, turned redesigning congressional
districts into a political art form. Gerrymandering upended the core
idea of democracy, that voters should elect their representatives. Now
politicians selected their voters.

Redrawing the map was not the only device that Republicans used
to rig elections in their favour. In 2005, Indiana and Georgia became
the first Republican-controlled states to pass more stringent voter ID
laws, requiring the presentation of a picture identification before a
person could vote. Drivers' licences, the most common form of ID,
cost money, and Blacks were five times less likely to possess them
than whites. John Lewis therefore described the law as a 'modern day
poll tax'.[35]

The Bush Justice Department, under the arch-conservative
attorney general, John Ashcroft, also made voter fraud a higher
order priority than protecting voting rights, a crackdown in search
of a problem. Five years after launching its campaign, the Justice
Department conceded it had turned up virtually no evidence of
any organised attempt to corrupt elections. Over the same period,
the Civil Rights Division relaxed their efforts to enforce the Voting
Rights Act, objecting to less than 50 voting changes out of more than
80,000 brought to their attention.[36]

Despite their efforts at the state level to erode enfranchisement,
the Republican Party continued to pay lip service to the Voting
Rights Act, which in 2006 was reauthorised for a further 25 years
with the unanimous consent of the Senate. And two years later came

its crowning achievement: the election of the country's first Black president. For the first time in US history, Black turnout was almost on a par with white turnout, which made Barack Obama's victory all the more symbolic. He even managed to win the southern states of Virginia, North Carolina and Florida, which would have been unthinkable prior to the civil rights revolution.

In what was becoming an ever more multiethnic democracy, the Democrats had now won the popular vote in four out of five presidential elections. Trapped in what looked like a demographic death spiral, the Republicans desperately needed a strategy to mount an electoral comeback. The scheme they came up with was dubbed 'REDMAP' – short for the 'Redistricting Majority Project' – which was targeted at winning control of state legislatures that would redraw congressional districts after the 2010 census.

Into these state races the Republicans poured millions, a splurge of political spending abetted by the Supreme Court, which at the start of 2010 handed down its controversial *Citizens United* decision. Reversing campaign finance restrictions dating back more than 100 years, the court opened the floodgates for corporations and other groups to spend unlimited funds on elections. Given the sway it handed to a small number of wealthy donors, soon the ruling was dubbed 'Plutocrats United'.

In that year's midterm elections, the Democrats received what Obama memorably described as a 'shellacking', which enabled the GOP to take back the House. What unfolded at the state level, where the party flipped 11 legislatures, was arguably more significant. REDMAP had worked spectacularly, and now it was put into literal effect. Gerrymandering on steroids was the result. Unfairly drawn congressional districts, studies have since suggested, swung 39 House seats in favour of the GOP.[37]

Redistricting went hand in hand with restricting voting rights. Voter ID laws proliferated. Nine states passed laws making it harder to register to vote. North Carolina, for instance, ended same-day registration, while Wisconsin placed new obstacles in the way of people who had moved home to remain on the electoral roll. Eight states passed laws curtailing early voting. Many states ended week-end and evening voting, times often favoured by minority voters. Not since the birth of Jim Crow had the country seen such a legislative assault on voting rights.[38] Not for the first time in US history, hard-won voting rights were prised away.

At least minority voters still had the Voting Rights Act as a safe-guard, and specifically its all-important Section Five, which forced jurisdictions with a history of racial discrimination to 'preclear' any proposed voting changes. But then, in 2013, came the single biggest blow to US democracy of the universal suffrage era, when the Supreme Court handed down its *Shelby County v. Holder* ruling. In a 5–4 judgement, the conservative justices decided that preclearance was now obsolete because voter registration in counties with a history of discrimination had shown such dramatic improvements. 'History did not end in 1965,' wrote Chief Justice John Roberts. 'Our country has changed.' Scalia had even likened the Voting Rights Act to a 'racial entitlement'. Yet as the liberal justice Ruth Bader Ginsburg pointed out in an unusually strong dissenting opinion, ending preclearance was akin to 'throwing away your umbrella in a rainstorm because you are not getting wet'. The court, she fumed, had brought about the 'demolition' of the Voting Rights Act.[39]

The effect of the *Shelby* ruling was instantaneous. Within two hours, Republican-controlled Texas put into effect new rules requir-ing a state-issued ID in order to vote that were clearly weighted in favour of the GOP. A gun permit was accepted as proof of iden-tification, for example, but not ID cards issued by the University of Texas, despite it being a state institution.[40] More than 20 states took advantage of the *Shelby* ruling to impose tough new voter restrictions.[41]

When Obama travelled to Alabama that year to mark the 50th anniversary of Bloody Sunday, there was still much to celebrate, not least the sight of him walking arm in arm with John Lewis across the Edmund Pettus Bridge. Yet Obama's speech that day was tinged with melancholy. 'Right now, in 2015, 50 years after Selma, there are laws across this country designed to make it harder for people to vote,' he warned, adding, 'The Voting Rights Act stands weakened, its future subject to political rancour.'[42] In 2016, Obama put it even more starkly: 'We're the only advanced democracy that deliberately discourages people from voting.'[43] What makes this all the more perturbing is that for four decades now, the Supreme Court has been presided over by two chief justices, Rehnquist and Roberts, with a long background in actively campaigning against voting rights.

The clearing of rioters from Capitol Hill on January 6th turned out to be a brief cessation rather than an end to the attack on democracy. That very night, as Congress reconvened to certify the election in chambers where only hours before lawmakers had been forced to barricade doors, crouch behind chairs and don gasmasks, came the second wave of the assault. One-hundred and forty-seven Republicans voted to overturn or challenge the election results, including almost two-thirds of the GOP House caucus and eight of the party's senators.

Mitch McConnell, the most powerful Republican on Capitol Hill, took no part in this coup attempt. Nonetheless, it had taken him more than five weeks to finally acknowledge that Biden had won the election, in which time the 'Big Lie' had grown to monstrous, uncontrollable proportions. Vice president Mike Pence acted bravely, given that the president had incited the mob to lynch him. But he waited until the morning of January 6th to publicly quash the specious theory propounded by Trump that a vice president could unilaterally overturn the votes of more than 150 million Americans.

The simple fact that so many Republicans traipsed into Congress that night and continued to do Trump's bidding demonstrated the extent to which the GOP had lurched from being an anti-Democratic Party party to being an anti-democracy party. Even the then House Minority leader, Kevin McCarthy, who only hours earlier had begged Trump to call off his mob, voted to challenge the election.

In the aftermath of January 6th came the usual bromides about how the Constitution had saved the day, and withstood its toughest stress test of modern times – a trope of the Trump years. However, it was not the Founding Fathers who rode posthumously to the rescue. Rather, the main safeguard was the simple mathematical fact that the Democrats had the numbers, and controlled the House of Representatives. Had the Republicans held sway in the House and Senate, they could legally have thrown the country into chaos.

If Mike Pence had sought to nullify the results of the election, he would have violated the Constitution, but who would have overruled him or held him to account? Maybe the Supreme Court would have intervened, but that is by no means clearcut given the constitutional authority granted to Congress to decide for itself how contested elections should be resolved. As the Black Mississippi Congressman Bennie Thompson, the chairman of the January 6th Committee, lamented in the preamble to its final report, 'Who knows what would have happened if Trump's mob had succeeded in stopping us from doing our job? Who knows what sort of constitutional gray zone our country would have slid into?'[44]

That is why January 6th was so doubly scary. It exposed how the US democratic system was based almost as much on norms as it was on laws. When those norms were violated, the Constitution was not a failsafe.

Nor was January 6th – and the votes that continued into the early hours of 7 January – the end of it. In the months afterwards came a third wave of the attack on democracy. This time it unfolded in state capitals, where Republican-controlled legislatures intensified their attempts to shrink the ever-more-multiethnic electorate. Texas restricted the number of drop-off boxes for postal ballots to one per county, which meant that Harris County, the home to Houston and its 4.7 million population, had the same number as Loving County, the least populous county in the entire country with only 64 residents.[45]

What made the latest onslaught from the states all the more disquieting was the opening up of a new line of attack. Traditionally, efforts had concentrated on voter suppression. Now there was a shift to election subversion: overturning the will of the people. Disturbingly, the 'Independent Legislature Doctrine', a fringe theory positing that state legislatures enjoyed enormous latitude in determining the outcome of federal elections, has gained intellectual respectability.

Right-wing think tanks, such as the Heritage Foundation, have endorsed it, pointing towards the passages from the US Constitution which give it credence. Article II Section 1 Clause 2 does indeed grant states the power to select presidential electors 'in such Manner as the Legislature thereof may direct', a loaded gun in the hands of anti-democrats. Backers of the Independent Legislature Doctrine have also cited the Supreme Court's ruling in *Bush v. Gore*, proving how easily its authors' shame-faced warning that it should never be used as a precedent could be disregarded. Back in 2000, the Supreme Court had ruled that state legislatures had the total authority to run presidential elections, and sided in Florida with Republican state lawmakers over the more liberal-minded Florida state Supreme Court.

There is a real danger that Article II Section 1 Clause 2 could be to US democracy what the Second Amendment has become to gun rights. If anything, the framers were clearer in decreeing that states should oversee federal elections than they were in defining the right to bear arms. At the time of the country's founding, James Madison understood this, and warned of the dangers in handing too much power to the states when it came to the conduct of elections. 'It was impossible to foresee all the abuses that might be made of the discretionary power', warned Madison during the Constitutional Convention in August 1787.[46] Repeatedly down the centuries, his apprehensions have been borne out.

At least in the 2022 midterm elections some of the most ardent Big Lie true believers were defeated. Overall, the elections seemed to indicate that the United States still harboured a majority of voters who remained committed to democracy. Yet the elections exposed worrying trend-lines. More than 150 election-denying House Republicans won their races, nearly 70 per cent of the GOP caucus. Republican election deniers won the Senate races in Ohio and North Carolina. Though he lost in Arizona, Mark Finchem, a former member of the militia group the Oath Keepers and a conspiracy theorist who claimed the Chinese Communist Party controlled US presidential elections, managed to garner 47 per cent of the vote in his bid to become the state Secretary of State, the post which oversees elections.

Following the midterms, Congress sought to strengthen some of the guardrails of democracy by passing the Electoral Count Reform and Presidential Transition Improvement Act. Amending legislation passed in 1887, it affirmed that the vice president had only a ceremonial role when Electoral College votes were counted, and could not overturn the election. By raising the threshold of votes needed to object, the legislation also made it harder for lawmakers to challenge the result, and prohibited state legislatures from overriding the popular vote by declaring 'a failed election'. But despite the bipartisan support offered by Mitch McConnell, more than half of Senate Republicans voted against, and in the House the measure attracted the support only of nine GOP lawmakers (none of whom made it into the new Congress which convened in 2023).[47]

In a fillip for democracy, the Supreme Court in June 2023 repudiated the most extreme form of the independent state legislature theory, and ruled that state legislatures did not have unchecked power in determining election rules. Thus it avoided what was seen as the democratic doomsday scenario that would have enabled Trump-supporting state legislatures to overturn the will of the people. Even so, the ruling penned by John Roberts included infuriatingly vague legalese that did not completely shut the door on a theory most constitutional scholars consider deranged being repurposed in the future.

So it is not as if the decades-long campaign of de-democratisation has suddenly ended, or the process of re-democratisation has begun. Moves by Congress to bolster democracy since January 6th have been outweighed by the ongoing efforts of Republican-controlled state legislatures to weaken it. As a result of this onslaught, America was remaining true to the quasi-democracy of its founding. Indeed, there are few better illustrations of the country's state of ceaseless contestation than the ongoing battle over voting rights and what sort of democracy America should be.

2

From July 4th to January 6th

'1776', the insurrectionists had chanted, as they stormed the US Capitol, believing themselves to be American patriots acting in the spirit of the revolution. Some carried the Betsy Ross flag, with its 13 stars and stripes signifying the original colonies, a popular banner amongst militia groups because it celebrates the era when Blacks and women were barred from voting. The VDARE flag was also brandished, an homage to Virginia Dare, who is thought to be the first white child born on 'New World' soil.[1]

Among the other militia groups to put boots on the ground that day was the Three Percenters, a far-right anti-government group established to 'push back against tyranny', which believes, erroneously and portentously, that it took only three per cent of the colonial population to overthrow the British. Present were members of the First Amendment Praetorian, a little-known group largely comprised of former Special Forces soldiers, intelligence officials and police officers, which was founded in 2020 to provide security at Trump rallies and offer close personal protection for far-right celebrities, such as Trump's former National Security Advisor Michael Flynn.

Some rioters turned up wearing memorabilia and carrying flags which appeared to have been purchased from 1776.shop, an online store set up by the neo-fascist militia, the Proud Boys. The birth-date of the republic had been used ahead of time in far-right memes promoting Donald Trump's 'Stop the Steal' rally. #1776 became a popular hashtag on social media, as did #1776Rebel. Previewing the rally, the newly elected Congresswoman Marjorie Taylor Greene, the far-right QAnon supporter who had turned up for her first day on the floor of the House of Representatives wearing a facemask reading 'TRUMP WON', described it as 'our 1776 moment'.[2]

An abiding memory from the morning afterwards was watching military engineers erect a wire fence around the Capitol, while a protester nonchalantly weaved his scooter down the street which runs between Congress and the Supreme Court hollering '1776!' in a high-pitched yelp. With so many insurrectionists wielding banners and standards from the past, January 6th became a deadly historical passion play.

'We're walking down the exact same path as the Founding Fathers,' claimed Stewart Rhodes, a former Army paratrooper with a Yale law degree and pirate-like patch over his left eye, who helped establish the Oath Keepers, a militia group launched on 19 April 2009 on Lexington Green, where the first shots of the Revolutionary War rang out. 'You've got pissed-off patriots who are not going to accept their form of government being stolen,' he told a reporter from the *Los Angeles Times*, as the riot raged around him. Another insurrectionist, Chris Hill, likened the uprising to the 'shot heard round the world' at Lexington and Concord in 1775. 'The second revolution begins today,' said the former marine.[3]

Many of the insurrectionists clearly believed they were descendants of a violent tradition that justified and legitimised their violence. In their minds, then, January 6th was a noble rebellion, a continuation of the armed struggle that had started almost 250 years hitherto. Like their revolutionary forefathers, they were militant nationalists rather than militant nihilists.

Many far-right extremists were inspired by words from Thomas Jefferson which, unlike the poetry of his Declaration of Independence, never made it into high school textbooks or onto the teleprompters of modern-day presidents. 'I hold it that a little rebellion now and then is a good thing, and as necessary in the political world as storms in the physical,' Jefferson had written to James Madison in 1787.[4] Nor was this an isolated or throwaway remark. Indeed, Jefferson, who was in Paris at the time, was one of the few Founding Fathers not to have been terrified by the Shays' Rebellion. 'The spirit of resistance to government is so valuable on certain occasions, that I wish it to be always kept alive,' he wrote to John Adams' wife, Abigail. 'I like a little rebellion now and then. It is like a storm in the Atmosphere.'[5]

In another letter, this time to Adams's son-in-law William Smith, Jefferson again endorsed the rebellion in New England. Lethargy, he said, was 'the forerunner of death to the public liberty ... And what country can preserve its liberties if its rulers are not warned from time to time that their people preserve the spirit of resistance? Let them take up arms.' Then he added a morbid concluding thought: 'The tree of liberty must be refreshed from time to time with the blood of patriots and tyrants. It is its natural manure.'[6]

Tragically, that maxim would echo down the centuries, and end up as something of a mission statement for extremists. On the day that Timothy McVeigh planted the truck bomb outside the Alfred P. Murrah Federal Building in Oklahoma City, which killed 168 of his fellow Americans, including 19 babies and children in a day-care facility, he wore a t-shirt with Jefferson's words printed on the back. His choice of explosive was also horribly, if inadvertently, symbolic. 'McVeigh's American fascist bomb was made largely out of fertiliser,' Christopher Hitchens reminded us in his short biography of Jefferson, 'which might also give pause to those who too easily compare blood with manure.'[7]

19 April, the date of McVeigh's attack, was also freighted with meaning. It was two years to the day since federal agents had raided the Branch Davidian compound in Waco, Texas, bringing the siege to a deadly end. Even more poignantly, it was Patriots' Day, the anniversary of the Battle of Lexington. Nor did McVeigh's historical allusions end there. On the front of his t-shirt was a portrait of Abraham Lincoln, along with the words 'Sic semper tyrannis': 'Thus always to tyrants.' The Latin phrase, which was adopted by the revolutionaries of 1776, was said to be the cry of John Wilkes Booth when he fired the fatal shots at pointblank range which brought Lincoln's life to an end. It also found

an echo on January 6th. As the Oath Keepers leader Stewart Rhodes rallied his militia, and revelled in reports from inside the Capitol that lawmakers were cowering behind their desks, he told them, 'Amen. They need to shit their fucking pants. Sic semper tyrannis.'[8]

Other quotes and sayings have been plucked from the revolutionary lexicon without much regard for who said them, or even if they were said at all. Cherished on the extreme right, for example, is the dictum: 'When the government fears the people, there is liberty. When the people fear the government, there is tyranny.' Alt-right websites sell t-shirts emblazoned with the slogan. Investigators found the words on a scrap of paper discovered in Timothy McVeigh's car, under which the terrorist had written, 'Maybe now there will be liberty.'[9] But although this mantra is frequently misattributed to Jefferson and the Bostonian revolutionary Samuel Adams, scholars have found no evidence that either voiced these words.

Turning misquotes of the Founding Fathers into far-right memes has become something of a cottage industry. 'The beauty of the Second Amendment is that it will not be needed until they try to take it,' Jefferson is purported to have said, another of his supposed quotes that has been used to validate violent extremism. Since it first appeared in print in 2007, however, scholars have drawn a blank in tracing its origin and deemed it spurious. Besides, Jefferson was an early proponent of gun control, having supported the decision to ban firearms from the campus of his beloved University of Virginia.[10]

These kinds of historical myths have fuelled the misinformation machine of the American far right. At the same time, however, one also has to acknowledge that much of the history which extremists have co-opted to justify their violence is accurate, not least Jefferson's assertion that a little rebellion now and then was good for the state of the union. In his famed 'tree of liberty' quote, for instance, he was not merely speaking figuratively. His words were supposed to be taken at face value. In a letter to Madison, he even suggested that insurrectionists should be dealt with leniently so as not to quell pre-emptively future rebellions. Governors should be 'mild in their punishment of rebellions, as not to discourage them too much', he said.[11] One thing of which the January 6th insurrectionists cannot be accused is a false reading of the words which Jefferson actually wrote or said.

Many of the January 6th insurrectionists were also motivated by 'Second Amendment extremism', or 'insurrectionism' as it is sometimes called. This is the belief that the framers embedded in the Constitution the right not merely to bear arms but to raise militias against the government. For decades now, this dangerous credo has festered within the conservative movement. As far back as the mid-1990s, the National Rifle Association's then CEO Wayne LaPierre argued that 'the people have the right, must have the right, to take whatever means necessary, including force, to abolish oppressive government'.[12] More recently, this thinking has taken firm hold on the Republican hard right. The Florida congressman Matt Gaetz, one of the more crazed members of the Republican House Caucus, has argued that the Second Amendment is 'about maintaining within the citizenry the ability to maintain an armed rebellion against the government, if that becomes necessary'. Ted Cruz, a graduate of Harvard Law School, who prides himself on his constitutional wherewithal, has described the Second Amendment 'as the ultimate check against government tyranny'.[13]

Validation for this dangerous interpretation of the Constitution has even come from the US Supreme Court. In the landmark *Heller* ruling in 2008, which affirmed for the first time that the Second Amendment provided a constitutional basis for the right of individuals to bear arms, the conservative justice Antonin Scalia observed that 'when the able-bodied men are trained in arms and organised, they are better able to resist tyranny'. Scalia was not fully embracing the insurrectionist theory, but, as one legal scholar put it at the time, he was nonetheless putting 'a sort of toe in the water'.[14] In a 2010 ruling, Samuel Alito, another ultra-conservative justice, approvingly cited a 19th century constitutional law textbook that described the Second Amendment as 'a strong moral check against the usurpation and arbitrary powers of rulers', which would 'enable the people to resist and triumph over them'.[15]

At a time when paramilitary extremists are casting themselves as liberty's true defenders, this kind of language has not only taken on a more sinister entendre but lent Second Amendment extremism a patina of legal respectability – the imprimatur of the highest court in the land. Yet the Second Amendment was never meant as a charter for vigilantism or insurrectionism. Indeed, the only crime explicitly spelt out in the pages of the Constitution is that of treason.

For the January 6th insurrections, the revolutionary era was not the only historical touchstone. Civil War revivalists carried the Confederate colours, a flag both of white supremacy and treason. Most infamously, it was wielded as a weapon by Kevin Seefried, a 53-year-old from Delaware, one of the first rioters to enter the Capitol, who jabbed it at a Black police officer and was later sentenced to three years in prison.

The Gadsden flag was also brandished, a yellow banner imprinted with a coiled rattlesnake and the slogan 'Don't Tread On Me', which had been designed by a South Carolinian slave owner, Christopher Gadsden. Those were the colours held aloft by a 34-year-old QAnon convert Rosanne Boyland, who, ironically, was killed on the steps of the Capitol after being trampled by the mob.

In the aftermath of January 6th, the narrative of the Lost Cause, the romanticised view that Confederate soldiers were valiant protectors of states' rights – as opposed to white supremacists defending enslavement – also found an echo. Rather than criminals or domestic terrorists, the rioters were cast as law-abiding citizens – patriots on 'a normal tourist visit', in the words of the Republican congressman Andrew Clyde. When in 2023 Fox News aired a documentary on January 6th presented by Tucker Carlson, it framed the deadly insurrection as a noble protest. 'They were peaceful, orderly and meek,' ran Carlson's honeyed commentary. 'They were not insurrectionists. They were sightseers.' The 41,000 hours of surveillance footage from security cameras that Carlson's film relied on was handed to him by the new House Speaker Kevin McCarthy, who was now acting as an accomplice to the falsification of history.[16]

There were claims that members of the leftist protest group Antifa and Black Lives Matter were responsible for the violence (by April, a poll suggested that more than half of Republicans thought January 6th was deliberately orchestrated by 'violent left-wing protesters trying to make Trump look bad').[17] Republicans accused the Democratic House Speaker Nancy Pelosi of knowing about the threat of violence before-hand, and allowing it to unfold in the hope of discrediting Donald Trump. The Republican congresswoman Elise Stefanik, a rising GOP star, stated that Pelosi 'bears responsibility' for January 6th, and accused her, perversely, of being 'an authoritarian who has broken the people's house'.[18]

Trump, by contrast, was absolved of blame. Seven days after the storming of the Capitol, more than 200 Republicans either voted against his second impeachment for 'incitement of insurrection' or did not vote at all. Only ten House Republicans voted in favour of him facing trial in the Senate. When the Republican Senator Rand Paul introduced a motion dismissing the case on the technicality that the Senate trial would take place when Trump was no longer in office, only five out of 50 Republicans voted to reject this manoeuvre.[19]

Rather than seeing January 6th for what it was, a day of infamy on a par with the attack on Pearl Harbor and September 11th, GOP leaders minimised its historical import. Republican leaders, with the exception of the Wyoming congresswoman Liz Cheney, refused to support the creation of an independent commission to investigate, and mounted a filibuster to block it. When the Democratic-controlled House appointed a January 6th committee regardless, the Republican leadership boycotted the panel. The two Republicans brave enough to join, Cheney and Adam Kinzinger, who on January 6th had holed himself up inside his office with a .38 calibre Ruger LCP pistol, were censured by their party.

Not only did conservatives seek to exonerate the insurrectionists, they sanctified them. Ashli Babbitt, a former US Air Force veteran, QAnon conspiracist and one-time Obama supporter, fatally shot by police on January 6th, was portrayed as a martyr. In a video recorded to commemorate what would have been her 36th birthday, Trump lauded her as 'a truly incredible person'.[20]

Each night, there are vigils now outside the DC Central Detention Facility where some 40 insurrectionists are awaiting trial. Speakers refer to their incarceration as 'the January 6th hostage crisis'. The name, 'Ashli Babbitt, Ashli Babbitt,' is chanted like a mantra. 'Slowly, inexorably, the J6 Cult of Martyrs is finding a place within the mainstream conservative pantheon,' wrote Laura Jedeed of the *New Republic*.[21] Trump even collaborated on a song performed by a self-styled 'J6 Prison choir', entitled 'Justice for All', in which he recited the words of the Pledge of Allegiance. The first major event of his 2024 presidential campaign, a rally in the menacingly symbolic setting of Waco, Texas, the site of the Branch Davidian siege, began with a video of the J6 song.

Drawing inspiration from the country's revolutionary ideology is by no means new. In more benign forms, the American conservative movement has been doing it for decades. As the GOP has lurched to the right, especially from the 1970s onwards, its invective has become more overtly rebellious. When hardliners in the NRA ousted moderates at their annual conference in 1977, it became known as the 'Revolt in Cincinnati'. 'The Sagebrush Rebellion' was the name given to the movement in western states in the '70s and '80s made up of ranchers, miners and loggers opposed to federal land control. 'Count me in as a rebel,' declared Ronald Reagan when he campaigned during the 1980 election in Utah, one of six conservative states which had passed legislation seeking to nullify 'federal colonialism' on the country's westernmost land. 'I happen to be one who cheers and supports the Sagebrush Rebellion,' he told a crowd in Salt Lake City. Eight years later, 'the Gipper' described his two terms in office as 'the Reagan Revolution'.

When Richard Nixon's former speechwriter, Pat Buchanan, mounted his attack on the Republican establishment in 1992, and sought to wrestle the presidential nomination from the incumbent president, George H. W. Bush, he revelled in his nickname 'Pitchfork Pat'. Two years later, the conservative landslide in the congressional midterm elections was dubbed the 'Republican Revolution'.

When a right-wing movement emerged in 2008, first in revolt at the big government conservatism of George W. Bush's response to the subprime financial crisis, and then as a backlash against America's first Black president, it called itself the Tea Party, in honour of the

Bostonians who had dumped chests of tea into the harbour to vent against the British. Tricolour hats, along with other costumes from the 1770s, became the uniform of protest. Political demonstrations looked more like Revolutionary War re-enactments, a form of historical cosplay.

The revolutionary strain has also been absorbed into the mainstream. To this day, 'Sic semper tyrannis' remains the official state motto of Virginia. 'Live free or die' is the motto of New Hampshire, a phrase inherited from a hero of the War of Independence. Even liberal-minded Washington DC has on its number plates the revolutionary *cri de coeur*, 'Taxation without Representation'.[22] The inscription, of course, is peaceful in intent, but speaks, too, of how the country glorifies rebellion. Each year comes further proof, with the fireworks of the 4th of July. Those pyrotechnics, so explosively metaphoric, celebrate a revolutionary ideology.

Racial advance would not have come without violent resistance, whether in the form of slave rebellions or John Brown's raid on the federal arsenal at Harpers Ferry, Virginia, in 1859 – part of a failed plan to ignite a wider revolt on southern plantations that ended up propelling the country further along the road to civil war. Harriet Tubman is best remembered as the great conductor of the Underground Railway, the network of clandestine safe houses and routes which helped enslaved African-Americans reach free states and Canada. Posthumously, it has earned her the honour of featuring on the new 20-dollar bill when it finally comes into circulation. Less well known is that Tubman helped Brown plan the Harpers Ferry raid, and would almost certainly have taken up arms herself had she not fallen ill.

Scholars have tended to frame the abolitionist movement as a nonviolent moral crusade, but as the historian Kellie Carter Jackson has pointed out, 'Though many abolitionists preached nonviolence and nonresistance for decades, force and violence became the most successful responses to combatting the institution of slavery.'[23]

A contradiction also lies at the heart of the civil-rights revolution. Its nonviolent heroes would never have made such progress had they not proven so skilled at provoking white supremacist violence. By targeting the most impregnable citadels of segregation, such as Birmingham and Selma, Martin Luther King knew that protesters would encounter the brute force of southern racism. This in turn would prick the conscience of white America and pressure the federal government to intervene. That became the movement's modus operandi. When police chiefs who understood this tactic of creative tension showed restraint – as in Albany, Georgia, a little-remembered campaign led by King in 1961 – the protests failed. In order for it to succeed, the Gandhian philosophy of nonviolence needed to be applied in places where Sundays were more likely to turn bloody. When John Lewis used to speak of 'good trouble', this was partly what he was alluding to.

Plainly, it is important to differentiate between the benign and malign of this twofold tradition. Of course, Americans should celebrate their independence from Britain. The motto 'Taxation without Representation', rather than inciting the residents of Washington DC to rebellion, makes an important political point that they have no voting representation on Capitol Hill, largely because such a high proportion of the city's population is African-American.

Yet a dangerous dualism is also at work which has contributed to the mutinous belief that political violence directed against the government is justifiable, historically legitimate and endorsed by the Founding Fathers. An origin story that, understandably, is rendered glorious is being used to validate violence. The ugliness of January 6th is closer to the spirit of July 4th than most Americans would care to admit. So when in the aftermath of the insurrection the then President-elect Biden issued a statement noting, 'The scenes of chaos at the Capitol do not reflect a true America, do not represent who we are', history suggested otherwise. In the minds of Donald Trump's army, Insurrection Day was a modern form of Independence Day.

Had it not been for Trump's decision in the summer of 2020 to hold his first rally since the Coronavirus outbreak in Tulsa, Oklahoma, on 'Juneteenth', the day which commemorates the end of enslavement in

America, the 100th anniversary of the city's race massacre would never have received so much attention. Tulsa was the site in 1921 of one of the country's worst hate crimes, when a white supremacist mob tore through the city's predominantly Black Greenwood district, killing perhaps as many as 300 African-American residents. In its reporting at the time, the Associated Press, the country's premier news agency, described it as a 'race clash', but this was a racist pogrom, aided and abetted by local police and troops from the National Guard.

Not just because of the scale of the death toll but because of the savagery of the violence, the massacre should instantly have become a landmark event in US history talked about for decades thereafter. An entire section of the city, a prosperous enclave known as 'Black Wall Street', was razed to the ground, including a hospital, a theatre, a newspaper office, a library, a number of churches, more than 600 Black-owned businesses and some 1,250 homes. Tulsa is also thought to have been the first American city ever to come under aerial bombardment. Eyewitnesses spoke of surveillance aircraft dropping incendiary devices, and firing indiscriminately on Blacks down below. The spark for this rampage was the allegation that a 19-year-old Black shoeshiner, Dick Rowland, had assaulted a 17-year-old white girl named Sarah Page, who worked as an elevator operator. His 'crime' that day, it is now thought, was to accidentally step on her foot as he got into the elevator.

Until recently, the Tulsa massacre was largely ignored by history. Oklahoma schoolchildren, in a deliberate act of official erasure, were not taught about it in school. Nationally, it never received anywhere near the same attention as, say, Little Rock, Birmingham, Selma, or the murder in Mississippi in 1955 of the Black Chicago schoolboy Emmett Till. Even the journalist Tim Madigan, who penned a fine book on Tulsa, *The Burning: Massacre, Destruction, and the Tulsa Race Riot of 1921*, was oblivious to this 'historic nightmare' until 2000, when he was handed some wire copy about the Tulsa Race Riot Commission by an editor who also had no inkling of what that body had been tasked with investigating. To my own shame, Madigan's book had sat on my shelf for well over a decade without me ever thumbing through its pages.[24]

In popular culture, this mass murder scarcely featured until the 2019 HBO series, *Watchmen*, staged a dramatic re-enactment. The show's director, Nicole Kassell, only learnt about Tulsa when she first read the screenplay, which was symptomatic of a gap of collective memory that she described as 'a crime upon a crime'.[25] Tulsa brought to mind that astute observation from the novelist Hilary Mantel, 'History's what people are trying to hide from you, not what they're trying to show you.'

This kind of concealment and disremembering is all too common when it comes to political violence and domestic terrorism in America. The Civil War, in which more than 750,000 are now thought to have lost their lives, has received microscopic attention. However, other acts of political violence, whether armed rebellions, riots or assassinations, have often been downplayed, ignored or whitewashed. Focusing on political violence has always contradicted the grand American narrative: that the United States is the most advanced democracy in the world, in which disputes are resolved in elections and legislative chambers, rather than with the noose, the guillotine or the gun. The result, then, has been collective memory loss and denialism. Perhaps we should call it the Tulsa syndrome.

Often it feels as if history has been redacted, and that even defining events have been concealed. Early revolts, such as the Shays' Rebellion, have been historically downgraded, because they muddy the legend that the intentions of the Founding Fathers were democratically pure. Other violent events early in the life of the republic, such as the Whiskey Rebellion, have been overlooked because they undermine the storyline of 'Hey presto, instant American nationhood'. Yet this revolt in Western Pennsylvania from 1791 to 1794, which involved more than 7,000 insurrectionists angry at the levying of an excise tax on whiskey, is especially significant because it showed early on that the spirit of revolution, and its resort to violence, would outlive the War of Independence.

To suppress the revolt, George Washington had to lead a federal force of some 13,000 men – the only time a US commander-in-chief has ever led his army in the field – a mission which succeeded without the firing of a single shot. But the rebellion was portentous nonetheless, serving both as a warning that national unity was by no means guaranteed and that the American people would be resistant, possibly violently so, to an overbearing central government. One of the reasons why Washington reluctantly agreed to serve a second four years as president was the fear that the United States of America was already tearing itself apart, and could easily descend into civil war.

Slave rebellions have also received short thrift, partly because they contradicted the prevailing narrative in the 19th century that Blacks imprisoned in chattel slavery were content and uncomplaining. A case in point is the German Coast Uprising of 1811, inspired by the successful Haitian rebellion where enslaved Blacks managed to overcome the army of Napoleon. What started as a revolt of 25 slaves on a sugarcane plantation 40 miles north of New Orleans quickly swelled into the largest slave rebellion witnessed on American soil. Singing Creole protest songs as they went, and burning down plantations and murdering their owners on the way, the aim was to march on New Orleans. Before they could reach the city, however, a force made up of militiamen and US soldiers brutally put the rebellion down. Almost 100 slaves were killed, the decapitated heads of the ringleaders placed on poles at intervals along the Mississippi River to act as a deterrent against further revolts. Yet despite being one of the bloodiest episodes in the early decades of the new republic, it has been largely overlooked by history. To this day, the only memorial to the rebellion is a brown plaque on a traffic island next to a strip mall in southern Louisiana, with the meagre inscription: 'Major 1811 slave uprising organised here.'[26] It is a history that is perennially invisible.

Race, needless to say, has often been the cause of historical blindness. Though we remember and memorialise the great battles of the Civil War, such as Antietam and Gettysburg, comparatively scant attention, for example, has been paid to the New York draft riots of 1863, where Blacks were primarily the victims. The spark for the violence, one of the deadliest civil disturbances in US history, was Lincoln's decision to enact the nation's first military draft. Thus, the bloodletting is often mischaracterised as an attack against the federal government. But the draft became the pretext for a four-day racist pogrom, in which at least 120 people were killed, and more than 2,000 injured. African-Americans became the target of a largely Irish immigrant mob, whose rage was fuelled not only by anger at being used by the Union army as cannon fodder, but the fear that freed Blacks would threaten their economic livelihoods. In the middle of New York City, African-Americans were lynched on lampposts and trees. The city's Orphan Asylum for Colored Children on Fifth Avenue was razed to the ground. A quarter of the city's Black population was displaced, as thousands fled in fear.

Martin Scorsese's 2002 epic, *Gangs of New York*, starring Daniel Day-Lewis and Leonardo DiCaprio, is perhaps the only time that the riots have entered into mass consciousness. Yet the film falsely depicted Irish immigrants as the heroes of the story: working-class warriors battling against middle-class white Protestants determined to cart them off to war. Ironically, many reviewers actually commended Scorsese for the super-realism of his attention to detail in costuming and set design, even though the storyline was a complete whitewashing of history.[27] To this day, there is no memorial in New York City to the African-Americans who were murdered. Moreover, the term 'draft riot' continues to be used, despite this being a racist massacre.

Greater attention has been paid to the campaign of lynchings conducted during the Reconstruction era. Between 1865 and 1876, more than 2,000 Blacks were killed (lynchings were rare before the Emancipation Proclamation, as Ta-Nehisi Coates has observed, 'because whites were loath to destroy their own property').[28] However, it could hardly be said that the mass lynchings which occurred across the states of the Old Confederacy have lodged in the American mind. In 1865 in Mobile County, Alabama, white mobs killed more than 130 Blacks. In Pine Bluff, Arkansas, the following year, 24 emancipated Black women, children and men were found hanging from the trees. In Millican, Texas, some 150 Blacks were killed by white mobs. But little of this has become household history, or a core part of the school curriculum.

The resurgence of the Ku Klux Klan in the 1920s has been well documented. The black and white photographs of thousands of Klansmen marching down Pennsylvania Avenue in 1926 wearing their conical, and comical, hats, have been widely published. As KKK membership swelled to between four and five million members, Klansmen occupied 11 governorships, 16 US Senate seats and possibly as many as 75 seats in the House of Representatives.[29] But the KKK was not the only home of violent extremism. By the mid-1930s, there were thought to be as many as 800 far-right groups, many of which have largely escaped historical notice. There was the Black Legion, which was largely made up of former Klansmen now decked in black gowns. The Silver Shirts Legion was an anti-Semitic hate group whose uniforms were modelled on the Nazi Brownshirts. There was the Christian Front, founded in 1938 at the urging of the Nazi-sympathising Catholic priest Charles Coughlin, which attracted support mainly from Irish and German-American Catholics. Coughlin spoke at a rally held by the Nazi German-American Bund at Madison Square Garden in February 1939 to mark George Washington's birthday, at which members of the 20,000-strong crowd chanted 'Sieg Heil' after reciting the Pledge of Allegiance.[30]

Most of the violence and extremism from the beginning of the 19th century onwards was repressive rather than revolutionary: whites savagely asserting their supremacy over Blacks and Native Americans; strike-breaking bosses making sure labour was put in its place; established immigrant groups maintaining their dominance over new arrivals. As the historian Michael Wallace has put it, 'We find in our racial history, the violent suppression of blacks by whites; in our economic history, the violent suppression of labor by capital; and in our ethnic history, the violent suppression of immigrant groups by more established ones.'[31]

Politics, too, frequently became a bloody arena. Attacks on members of Congress are as old as Congress itself. Back in 1796, in the midst of the dispute over whether the new republic should ratify the much-hated Jay Treaty negotiated with the British, the country's first House Speaker, Frederick Muhlenberg, came close to being murdered. Shortly after casting the tie-breaking vote in favour of the treaty, he was stabbed by his brother-in-law, who opposed any rapprochement with King George.

Capitol Hill was also the site of the first presidential assassination attempt, when in 1835 a gunman approached Andrew Jackson brandishing two pistols, both of which misfired. Jackson, an accomplished dualist and gunfighter himself, beat the assailant with his cane, while 'Davy' Crockett, the backwoodsman turned congressman, also muscled in. The assassination attempt on Jackson spawned one of the many early-American conspiracy theories, that the deranged house painter who carried out the attack was actually an agent of Jackson's political opponents, the Whigs.[32]

Regularly, the halls of Congress witnessed physical political combat. The story most often told is of the caning of the anti-slavery campaigner Senator Charles Sumner, who was set upon by Congressman Preston Brooks of South Carolina in May 1856, as the country spiralled towards Civil War. Brooks walked into the Senate chamber, pummelled Sumner's skull with the butt of a gold-topped cane, and kept up the attack even after his cane snapped in two. Sumner's near murder, and his convalescence afterwards, kept him from the Senate for more than a year. Yet his attacker became a hero. A number of southern towns were renamed in his honour, while hundreds of new canes were sent to the congressman, one of which was inscribed with the words 'hit him again'. Pro-slavery Democrats even wore necklaces from which dangled fragments of Brooks' splintered cane.[33]

The attack on Sumner was far from being an isolated assault. Violence was commonplace in the lead-up to the Civil War. Between 1830 and 1860, as the historian Joanne Freeman has chronicled, 'There were more than *seventy* violent incidents between congressmen in the House and Senate chambers or on nearby streets and duelling grounds, most of them long forgotten.' These included canings, the brandishing of pistols and knives, fistfights and duels.[34] In 1841, the entire House chamber erupted into a mass brawl.

Washington DC has intermittently been the target of campaigns of intimidation and rebellion. In September 1939, after Hitler had invaded Poland, Charles Coughlin incited his followers to march on

Washington to harass lawmakers into upholding the neutrality laws which made it harder for Franklin Delano Roosevelt to aid America's eventual allies. Earlier in the 1930s, a group of wealthy businessmen plotted a fascist coup d'état against Roosevelt with the aim of installing a retired Marine major-general, Smedley Butler, as dictator. In what became known as the 'Wall Street Putsch' or 'Business Plot', the plan was for Butler to raise an army, strike at Washington and seize control of the capital.

Deadly violence has been a recurring feature of presidential politics. Sixteen years after the assassination of Abraham Lincoln came the murder in 1881 of James Garfield, who was shot twice at a railway station in Washington and who died 11 weeks later from his wounds. In 1901, William McKinley became the third president to be assassinated, after he was shot twice in the abdomen while attending the Pan-American Exposition in Buffalo. In 1963, Kennedy became the fourth.

Then there were the failed assassinations. Lincoln had survived at least one previous attempt on his life, when the bullet from a sniper's rifle reportedly passed through his hat as he rode one evening from the White House to his personal residence, the Soldiers' Home, on the outskirts of Washington. Confederate sympathisers are also thought to have hatched a plot to kill him en route to his first inauguration.

Only the 50 pages of a speech he was due to deliver saved the life of the former president Theodore Roosevelt, when a gunman shot him in the chest as he campaigned in 1912 for a return to the White House. Franklin Delano Roosevelt, shortly before taking his first oath of office in 1933, came close to being gunned down in a Miami park when an armed attacker fired five rounds from his handgun. Harry Truman also survived an assassination attempt in 1950, when two pro-independence Puerto Rican nationalists tried to kill him outside Blair House, the residence on Pennsylvania Avenue where the president was living while the White House was being renovated.

John F. Kennedy was targeted in Palm Beach, Florida, during his presidential transition, when a retired postal worker, Richard Paul Pavlick, packed his car with explosives as part of a suicide plot to ambush the president-elect's motorcade on its way to mass. Pavlick only aborted the attack when he realised that Jackie Kennedy, and the couple's two young children, Caroline and John Jr, would also end up being killed.

Richard Nixon was the target in 1972, when an army veteran attempted to hijack a plane at Baltimore/Washington International Airport with the intention of flying it into the White House (in the aftermath of September 11th, US intelligence services were criticised for their lack of imagination in failing to anticipate the weaponisation of commercial aircraft, but what they were truly guilty of was a fatal lapse of memory). In the spring of that year, the former Alabama governor George Wallace was critically wounded while campaigning at a shopping mall on the outskirts of Washington.

Within a 17-day period in 1975, President Gerald Ford survived two separate attempts on his life. In both instances, the would-be assassins were women. In his first year as president, Ronald Reagan skirted death as he was leaving the Washington Hilton Hotel, when a bullet fired by John Hinckley Jr ricocheted off the armour-plating of his presidential limousine and hit him in the left underarm. Hinckley had been inspired by the hit movie *Taxi Driver*, whose central character, a troubled young Vietnam war veteran named Travis Bickle, had become something of an anti-hero after the film premiered in 1976 for trying to assassinate the fictitious presidential candidate, Senator Charles Palantine.

Post-mortems into these assassination attempts tended to focus on the psychiatric profiles of the gunmen and women, and to lump them together as deranged lone wolves. Theodore Roosevelt's would-be assassin, the exotically named John Flammang Schrank, claimed to be acting on the orders of the ghost of William McKinley. John Hinckley Jr had an unhealthy fixation with the actress Jodie Foster, the star of *Taxi Driver*. After watching the film at least 15 times, he wanted to impress Foster by trying to kill the president, as Travis Bickle had done to such acclaim. By focusing on the psychiatric state of the assassins, however, we have not always delved sufficiently deeply into the psyche of the nation.

In the aftermath of the assassination of Robert Kennedy, there was an attempt to do just that. The murders of the Kennedy brothers, Martin Luther King, Malcolm X, Medgar Evers, the civil-rights workers James Chaney, Andrew Goodman and Michael Schwerner, and George Lincoln Rockwell, the founder of the American Nazi Party, had made the 1960s a particularly, if not uniquely, violent decade. In a quest for understanding, President Lyndon Johnson appointed a blue-ribbon panel of scholars, the US National Commission on the Causes and Prevention of Violence. Remarkably, it was the first comprehensive academic study of collective violence throughout American history.

Racism, the panel concluded, explained much of the violence directed against 'ethnic scapegoats' by white supremacist and nativist groups. The 'frontier experience' of suppressing Native Americans and Mexicans had created a tradition of vigilante justice and nurtured a sense of popular sovereignty, the principle that the consent of the people is paramount. The manner of the country's founding, through violent revolution, had also made it more prone to political violence. '[T]he revolutionary doctrine that our Declaration of Independence proudly proclaims is mistakenly cited as a model for legitimate violence,' it noted. This was overlaid by a pervasive fear of governmental power which 'reinforced the tendency to define freedom negatively as freedom *from*'. Again, this had validated the idea that 'violent local and state resistance' to unpopular federal actions was 'a legitimate response'.

Memory loss added to the problem. Like all nations, the report concluded, the United States suffered from 'a kind of historical amnesia or selective recollection that masks unpleasant traumas of the past, but Americans have probably magnified this process of selective recollection, owing to a historic vision of ourselves as a latter-day chosen people, a new Jerusalem'. In other words, a positive sense of American exceptionalism blinded it to the negative aspects of American exceptionalism, in this instance a populace of 'rather bloody-minded people in both action and reaction'. One upside of the turmoil of the 1960s, the panel concluded, was 'maybe to force a harder and more candid look at our past'.[35]

A year after the panel brought out its report, Richard Hofstadter edited a book entitled *American Violence: A Documentary History*, which identified the same disease of the national mind, a problem of forgetfulness when it came to the country's bloody history. '[W]e have a remarkable lack of memory where violence is concerned and have left most of our excesses a part of buried history,' he wrote. 'Shirked by historians, the subject has been repressed in the national consciousness.'[36] After compiling more than 100 episodes of large-scale violence, the majority of which were hitherto little known, Hofstadter predicted that 'much of this inattention will be remedied' in the future. Yet the political violence continued and so, too, did the historical amnesia.

This was evident in the aftermath of January 6th. Looking for historical antecedents, most reporters, myself included, reached back to 1814, when the British ransacked Washington, which we all reckoned to be the last time that the US Capitol had been breached. In doing so, we overlooked an attack in March 1954 carried out by a posse of Puerto Rican nationalists, who made it into the Ladies Gallery of the House of Representatives, and showered lawmakers down below with a hail of semi-automatic gunfire. Five congressmen were injured, although remarkably no-one was killed.

Likewise, we underplayed the bomb attacks targeting the Capitol. In 1915, a former Harvard professor and German sympathiser, Eric Muenter, had planted three sticks of dynamite beneath the desk of the Senate switchboard room, set the time for midnight and then watched them explode from Union Station before boarding a train to New York.[37] In 1971, the domestic terror group the Weather Underground left a bomb in a Senate bathroom. In 1983, members of an all-female leftist terror group, the May 19th (M19) Communist Organisation, planted an explosive device in protest at Ronald Reagan's decision to invade Grenada. The Senate was not in session when the bomb exploded, and no-one was injured, but the pictures of blown-out windows amidst the columned facade were shocking nonetheless – though quickly forgotten.

These omissions from our reporting on January 6th revealed what happens when a failure of collective memory and historical understanding meets the hive mind of the modern media. It ended up producing a false narrative passing over previous acts of political violence. That may have been excusable after the storming of the Capitol, because the violence was so extreme, and its ringleader was a sitting president. Nonetheless, it spoke of a broader problem. Always there has been a tendency to downplay the full extent of American violence and extremism. Always there has been a false narrative.

Since the January 6th insurrection, greater attention has naturally been paid to the origins of modern-day militia violence, which are ordinarily located in the early 1970s. At the beginning of that decade it was groups on the far left that posed the gravest threat. The domestic terror group the Weather Underground Organisation, originally known as the Weathermen, carried out bombings targeting at least 25 government buildings, including the Capitol and the Pentagon. The Black Liberation Army, a Marxist-Leninist Black nationalist group, was responsible for more than 70 attacks, many involving the assassination of police officers. By the end of the 1970s, however, far-right militia activity and domestic terrorism were more dangerous.

The white power movement, which brought together neo-Nazis and white supremacists from groups such as the KKK, National Alliance and White Aryan Resistance, was partly a backlash to the civil rights and immigration reforms of Lyndon Johnson's Great Society. Vietnam and Watergate heightened hostility towards the federal government. 'Unlike previous iterations of the Ku Klux Klan and white supremacist vigilantism, the white power movement did not claim to serve the state,' the historian Kathleen Belew has observed. 'Instead, white power made the state its target.'[38] It was a crucial difference.

The vilification of government was at the heart of the Sagebrush Rebellion in those western states. The 1970s saw the emergence of what was called the constitutional sheriff movement, founded on the fringe theory that the ultimate law-enforcement authority in America was the lowly country sheriff. In 1977, David Duke of the

KKK announced the formation of a 'Klan Border Watch' along the California-Mexico border, a forerunner of militia outfits, such as American Patrol, that arose in the '90s.

For the white power movement, perhaps the most significant event of the late 1970s was the publication of a novel, *The Turner Diaries*, by the neo-Nazi leader, William Luther Pierce, which centred on a fictitious white supremacist group called The Order. Not only did the book feature an attack on the US Capitol but also a 'Day of the Rope', when 'traitors', including members of Congress, newscasters, journalists, school teachers and judges, were murdered in mass lynchings. Pages of *The Turner Diaries* were discovered in Timothy McVeigh's truck. The Oklahoma bomber had also sold copies of it on the gun-show circuit.[39] The novel even spawned a copycat group, which called itself The Order. Since first coming out in 1978, it is thought to have been the inspiration for at least 40 hate crimes and terrorist attacks. The FBI has described the novel as 'the bible of the racist right', and on January 6th it became something of an operations manual.

The 1990s, which are often miscast as a period of unprecedented peace, prosperity and domestic tranquility, saw an uptick in militia activity. The spark came from a remote corner of northern Idaho, where in the summer of 1992 the Ruby Ridge stand-off played out. What began as an attempt by US marshals to arraign Randy Weaver, a gun enthusiast and army veteran who had been holed up in a cabin with his family for more than a year-and-a-half to avoid attending his trial on firearms charges, turned first into a fatal firefight, in which his son was killed, and then an 11-day siege. Soon satellite trucks had converged on the scene, lending it the feel of a media circus. So, too, neo-Nazis from a nearby Aryan Nations compound, an explosive combination. Though the stand-off eventually ended peacefully, Ruby Ridge instantly became shorthand on the far right for how an overbearing federal government was trampling on the rights of a little guy and his family. Tyranny was snuffing out freedom.

The Waco siege the following year, which unfolded at a compound in Texas run by the religious sect the Branch Davidians, embellished this conspiracist narrative. Like Ruby Ridge, the stand-off started with a fatal firefight after federal agents from the Bureau of Alcohol, Tobacco and Firearms attempted to execute a search warrant. It ended 51 days later when the FBI launched an assault on the property. Fire soon engulfed the compound, which claimed the lives of 76 Branch Davidian sect members, including 25 children.

Fury over Ruby Ridge and Waco combined with rage over gun controls pushed by the new Clinton administration: the 1993 Brady Act and the 1994 federal assault weapons ban. As the Cold War came to an end, George H. W. Bush's talk of a 'new world order' also revived anti-Semitic conspiracy theories which had swirled since early in the 20th century about a secretive global cabal intent on forming a worldwide government.

To add to this toxic brew, the conservative movement's anti-government rhetoric had become more shrill and war-like. No-one was more fluent in this combative new tongue than the Georgia congressman Newt Gingrich, a one-time history professor with a fascination with dinosaurs, who became the figurehead of the Republican Revolution and the country's 50th House Speaker. The Clintons and the Democratic Party, he protested, were 'the enemy of normal Americans'. A 'war' needed to be fought, he warned in a speech to the right-wing Heritage Foundation in 1988, 'with a scale and duration and a savagery that is only true of civil wars'.

America was a tinderbox. A 'United States of Anger', it was dubbed by my then BBC colleague Gavin Esler.[40] Then came Oklahoma City. McVeigh had plotted the attack on the federal office building in revenge for the deaths at the Branch Davidian compound and Ruby Ridge and the passage of the 1994 assault weapons ban, which he equated with the 'Cohen Act', the fictitious gun-control law outlawing the private ownership of firearms that appeared in *The Turner Diaries*.

Horrendous though it was, the Oklahoma bomb attack was not the end of it. The following year, Eric Rudolph, a domestic terrorist from the self-styled Army of God – an outfit which believed it had the blessing of the Almighty to target abortion clinics – mounted a bomb attack on the Centennial Olympic Park during the Atlanta Olympics, which ended up claiming the lives of two victims. The bombing is perhaps best remembered for the false accusations levelled against Richard Jewell, the security guard who discovered the pipe bombs, whose story was made into a 2019 movie, *Richard Jewell*. Thus we recall it for the wrong reason. What should have stuck in our minds was how Atlanta became the target of yet another deadly act of white domestic terrorism.

The militia movement spiked in 1996, with 370 different groups active across the country. However, with domestic terrorism now a higher priority for law enforcement agencies, the number plummeted to 68 by the end of the century.[41]

This lull in militia activity during the early years of the 21st century ended with the emergence of Barack Hussein Obama in 2008. The country's first Black commander-in-chief became a recruiting sergeant for far-right militia groups. The Three Percenters were founded that year. The Oath Keepers were formed in 2009, months after Obama had taken his oath of office. Political violence again came to the fore. As president, Obama received three times more death threats than his predecessors – 30 death threats a day.[42] Michelle Obama became the first First Lady to have assigned to her motorcade a Counter Assault Team, the helmeted agents who wear the full black battle dress uniform.[43] The rise of the Tea Party meant the mood was not just febrile but fissile.

Despite this uptick in threats of political violence, it still came as a shock when in January 2011 news came through from Arizona that the Democratic congresswoman Gabby Giffords had been shot in the head outside a Safeway store in Tucson, an attack in which six other people were killed, including a US district judge and a nine-year-old girl. The shooter was a mentally ill white, skin-headed gunman, who believed in various New World Order conspiracy theories. During the midterm elections, held two months earlier, the website of a political action committee run by the former vice-presidential candidate Sarah Palin had featured Giffords and other House Democrats with stylised crosshairs over their districts. Though no direct connection was established between the graphic and the shooting, Giffords herself had complained at the time about the inflammatory rhetoric:

'When people do that, they have got to realise there's consequences to that.'[44] Four days after the Tucson shooting, a white supremacist tried to detonate a pipe bomb along the route of a Martin Luther King Day parade in Spokane, Washington.

The Obama years also witnessed the rise of the alt-right. The term 'alternative right' was first coined in 2009 by the neo-Nazi conspiracy theorist Richard B. Spencer, and combined anti-Semitism, nativism, anti-feminism, white nationalism, a belief in the mass deportation of all non-white immigrants and the repatriation of the descendants of enslaved people. Its ideas found a home on Breitbart News, a website described by its former chairman, Steve Bannon, as 'the platform for the alt-right'.

In August 2016, Bannon was appointed chief executive of Donald Trump's then-faltering presidential campaign, and became his chief White House strategist after the election. An alumnus of Harvard Business School and Goldman Sachs, Bannon summed up his approach to politics in a conversation with the left-wing firebrand Michael Moore. Democrats favoured pillow fights, he quipped, Republicans came ready to deliver a head wound.[45] By the end of January 2021, Bannon had an office in the West Wing of the White House, right at the heart of the 'administrative state' which he vowed to destroy.

For Donald Trump the menace of violence not only differentiated his hypermasculine politics but also came to define them. Frequently during his insurgent campaign, as he encouraged supporters to 'knock the crap' out of protesters, he evoked the bare-knuckled brutality of the 1930 German beer hall. His statement that 'Second Amendment people' might deal with Hillary Clinton sounded like an open invitation to anyone with a handgun or AR-47. Boasting about personally meting out violence became a leitmotif. Tellingly, his signature line from the 2016 campaign involved violence. 'I could stand in the middle of Fifth Avenue and shoot somebody and I wouldn't lose voters,' he bragged on the eve of the Iowa caucus, in his most astute piece of self-analysis during the entire campaign.

Violence became central to his grievance-fuelled politics. Between Trump and the MAGA diehards, it served as a bonding mechanism, a marker of cultural affinity. Machismo demonstrated his vitality and strength, accentuated how he was prepared to say the unsayable, and served also a rejoinder to the 'wokeism' of the Obama years. It also helped him survive the biggest scandal of his candidacy, the emergence of the *Access Hollywood* tape in which he boasted of grabbing women by the pussy. Sexual violence against women, for many of his supporters, was no more problematic than his bullying of protesters or his verbal attacks against Hillary Clinton.

White supremacist militia groups clearly believed they had found their man. The neo-Nazi news site The Daily Stormer quickly endorsed him.[46] When David Duke, the former Grand Wizard of the Knights of the Ku Klux Klan, expressed admiration, Trump refused to disavow him. After his victory, the far right claimed the president-elect as their own. 'Our Glorious Leader has ascended to God Emperor,' The Daily Stormer's neo-Nazi editor Andrew Anglin wrote. 'Make no mistake about it: we did this.'[47] Believing that America had moved closer towards the establishment of a white ethno-state, Richard B. Spencer proclaimed during a speech in Washington, 'Hail Trump, hail our people, hail victory!' Some in his audience then raised their arms in Hitler salutes.[48]

As president, Trump continued in his extremist vein. I was at the press conference held on Fifth Avenue, in the lobby of Trump Tower, when he stated, to the incredulity of reporters shouting questions, that there were 'very fine people on both sides' in the disturbances following the neo-Nazi torch rally in Charlottesville, Virginia. At a rally in Montana in 2018, he praised the state's then Republican congressman, Greg Gianforte, who had body-slammed a reporter from the *Guardian* to the floor. 'Any guy that can do a body slam, he is my type!' proclaimed the president.[49]

Trump loved reinforcing the impression that he was a presidential pugilist, even tweeting a photoshopped image of his head superimposed on the body of Sylvester Stallone playing Rocky. Much of the early Trump iconography depicted him as Rambo, and the Terminator, imagery in which he revelled. Trump had managed to avoid serving in Vietnam, because bone spurs in his heels granted him a medical exemption, but loved portraying himself as a warrior.

Frequently throughout his presidency, he threatened protesters with a violent response from law enforcement or even the military. 'When the looting starts, the shooting starts,' he tweeted after the rioting in Minneapolis sparked by the murder of George Floyd. Black Lives Matter protesters who breached the White House grounds, he warned, would be met with 'ominous weapons' and 'vicious dogs', which instantly revived memories of Bull Connor's police dogs in Birmingham.

When during the George Floyd protests Trump ordered the park opposite the White House to be cleared of protesters by police firing tear gas and rubber bullets, it was dubbed the Battle of Lafayette Square. But this was no battle. The demonstration that day had been peaceful. Trump turned it into a one-sided show of force, a presidential act of violence. The intention appeared to be to manufacture a historical event, which was capped when Trump marched across this faux battlefield with the Chairman of the Joint Chiefs of Staff, General Mark Milley, dressed in combat fatigues at his side. Then he stood defiantly outside the church opposite the White House, St John's, that had been partially damaged earlier in the protests holding aloft a bible.

In the early days of his candidacy, perhaps the sharpest piece of commentary came from *The Atlantic* writer Salena Zito, who posited that Trump supporters took him seriously though not literally, while detractors took him literally but not seriously. When it came to political violence, however, this formula broke down. From the outset it was clear that MAGA diehards were prepared to act on his violent directives. Just weeks after Trump suggested that protesters should be taken out on a stretcher, a 78-year-old white male Trump supporter punched a Black protester in the face, as the heckler was being escorted from a rally in Fayetteville, North Carolina. After his targeting of Muslims and Mexican immigrants, hate crimes showed a sharp and immediate spike. A 2019 report, mapping violence and Trump rally appearances, showed a staggering 226 per cent increase in hate crimes in those areas.[50]

Violence had the imprimatur of the President of the United States, and his words travelled. Months after laughing when a rally-goer in Florida cried out during a speech that immigrants should be shot – 'only in the [Florida] Panhandle can you get away with that statement,' joked Trump – a 21-year-old gunman slaughtered 23 shoppers at a Walmart in El Paso. The gunman, Patrick Wood Crusius, whose online manifesto railed against a 'Hispanic invasion', deliberately targeted Latinos. After Trump posted a bizarre video of himself wrestling and punching a figure whose head had been replaced with a CNN logo, one of his self-styled superfans, Cesar Sayoc, sent pipe bombs to the news organisation's headquarters in New York. Following his arrest on charges of domestic terrorism, Sayoc described Trump as his 'surrogate father'.[51]

During the Trump years, threats against lawmakers increased dramatically. In 2016, the year before he took office, the Capitol Hill police investigated 902 threats. In 2017, that number had skyrocketed more than four times to 3,939.[52] Not all of them came from Trump supporters. A quarter came from Democrats threatening Republicans. Moreover, it was a Bernie Sanders supporter who carried out a gun attack in June 2017, targeting Republican lawmakers training for the annual congressional baseball match in Alexandria, Virginia. Nonetheless, this was predominantly a problem on the right.[53] By the final full year of his presidency, the number of domestic terror plots had risen dramatically, reaching their highest level since 1994.[54]

When the Covid pandemic hit, Trump's repeated use of the terms 'China virus' and 'Chinese flu' – 'Kung Flu' was the phrase used privately – made Asian-Americans more vulnerable to attack. In Midland, Texas, a 19-year-old stabbed to death three members of an Asian-American family, including a two-year-old and six-year-old child, because he thought they were Chinese and therefore spreading the virus.

Covid also led to a spike in militia activity. Between 2020 and 2022, 228 separate militia groups organised 2,335 events.[55] This I witnessed firsthand when reporting on the anti-lockdown protests on the lawns of the State Capitol in Lansing, Michigan. Some militia groups turned up in full combat fatigues. Other protesters were dressed more casually, as if they were off to watch a college football game, albeit with AR-15s slung over their shoulders. One middle-aged lady was particularly striking, dressed as she was in designer jeans with a revolver strapped into a black leather thigh holster. Militia chic. Given the relatively light police presence that day, the mob could easily have rushed the Capitol, which is precisely what had happened in April 2020, when gun-toting protesters entered the building two days after Trump urged his Twitter followers to 'liberate Michigan'. That afternoon, protesters had merely occupied the balconies of the House and Senate chambers, peering menacingly down at state lawmakers who, remarkably, continued their deliberations. But it was a fearsome mob. One protester brandished a sign, seemingly inspired by *The Turner Diaries*: 'Tyrants get the rope.'[56]

Revisiting press coverage of the anti-lockdown protests, it is noticeable how much reporting focused on the health risk they posed: of how they were potentially super-spreader events. Less attention was paid to the propagation of something more sinister: the idea that it was acceptable to mount shows of armed force at state legislatures. In the 12 months leading up to January 6th, far-right extremists held at least 39 armed demonstrations at legislative buildings that in retrospect look like dress rehearsals for January 6th.[57]

A lesson of the Trump years was that when the president identified a target, his supporters attacked it. That is why his comments during the 2020 presidential debate with Joe Biden about the Proud Boys were so chilling. When he told them to 'stand by and stand back', he knew he had a personal militia ready to act on his orders. At the Stop the Steal rally on January 6th, America's commander-in-chief knew precisely what sort of armed force was amassing. Beforehand, the Secret Service had advised him that many in the crowd had come wielding firearms, which explained why his protective detail resisted

Trump's orders to remove the walk-through metal-detectors that surround every presidential appearance. Yet as Trump explained to his harried security team, those weapons posed no threat to him, and would only be trained on lawmakers on Capitol Hill.

As he urged the mob to march on Congress and to 'fight like hell', he was acutely aware that his supporters took him seriously and literally. Determined to observe the rebellion unfold, he even ordered his Secret Service chauffeur to drive him to Capitol Hill, and then tried to seize control of the steering wheel when this order was disobeyed. 'I'm the fucking president,' he shouted, 'take me up to the Capitol now.'

When the Secret Service returned him to the White House instead, he watched live coverage of the insurrection, and delighted in its chaos and bloodshed. Finally, after pleadings from White House aides, Republican lawmakers and even hosts at Fox News, he called off his dogs. Still, though, he felt no compulsion to reproach them. 'We love you,' he said in a video message. 'You're very special.' The rebellion was righteous.

The poster boy of the January 6th insurrection turned out to be Jacob Anthony Angeli Chansley, a bare-chested 33-year-old former actor, decorated Navy seaman and vegan, better known as 'the QAnon Shaman'. His outfit that day could scarcely have been more eye-catching: animal pelts draped from his shoulders, low-slung trousers, no shirt, and, his crowing flourish, a bison-horned headdress. His face was daubed with red, white and blue warpaint. Inked into his torso was the hammer of Thor. Norse mythology was also the inspiration for other tattoos on his body, many of them symbols appropriated by the Nazis in the '30s which had now been co-opted by American white supremacists.[58]

That an eccentric such as Chansley should come to enjoy such instant celebrity revealed a clutch of modern-day media traits. A tendency to focus on the most extreme and outlandish character in the story (to his credit, and later regret, a BBC colleague had noticed Chansley at a protest outside a vote-counting centre in Arizona a few weeks before and decided that he was simply too cartoonish a figure to feature in his report). The habit of turning even the gravest of events into comedy, whether in the form of a late-night monologue, a skit on *Saturday Night Live*, a meme on social media or, months later, a Halloween costume.

Chansley did not completely monopolise media attention. Afterwards, we naturally focused on the militia groups present that day: the Proud Boys, the Oath Keepers and the Three Percenters. But making these paramilitary outfits and QAnon Shaman the centre of attention betrayed a fundamental misunderstanding about the horde that stormed the Capitol: that it was a fringe mob made up of violent outliers.

As the FBI rounded up more than 800 suspects, and the names of those indicted entered into the public record, the crowd profile changed dramatically. Nearly 90 per cent of those arrested had no connection with a militia or fringe group, according to a study conducted by the University of Chicago. Some 28 per cent were white collar workers. The mob included doctors, nurses, an airline pilot, a florist, an attorney, a teacher, a chiropractor, a field operations manager for Google, a bank manager, and even an actor who had appeared on the folksy all-American drama *Friday Night Lights*. Almost a quarter were business owners. This, as the study suggested, was the 'American face of insurrection'.[59]

Some 13 per cent of those arrested had military or law enforcement backgrounds, according to an investigation conducted by National Public Radio. These included police officers currently serving, veterans of the 9/11 wars, and at least one recipient of the Purple Heart.[60] A former NYPD officer, Thomas Webster, was sentenced to ten years for brutally assaulting a DC police officer, a blue-on-blue attack.[61]

Even within the FBI, there was support for the January 6th rebellion. 'There is no good way to say it so I'll be direct,' an unnamed FBI employee wrote to the agency's second-in-command, Paul Abbate, a week after the attack: 'from my first and second-hand information from conversations since January 6th, there is, at best, a sizeable percentage of the employee population that felt sympathetic to the group that stormed the Capitol.'[62] One FBI agent, who has since retired, embraced the conspiracy theory that the storming of the Capitol was a false flag operation mounted by Trump opponents. 'Insurrection my a$$,' he tweeted. 'It was a set-up.'[63]

When, in May 2021, a group of more than 200 retired admirals and generals calling themselves 'Flag Officers of America' published an open letter questioning the legitimacy of the 2020 election, it raised the spectre of rogue units in the US military supporting armed rebellion. Fearful also that far-right extremists were using the military in order to get weapons training, the Defense Secretary Lloyd Austin instructed his forces chiefs to root out extremists.

Christian evangelical Republicans had also become 'outsized' supporters of political violence and QAnon, according to recent research from the academic Rachel Kleinfeld. 'The bedrock idea uniting right-wing communities who condone violence,' wrote Kleinfeld, 'is that white Christian men in the United States are under cultural and demographic threat and require defending – and that it is the Republican Party and Donald Trump, in particular, who will safeguard their way of life.'[64]

As well as representing a cross-section of conservative America, the January 6th rebellion had sizeable public support. Even afterwards, polling suggested one in three Americans thought violence against the government was justified.[65] A poll conducted by the University of Chicago suggested that 38 per cent of conservatives thought it may soon be necessary to take up arms against the government.[66]

This mainstreaming of violent extremism is sometimes reported as if it is a new, Trumpian phenomenon. Yet there is no shortage of antecedents. In the late 19th century, the Louisiana-based terror group, Knights of the White Camelia, was made up of upper-class southerners, including landowners, physicians and newspaper editors. The White Citizens Councils, formed in response to the *Brown* decision, considered themselves more respectable than the Klan, and attracted members from the more well-heeled echelons of southern society – 'the quintessence of the civic luncheon club,' observed the journalist David Halberstam in the mid-1950s.[67] Yet although economic coercion was their preferred mode of intimidation, the councils also incited lynchings, arson and killings. Byron De La Beckwith, the racist who murdered the NAACP activist Medgar Evers, was a member of a White Citizens Council.

The ultra-right John Birch Society, a group named in tribute to a US intelligence officer killed at the end of World War II by Chinese communists, offers another case study in mainstream extremism. When the candy manufacturer Robert Welch founded it in 1958, leading businessmen made up its small cabal of early backers. Thereafter, its membership, which reached some 100,000 at its peak in the early 1960s, included 'highly substantial figures in local communities', according to an investigation by *Commentary* magazine in 1961: 'physicians, stockbrokers, retired military officers, lawyers, businessmen (particularly small and middle-sized manufacturers in the Midwest and South) and professionals.'[68] When, ahead of the 1964 presidential contest, the conservative intellectual William F. Buckley Jr tried to persuade the Republican presidential nominee Barry Goldwater to disown the Birchers, the Arizona senator responded, 'Every other person in Phoenix is a member of the John Birch Society. I'm not talking about commie-haunted apple pickers or cactus drunks. I'm talking about the highest caste of men of affairs.'[69]

Given its recurrence throughout history, it should come as little surprise that January 6th has not brought an end to political violence. Ahead of the 2022 midterms, there was a failed kidnap attempt on the then Speaker Nancy Pelosi, when a 42-year-old man broke into her San Francisco home brandishing hammers, tape, rope and zip ties. 'Where's Nancy?' shouted David DePape, echoing the cry on January 6th of insurrectionists who roamed the corridors in search of her. Then, when he realised she was not there, he clubbed her husband, Paul Pelosi, smashing the hammer into the 82-year-old's skull. In 2023, a gunman targeted the Democratic Governor of Wisconsin, Tony Evers, twice on the same day. First the assailant turned up at the State Capitol in Madison carrying a handgun. Then, after being arrested and bailed, he returned later on, carrying an AK-47-style rifle.

Physical threats to themselves and their families was a central reason cited by Republican lawmakers for retiring from Congress in 2022, rather than seek re-election. This marked a disturbing new trend. Though it was routine for moderates to be 'primaried' out of politics, now they were being terrorised into early retirement.

Donald Trump has continued to threaten political violence, and his supporters have continued to act on those threats. When faced with federal indictment after the FBI raided his mansion at Mar-a-Lago to retrieve top secret documents, Trump told the right-wing radio host Hugh Hewitt, 'I think if it [an indictment] happened, I think you'd have problems in this country the like of which perhaps we've never seen before.' Days afterwards, the FBI shot dead an armed man who was trying to attack its office in Cincinnati, Ohio, and since then threats against FBI agents and facilities have increased by 300 per cent.[70] Ahead of his arraignment in New York, where he became the first current or ex-president ever to be indicted, Trump again warned of 'death and destruction', which fortunately did not eventuate.

Often it is said that Trump did not change the modern-day Republican Party, he simply revealed it. The same could be said of American political violence.

3

The demagogic style in American politics

Just seven weeks after the storming of the Capitol came the consecration of Donald Trump at a conservative conference in Orlando that felt more like a cult conclave. Under the palm trees that lined the sidewalk outside, flora that seemed fittingly apostolic, Trump followers bellowed the former president's name through Stars and Stripes bullhorns and cheered when a mobile billboard was driven past illuminated with what was meant to be a trolling taunt: 'January 6th Reunion.' As I myself discovered, journalists who interviewed members of the crowd, and pushed back against the fantasy that Trump had been the victim of some terrible electoral fraud, were encircled by angry supporters with the manic energy of Big Lie true believers. More so than ever, the press were the enemies of the people. It was the first time during the Trump years that I actually felt physically at risk.

All religions need demons as well as prophets, and inside the convention hall delegates could purchase Nancy Pelosi toilet paper and 'Not my Dictator' t-shirts, portraying Joe Biden with a Hitler-style moustache. There was also the usual Trump paraphernalia: 'Trump 2024' baseball caps; flags and fridge magnets; pennants emblazoned with mantras such as 'Jesus is my Saviour. Trump is my president'; and 'The best part of waking up is Donald Trump'. But here, a gleaming coup de grâce, was something we had not cast eyes on before: a gold-plated statue of Donald Trump wearing garish 'Old Glory' swim shorts, which looked like the 1980s had thrown up all over it. Delegates queued up to have their photographs taken alongside it, like giggling nuns posing next to the Pope.

The climax of the event came on the final afternoon of the conference – a Sunday, fittingly – when his arrival on stage, to deliver his first speech since leaving the White House, felt like a celestial event. It was not so much his resurrection, however, because it was clear by now that January 6th had not brought about his political death.

What made this appearance all the more momentous was Trump's ouster of Ronald Reagan as the object of worship. The Conservative Political Action Conference (CPAC) had long been a church of Reaganism. At its inaugural gathering in 1974, the then Governor of California became its first keynote speaker, delivering an address entitled 'We Will Be a City Upon a Hill'. As the former actor brought together the modern-day conservative movement – the alliance of evangelical Christians, trickle-down economists, constitutional originalists, gun enthusiasts and working-class Reagan Democrats – CPAC's annual conclave provided the big tent. The Ronald Reagan Dinner, which was held on the Saturday evening, remained the social centrepiece of the conference.

Tucking into their rubber chicken dinners that night were a good many traditionalist conservatives unhappy at Trump's role in inciting the insurrection. By then, his purge of the party had not yet cranked into full gear. Yet when a straw poll was held, 68 per cent of the CPAC delegates indicated they wanted Trump to run again in 2024. This thrice-married, twice-impeached, Putin-admiring former playboy, who only a few weeks earlier tried to engineer an American coup, had become the leader of a quasi-religious movement. A messiah complex came together with a martyrdom complex, the sense of shared victimhood that went a long way towards explaining his visceral connection with followers. It was Trump as godhead, and Trumpism as creed.

The deification of American political figures was hardly unprecedented. The January 6th rioters could have seen that for themselves had they peered up at the fresco in the eye of the Capitol rotunda, an artwork which looks like it belongs more in the Vatican or a Roman palazzo. Painted by Constantino Brumidi, a Greek-Italian immigrant who worked in the Eternal City, it portrays a God-like figure ascending to the heavens. This demiurge is surrounded by 13 maidens, representing the original US states, and flanked by two voluptuous female figures, the goddesses of liberty and victory. He is floating weightlessly above a Wonder Woman-like Columbia carrying a shield emblazoned with the Stars and Stripes and wearing a golden helmet crowned with a sculptured eagle. What looks like an American rendering of the *Adoration of the Magi* is actually *The Apotheosis of George Washington*. It was painted in 1865, the year that the Civil War came to an end, when the country was in desperate need of transcendent figures.

From the outset, as the idolatry of Washington served to show, America was ripe for demagoguery. Watching the crowds make the pilgrimage after Washington's death in 1799, John Adams complained that Mount Vernon, the late president's estate on the banks of the Potomac, had become 'the new Mecca or Jerusalem'. This he found unnerving, fretting, 'The feasts and funerals in honor of Washington is as corrupt a system as that by which saints were canonized and cardinals, popes, and whole hierarchical systems created.'[1]

Though Washington was not without his airs and graces – during the Revolutionary War, he insisted on being called 'your excellency', while as president visitors were expected to stand in his presence – at least he never encouraged this kind of hero worship. Like Adams, he feared that demagoguery posed a threat to the new republic. In the early weeks of the Constitutional Convention, he wrote to his friend and former comrade-in-arms, the Marquis de Lafayette, that the 'anarchy and confusion' that followed the American Revolution could be exploited 'by some aspiring demagogue who will not consult the interest of his country so much as his own ambitious views'.[2]

Part of the reason the framers were so resistant towards direct democracy was their fear of the emergence of a demagogic populist. 'History will teach us that ... of those men who have overturned the liberties of republics,' wrote Alexander Hamilton in *Federalist No. 1*, 'the greatest number have begun their career by paying an obsequious court to the people; commencing demagogues, and ending tyrants.'[3] James Madison concurred, warning in *Federalist No. 10*, 'Men of factious tempers, of local prejudices, or of sinister designs, may, by intrigue, by corruption, or by other means, first obtain the suffrages, and then betray the interests, of the people.'[4] The Electoral College was designed to prevent such a possibility. Yet this noble idea of the president as a statesman inoculated from popular passions, as an independent leader detached from partisan politicking, was never likely to survive long.

The first 'master of the masses' was Andrew Jackson. This unabashed populist traded on his rags-to-riches reputation as an orphan boy made good, and as a military hero who had vanquished the British at the Battle of New Orleans in 1815 and slain Native Americans during the first Seminole war in Florida. War turned him into a celebrity, and in fiery stump speeches he railed against the privileged eastern aristocracy, and presented himself as a man of the people.

At the 1824 presidential election, his first attempt to reach the White House, his main opponent John Quincy Adams became the perfect foil. Not only was Adams the darling of the wealthy, as the son of the country's second president he also had the born-to-rule air of hereditary privilege. Jackson won the popular vote, but not, crucially, a majority in the Electoral College, which meant the election was decided by the House of Representatives. There, the then House speaker Henry Clay colluded with Adams to help win him the presidency in return for being appointed as Secretary of State in the incoming administration. The 'corrupt bargain' was how this stitch-up came to be known. With Jackson claiming he had been swindled out of the presidency, he won four years later by pioneering an early form of grievance politics.

The 1824 campaign was the ugliest and most vicious that the new republic had seen to date, featuring allegations that Jackson was the mixed-race offspring of an English prostitute and a 'Mulatto man' of African heritage. Opponents claimed he had massacred his own soldiers for desertion during the War of 1812, and devoured the dead bodies of Native-American women and children. Often the 1824 contest is referred to as 'the first modern presidential election', because Jackson was the first candidate to actively campaign – something which had previously been regarded as suspiciously demagogic. But its conspiratorial fervour also made it foreshadowing. Despite all the mudslinging, Jackson romped to a landslide victory, winning 55 per cent of the vote.

So strong was his everyman appeal that it is tempting to see Old Hickory's election as a popular uprising, a view reinforced by the raucous scenes at his inauguration, which were likened to the 'inundation of the northern barbarians into Rome'.[5] After an outdoor ceremony at the East Portico of the US Capitol, the first inauguration held there, the moshpit of Jackson supporters celebrating the triumph of 'the people's president' converged on the White House. As supporters rampaged from room to room in search of liquor, the new president had to escape out of fear of being crushed in the melee. Evidently, it was too much even for a president who famously remarked, 'I was born for the storm, and a calm does not suit me.'

Small wonder that Donald Trump viewed him as his presidential soulmate, placing his portrait in the Oval Office and making a pilgrimage to Jackson's Tennessee plantation, The Hermitage, to mark the 250th anniversary of his predecessor's birth. 'Inspirational visit,' Trump commented afterwards, 'I have to tell you, I'm a fan.' Steve Bannon even modelled Trump's inauguration on the saturnalia of Jackson's swearing in. Certainly, there was something Jacksonian about the MAGA hordes gathered at the base of Capitol Hill, who booed when Hillary Clinton, an Adams-like doyenne of the political establishment, made her entrance onto the inaugural platform and whooped when Trump spoke of 'American carnage'.[6]

More demagogues tried to follow in Jackson's path. Later in the 19th century came the prairie populism of William Jennings Bryan, a mesmerising orator known as 'the Great Commoner', who in 1896, aged just 36, became the youngest-ever presidential nominee of any major party. 'Bryan the Demagogue' ran the headline in the *New York*

Times from July that year, in a report which likened him to a French revolutionary.[7] Yet Bryan's progressive populism, which took aim at the East Coast financial establishment, could not win him the presidency on the three separate occasions on which he tried.

The 1930s witnessed the rise of 'the demagogues of the depression', a rogues gallery that came into much sharper focus during the Trump years as commentators looked for his antecedents. The Catholic priest Father Charles Coughlin parlayed his hatred of Jews, and his admiration of Nazis, into national celebrity. At his peak, Coughlin's radio show attracted an audience of 20 million and a postbag filled with 10,000 letters a day. The Governor of Louisiana, Huey Long, known simply as 'Kingfish', also became a darling of the masses, again by attacking the East Coast financial and political elite. In inflammatory speeches, which pre-empted some of the rhetoric of Donald Trump, he raised the spectre of a popular rebellion. 'Unless we provide for the redistribution of wealth in this country, the country is doomed; there is going to be no country left here very long.' A 'backwoods demagogue' is how the journalist H. L. Mencken described him, but his appeal was broader, and included members of the middle as well as working class.

The threat proved short-lived. Long was assassinated in September 1935. By the end of the '30s, Coughlin had dug his own grave, after plagiarising a speech by Joseph Goebbels which he published under his own byline. Yet the appetite for demagoguery remained unsated, as the political ascent of the aviator Charles Lindbergh attested. The first airman to fly solo across the Atlantic, Lindbergh demonstrated the ease with which fame could be transferred into the political realm. Claiming to speak on behalf of 'the silent majority', Lindbergh became the leading light in the America First movement, a group opposed to US involvement in World War II. Even being awarded the Service Cross of the German Eagle by the Nazi propaganda chief Hermann Goering in 1936 had failed to dent his popular appeal.

The horrors committed by Hitler and Mussolini should have annulled any lingering appeal of demagogues. Yet in the post-war years the rise of a Russian totalitarian, Joseph Stalin, fuelled the ascent of the red-baiting anti-communist Joe McCarthy. No-one better embodied the paranoid style of American politics than 'Tail Gunner Joe', the senator from Wisconsin, who spied communist subversion in every American institution, whether it be the labour movement, the State Department, the Pentagon, Capitol Hill or Hollywood. Eleanor Roosevelt likened him to the Third Reich Führer, noting, 'McCarthy's methods, to me, look like Hitler's.'[8] In a private letter, President Harry Truman opined, 'There is no difference in kind between Hitlerism and McCarthyism, both being the same form of bacteriological warfare against the minds and souls of men.'

Despite these dark warnings, the era of McCarthyism lasted seven years, and only ended in 1954, when it was felt, finally and belatedly, that the senator had infringed too many democratic norms and transgressed too many behavioural boundaries. 'Have you no sense of decency, sir?' asked the counsel for the army, Joseph Welch, at a televised congressional hearing in 1954, after McCarthy had accused a young attorney in Welch's law firm of having communist sympathies.

Southern demagogues were two a penny. 'A fantastic parade of charlatans has marched across the hustings of the South since the Civil War,' wrote Allan A. Michie and Frank Ryhlick in their 1939 study, *Dixie Demagogues*. But, like Long in the 1930s, George Wallace, the bantam-sized governor of Alabama, demonstrated that they could attract a national audience. 'I'm gonna make race the basis for politics in this state, and I'm gonna make it the basis of politics in this country,' vowed Wallace ahead of his inauguration as governor in January 1963, a statement that became even more politically resonant as the decade wore on.[9] By 1968, when he stood as the presidential candidate of the American Independent Party, polls suggested that 40 per cent of Americans approved of him. In 1972, when he sought the Democratic presidential nomination, Wallace was on track to do even better. And though at the outset of his campaign, he tried to convince reporters that he was not the race-baiting segregationist of old, opposition to court-ordered busing quickly became his signature issue, while privately he bemoaned not giving white crowds enough 'n***er talk'. In the Florida primary, he trounced his Democratic opponents. By mid-May, he had accumulated 3.35 million votes, a million more than his closest rival, George McGovern, the eventual nominee. When Wallace crossed the Mason-Dixon Line to campaign in northern primaries, it immediately became clear his vote-winning capabilities extended beyond Dixie. In the Wisconsin primary, despite entering the race at the 11th hour, he came an impressive second.[10]

When recalling Wallace's 1972 bid for the presidency, the attempt on his life in Maryland, which left him wheelchair-bound and forced his withdrawal from the race, is inevitably the focus. But we tend to forget how close he came to winning the Democratic presidential nomination. Even while convalescing in hospital, Wallace swept the Michigan and Maryland primaries.

In the post-war years, changes to the way major parties selected their presidential nominees opened the door wider for demagoguery. From the mid-19th to the mid-20th century, the choice had been left to party bosses meeting in smoke-filled rooms, a process that was hardly democratic, but which weeded out extremist candidates. Starting in the 1950s, when the folksy Tennessean, Senator Estes Kefauver, challenged President Truman in New Hampshire, a state he traversed wearing his trademark coonskin cap, the influence of the primaries grew. In 1964, the Arizona senator Barry Goldwater had racked up enough primary victories by the time Republicans gathered for their convention at the Cow Palace in San Francisco that he secured the nomination on the first ballot. Goldwater, who proclaimed during his acceptance speech that 'Extremism in the pursuit of liberty is no vice', showed how a politician from the fringe of his party could emerge from the primary process at its centre.

Economic hard times in the early 1990s provided the seedbed for another wave of demagoguery. Pat Buchanan, who also used the primary process to mount an assault on the Republican establishment, was an old-style populist offering simple solutions to complex problems. 'Pitchfork Pat' laid the blame for the country's economic woes on mass immigration, and framed politics as a battle between ordinary Americans and an East Coast political, economic and cultural elite, a now-familiar script. Even though he had once described Hitler as 'an individual of great courage' and saw apartheid

South Africa as 'an outpost of Western empire and Western civilisation', he still won the 1992 New Hampshire primary.[11]

When Buchanan faded thereafter, Ross Perot took on the demagogic mantle. His anti-elitist rhetoric was much the same. 'The British aristocracy we drove out in our Revolution has been replaced with our own version', he harangued, 'a political nobility that is immune to the people's will.' His folksy style, glib answers, talent for oversimplification and anti-Washington broadsides created a 'Perot phenomenon'. Never before in the history of Gallup polling had a third-party candidate led the national polls, a feat he achieved in the summer of 1992. Both Buchanan and Perot were harbingers of Trump.

Sarah Palin, the former governor of Alaska who was the surprise choice as John McCain's running mate in 2008, broke something of a glass ceiling when she became the country's first female demagogue. But she displayed the hallmarks of her male forebears. There was her folksy populism (she mocked the 'Yes We Can' idealism of Barack Obama as 'hopey, changey stuff'), fear mongering and truth-twisting, all of which came together when she claimed that Obamacare would lead to the creation of 'death panels' to determine whether the elderly would receive care.

A pin-up of the Tea Party, she claimed to be the mouthpiece of 'real America' and 'real Americans', and looked in 2012 like she might be able to mount a viable bid for the Republican presidential nomination, despite being so manifestly unqualified for high office. Crucially, this did not matter to her followers. When she failed to answer even the simplest questions from reporters, it was viewed as proof that the liberal elite were out to get her.

American demagoguery is not solely the preserve of the populist, paranoid or racist right. Andrew Jackson founded the modern-day Democratic Party, and was celebrated at annual Jefferson-Jackson fundraising dinners. William Jennings Bryan was a leading progressive, who eventually served as Woodrow Wilson's vice president. Blue America, as it came to be known, was also prone to hero worship, as the political aphorism 'Democrats fall in love, Republicans fall in line' suggests.

There was the cult of the Kennedys, which for decades spurred the quadrennial search for a candidate to head the Democratic ticket who matched the winsomeness and charisma of JFK and RFK. Barack Obama, almost from the moment he delivered his break-through speech at the 2004 Democratic convention, became an object of devotion. 'Obamamania' was quasi-religious in its intensity, what with the iconography of Shepard Fairey's HOPE poster, and the hymnal from the Black Eyed Peas front man, will.i.am, based on the Obama mantra, 'Yes We Can'. Nor was the euphoria surrounding his candidacy restricted to America, as the people of Berlin demon-strated in the summer of 2008, when Obama drew a crowd some 200,000 strong.

If not the content, the staging of these events bordered on the demagogic. In Berlin, the Obama advance team placed him at the foot of the Victory column in the Tiergarten. Denver's Mile High Stadium became the outdoor setting for his acceptance speech at the 2008 Democratic convention, which the candidate delivered on a pillared stage which was meant to mimic the White House, but which looked like the Parthenon. Had a right-wing candidate appeared in such an imperious setting, the press would have had a field day. But, for the most part, reporters present seemed spellbound, and did not focus too much on this audacity of hype. Obama was no more a demagogue than Kennedy. He didn't adhere to the populist playbook of using emotion and prejudice over reason. Like Kennedy, a sense of cool detachment was central to his appeal. Nonetheless, both bene-fited from the adulatory strain in US politics, the tendency to laud, lionise and idolise.

Nor was it just Obama, and nor was it just politics. The end of the Fairness Doctrine during the Reagan years, the regulatory require-ment for broadcasters to air a parity of opposing political views, paved the way for the rise of demagogues of the airwaves, such as Rush Limbaugh. Believing that the talkback formula would be just as profitable on cable as it was on radio, Rupert Murdoch and Roger Ailes then founded Fox News in the mid-1990s. Its most profitable stars were invariably its most outspoken anchors, blowhards such as Bill O'Reilly, Sean Hannity and Tucker Carlson.

On his website, Infowars, Alex Jones achieved the same success online with his nonstop stream of paranoia. All peddled the same populist nationalism riven with grievance, nativism, anti-elitism and conspiracy. Demagoguery had entered the digital era, and the algorithms loved extremism. The princes of Silicon Valley, like Steve Jobs of Apple, also encouraged this kind of demagoguery with their showy product launches and corporate cults of personality. Many of them embraced this messiah complex. In the early days of Amazon, Jeff Bezos was once asked whether he could spell profit. He replied 'P-R-O-P-H-E-T'.[12]

In all of these demagogic political figures we find common traits. Even if not pious or overtly religious, many draped themselves in religiosity. Often they used a low church form of liturgy at rallies which strengthened the sense of communion with their followers. William Jennings Bryan, who has been labelled 'God's demagogue', was a preacher politician. His most famous 'Cross of Gold' speech, which demanded that America detach itself from the gold standard, recalled the crucifixion: 'You shall not press down upon the brow of labor this crown of thorns: you shall not crucify mankind upon a cross of gold.'

Father Coughlin was a man of the cloth, even if his church in Michigan was nicknamed 'The Shrine of the Little Führer'. Campaigning for the presidency in 1972, George Wallace wore colourful suits and had slicked-back hair, the mien of the TV evangelist: as the journalist Theodore White observed, the former governor had cast off the 'undertaker's uniform' he wore in the early 1960s. Wallace's second wife, Cornelia, a former Alabama beauty queen, was dubbed by his campaign manager, 'the Jackie Kennedy of the rednecks', but there was something of the Tammy Faye Bakker about her as well. His rallies began with a 'foot-stomping rendition of "Give Me That Old Time Religion",' wrote a reporter with the Associated Press who was assigned to his campaign, and felt 'more like a revival than a political appearance'.[13] When Pat Buchanan ran in 1992, his

Catholic social conservatism became a hallmark of his brand. Some of his most enthusiastic support in New Hampshire came at prayer breakfasts.

Americans have long had a weakness for conviction politicians who speak with the certainty of prophets. It should therefore have come as no surprise when Trump attracted so much support from white evangelical Christians – more than 80 per cent in 2016. Trump happily retweeted comments suggesting his presidency was akin to the 'second coming of God', while the fact that he descended a golden escalator to announce his run for president, a heavenly portal in the minds of some of his supporters, suggested he was the 'chosen one'.

One of the most striking images of his presidency came when evangelical preachers visited him in the Oval Office, and laid multiple hands on him as they prayed. It looked like a scene from *The Exorcist*. Indeed, anyone who struggled to comprehend how a twice-divorced Manhattan playboy could win so much support in the Bible Belt had not been watching Christian cable.

Most demagogues were skilled at manipulating the media. Coughlin and Long understood the intimacy of radio – as did FDR, whose fireside chats brought charges of demagoguery. Joe McCarthy learnt the daily rhythms of the news cycle, timing his public statements to coincide with important news junctions and reporters' deadlines. Not only did Tail Gunner Joe understand the power of television, but also the vacuousness of the new medium. 'People aren't going to remember the things we say on the issues here, our logic, our common sense, our facts,' he once told Roy Cohn, his aide who went on to tutor Donald Trump. 'They're only going to remember the impressions.'[14]

What was striking about the demagogues of the 20th century was how easily they won mainstream acceptance. Lindbergh's America First movement enjoyed support from Walt Disney and Henry Ford. McCarthy was a close friend of Joe Kennedy, dated both Patricia and Eunice Kennedy, and became a regular visitor to the family compound at Hyannis Port. Robert Kennedy served as an aide for the notorious Senate Permanent Subcommittee on Investigations chaired by McCarthy – although he resigned five months later in protest at his guilt-by-association tactics. Jack Kennedy was a friend. When the Senate voted in 1954 to censure McCarthy, after tiring of his crackbrain tirades, Kennedy was in hospital recuperating from life-threatening surgery on a wartime spinal injury. Yet unusually for a senator absent from a critical vote, he did not seek a pair. His reticence on McCarthyism partly explained why leading liberals, such as Eleanor Roosevelt, doubted his progressive credentials. But JFK understood that McCarthy was hugely popular with his blue-collar Massachusetts constituents.

After George Wallace was forced from the race in 1972, George McGovern, the most left-wing presidential candidate the Democratic Party had ever fielded, tried repeatedly to secure his endorsement. George H. W. Bush had to offer Pat Buchanan a keynote speaking slot at the 1992 Republican convention, which Pitchfork Pat used to deliver his famed 'Culture War' speech in which he claimed, 'There is a religious war going on in this country. It is a cultural war so critical to the kind of nation we shall be as the Cold War itself, for the war is for the soul of America.'

Frequently, these populist extremists shaped public policy. Coughlin and Long heavily influenced Roosevelt's New Deal, forcing him to drift leftwards after his early policies were deemed too Wall Street-friendly. The so-called 'Second New Deal', from 1935 to 1936, which included interventionist economic reforms that Roosevelt initially opposed, came partly in response to Long and Coughlin's anti-business populism. 'Roosevelt owes his liberal sainthood,' noted the veteran journalist Robert Sherrill, 'to having been goaded by ideological roughnecks like Long and Coughlin into advocating reforms he was basically rather cool to.'[15]

The virulent anti-communism of McCarthyism shaped US foreign policy for decades after his demise. No president wanted to be accused of being soft on communism, which was partly why Truman waged war on the Korean Peninsula, a conflict in which more than 36,000 Americans lost their lives, and why Eisenhower, Kennedy, Johnson and Nixon Americanised the war in Vietnam.

Though Barry Goldwater was buried by a landslide in 1964, his hardline campaign provided the blueprint for Republican victories in five of the next six presidential elections. As the columnist George Will once so memorably put it, 'He lost 44 states but won the future.'[16]

Likewise, George Wallace shifted the parameters of political acceptability. Prior to his success in the 1972 Florida primary, as his biographer Dan T. Carter has noted, the White House had ruled out President Nixon ever going on national television to make a speech that was anti-busing. Less than 48 hours after Wallace's victory in the Sunshine State, however, the president did just that by calling for a moratorium. Pat Buchanan's overt nativism made the Republican Party more hostile towards immigrants. Joe Biden has resumed construction of a section of Donald Trump's fabled border wall (although, pre-Trump, the Bush and Obama administrations had erected hundreds of miles of walls and fencing along the southern border).

Always there has been a tendency to relegate American demagogues. To view them as fringe figures. To see them as bit players in some historical sideshow. But, as the rise of Trump served to show, they were more central to the story.

———

Nine months before Donald Trump descended his golden escalator came another foretaste of how a demagogue with extreme nationalistic views could fill a stadium. The setting was Madison Square Garden, the venue for that Nazi rally in 1939. The capacity crowd came decked out in fanwear. The object of devotion was the Indian prime minister, Narendra Modi, a Hindu extremist who doubtless could have shot someone on Fifth Avenue, two blocks away, on his way to the rally without much affecting the size of the crowd. Certainly, his Indian-American supporters seemed unperturbed by longstanding allegations of complicity in Gujarat's anti-Muslim pogrom in 2002 during his tenure as chief minister of the state (Modi had been cleared of wrongdoing by an investigative team appointed by India's Supreme Court but could have done more to stop the bloodshed).

Back then, the Bush administration had banned him from enter-ing the United States, let alone granting him access to the country's most storied sports arena. But for this Sunday afternoon rally, the joke was that the venue had become 'Modison Square Garden'. The colour, vibrancy and Bollywood panache of Indian political theatre had been fused with the stage management of a US convention – this was the arena where Bill Clinton accepted the Democratic nomination in 1992, and where the Republicans held their 2004 convention in order to tap into the nationalism aroused by September 11th. Red, white and blue balloons were primed to fall at the rally's finale. A portrait of Modi modelled on the Obama HOPE poster became the event logo.

My lasting memory from the rally was not so much the wild reception that Modi received as he entered the arena from a side door, surrounded by a phalanx of bodyguards in the manner of a prize fighter shuffling his way to the ring. Rather, it was the greeting bestowed on him by US politicians, including the African-American Senator for New Jersey, Cory Booker, and Bob Menendez, then the chair of the Senate Foreign Relations Committee. Lined up around the perimeter of a stage erected in the heart of the arena, they formed what looked like an honour guard. Then they applauded as Modi passed them by and gladly, if somewhat awkwardly, returned his namaste gesture with ingratiating bows.

So fawning was this charm offensive – India had become a useful counterweight to China – that when Modi visited Washington after-wards, President Obama gave him a surprise tour of the Martin Luther King memorial, where they peered up at the towering white sculpture of the slain civil-rights leader who had been a disciple of Gandhi. Later, when he penned a tribute to Modi for *Time* magazine's '100 Most Influential People' series, Obama wrote fondly of that visit, noting how this one-time tea-seller had risen from 'poverty to Prime Minister', an improbable story that mirrored his own.[17]

Modi's visit should have been a warning sign, a timely reminder about how easily an extremist could infiltrate the mainstream. Not only did this Hindu Nationalist co-opt the props of American politics – the balloons, the portraiture and the VIP surrogates. Modi tapped into national nostrums such as the American dream and even, with his visit to the MLK Memorial, the Black freedom struggle.

That very month, I had interviewed Donald Trump in the board-room of his eponymous tower, a conversation centred on the demise of his old gambling empire in Atlantic City, which hinted at how his glory days might be in the past. The possibility of a successful pres-idential run did not even arise; partly because it seemed risible to me, and partly, I suspect, because it was somewhat far-fetched even to him. Not for one moment did I think he would soon be packing stadiums with adoring followers, or lead a political cult.

Yet from 2015 onwards, Trump tapped into precisely the same anxieties as his demagogic forebears. A deep-rooted suspicion of central government; a collective sense of victimhood; an ugly nativ-ism, racism and hostility towards the other; an anti-intellectualism; an anti-elitism; a populist anti-capitalism; a nostalgic nationalism; and the drawing of battlelines which portrayed him as a David up against a Goliath. Trump benefited from the same extreme hatred of East Coast elites and the political establishment – a blinkered rage which allowed him to get away with ideological inconsistencies and all manner of other sins. Like previous American demagogues, he could tap into an unholy trinity of racism, religious fundamen-talism and the mass media's partiality towards a ratings-winning rabble-rouser.

In many ways, then, Trump became an amalgam of this dangerous tradition. The raucousness of Andrew Jackson. The racism of Father Coughlin. The economic populism of Huey Long. The America First isolationism of Lindbergh. The conspiratorialism of McCarthy. The 'angry white man' rage of Wallace. The nativism of Buchanan. The billionaire chutzpah of Perot. The serial stupidity of Sarah Palin. Throughout history, Americans had always been susceptible to demagogues promising to make their country great again, whatever their qualifications for the job.

4

American authoritarianism

Just as the rise of Donald Trump demonstrated the enduring appeal of an American demagogue, his four years in office testified to the allure of an American strongman. As president, he revived a kindred tradition, an authoritarian style of leadership which had been exhibited by a surprising number of his predecessors.

This became evident from the moment he raised his right hand to take the oath of office. Indeed, his first 36 hours in charge were his presidency in microcosm. His inaugural address had the ranting, ultranationalist tone of a rally speech, more potentate than fledging president. His inaugural parade he had wanted to display martial trappings. 'Make it look like North Korea,' he declared at one of the planning sessions, 'tanks and choppers' rather than floats and high school marching bands.[1] He even attempted to gaslight his compatriots into believing his inaugural crowd was the largest in history, demanding that they discount the evidence of their own eyes. All authoritarian regimes begin with an act of repression, and Trump was trying to quash the truth.

As this lunatic row flared, senior White House officials were dragooned into becoming propagandists. Sean Spicer, his barrel-chested new press secretary, was dispatched by the president to the White House briefing room, not to take questions from reporters, as ordinarily would be the case, but to bark out a statement with untrue claims about the meagre crowd size. Appearing on *Meet the Press* that same weekend, the White House aide Kellyanne Conway introduced into the lexicon the term 'alternative facts'. Trump's Washington instantly felt like Pyongyang on the Potomac.

On his first full day in charge, Trump tried immediately to co-opt one of the nation's 'power ministries' by heading over to the CIA headquarters in Langley, Virginia. 'Probably almost everybody in the room voted for me,' he claimed, 'because we're on the same wavelength, folks.' Then, standing in front of the honour wall commemorating agents killed defending freedom, he verbally bludgeoned the media, blasting members of the press pack as being 'amongst the most dishonest human beings on earth'. Undermining trust in the Fourth Estate, the monitors of baseline facts, was another classic authoritarian play.

More worrying, but less prominently reported than his crowd size deception, was his empty claim that up to five million votes had been cast illegally for Hillary Clinton in the 2016 election, which explained why she had outpolled him by three million votes. Even in victory, Trump defamed democracy, going as far as to appoint a Presidential Advisory Commission on Election Integrity, which, needless to say, found no evidence of widespread fraud.

Down the centuries, assuming the powers of the presidency had a chastening effect on incumbents. Washington spoke of his 'inability to perform' such an arduous role. 'The magnitude of the job dwarfs every man who aspires to it,' observed Lyndon Johnson, adding, 'I believe that every man who ever occupied it, within his inner self, was humble enough to realise that no living mortal has ever possessed all the required qualifications.'[2] Trump experienced the polar opposite of imposter syndrome. In his first television interview, with David Muir of *ABC News*, he put himself on the same pedestal as Abraham Lincoln.

Trump believed that power flowed through the tip of his Sharpie pen. Rather than focusing on advancing a legislative agenda, which he should have been able to accomplish given that the Republicans initially controlled both houses of Congress, he instructed his White House aide Stephen Miller to draft 200 executive orders that he could sign during his first 100 days. When the courts blocked one of his first executive orders, the Muslim travel ban, he harangued the federal judges who thwarted him, an unprecedented attack on the judiciary.

From continuing to hold campaign-style rallies throughout his presidency, which no incumbent had done before, to using his Twitter feed not just as a propaganda tool but an instrument to project his omnipresence (he sent more than 25,000 tweets during his four years in office), Trump continued in this authoritarian vein. New federal buildings should be designed in the classical style, he decreed, the architecture of authoritarians. Symbols of his power became something of an obsession. Treating them almost as executive toys, he was fixated with the purchase of new planes to replace the ageing Air Force One fleet, insisting on a red, white and blue colour scheme reminiscent of his old Trump Airlines to replace the stylish baby blue livery chosen by John F. Kennedy.

On July 4th in 2019, he orchestrated a 'Salute to America' military tattoo on the steps of the Lincoln Memorial, 'the show of a lifetime' featuring Abrams tanks, Bradley armoured personnel carriers and a fly-past including a B-2 stealth bomber, F-22 Raptor fighters and even one of the jumbo jets used as Air Force One (Trump had wanted a grand parade through the streets of Washington, but was told the tank traps would tear up the city's avenues).

Trump fired his FBI director, James Comey, something even Nixon did not do – a point underscored by the Nixon Presidential Library in a tweet after the sacking featuring the hashtag '#notNixonian.'[3]

When the Justice Department appointed the former FBI chief Robert Mueller to investigate allegations of collusion between the Trump campaign and the Kremlin during the 2016 campaign, the president claimed that Article II of the US Constitution granted him the power to fire the special counsel. In the summer of 2018, when it was thought, incorrectly, that Mueller was about to hand down an indictment of a sitting president, Trump claimed he was above the law. 'I have the absolute right to PARDON myself,' he tweeted in June 2018, a view that contradicted a Justice Department memo from 1974, which stated that no president could pardon himself because 'no one may be judge in his own case'.

When Congress thwarted his attempts to build a wall along the Mexican border, he declared a 'national emergency' so as to seize control of the purse strings. Seeking to barter US assistance for dirt on the Biden family, he held back military aid for Ukraine, even though it had been authorised by Congress, a blackmail scheme which led to his first impeachment.

Trump tried to create a continuous sense of crisis, whether it came in the form of the 'invasion' of immigrants crossing the southern border, disturbances in Portland, Oregon, gang-related murders in Chicago or the nuclear threat posed by North Korea. Trump's 'fire and fury' sabre-rattling, in which he threatened both North Korea and Iran with annihilation, was of particular concern, because the president has the sole authority to launch America's arsenal of atomic warheads – although his four years in office ended without him initiating any new wars.

The irony of Trump's crisis peddling was that when the country was confronted with a truly national emergency, during the Covid-19 pandemic in early 2020, he did his damnedest to downplay it.

His behaviour after succumbing to the virus became even more imperious. First, he insisted on being paraded in a presidential drive-past before supporters gathered outside the hospital. Then he choreographed a triumphant return to the White House, in which he came across as an American Il Duce, right down to the lordly balcony scene at the end. This primetime spectacular looked like bad comic opera, but we learnt afterwards that it could have been even more absurdist. Trump had entertained the idea of ripping off his shirt to reveal a Superman costume, the apotheosis of his hypermasculine style. Aides thought he was joking, but with Trump it was difficult to know for sure.

In private, Trump could be even more extreme than he was on Twitter. To deter immigrants from crossing the Mexican border, he suggested building an alligator moat stocked also with venomous snakes – aides even conducted a cost estimate – and that migrants could be shot in the legs to hamper their advance.[4] Journalists, he told his then National Security Advisor John Bolton and Defense

Secretary James Mattis, should not merely be imprisoned, but eliminated. 'These people should be executed,' he said, 'they are scumbags.'[5] When protesters gathered outside the White House at the height of the George Floyd protests, he asked his then Defense Secretary Mark Esper, 'Can't you just shoot them? Just shoot them in the legs or something?'[6] Trump also wanted to invoke the 1807 Insurrection Act, the law which allowed a president to use active duty troops on US soil to crush the protests.

Little of this should have come as a surprise, since one of the most blatant manifestations of his autocratic leanings was his unconcealed adulation of homicidal tyrants: the Philippines president, Rodrigo Duterte, the Saudi prince, Mohammed bin Salman, Kim Jong Un, and his friend and hero Vladimir Putin. I was travelling with Trump in 2019, when he invited the despot he once ridiculed as 'Little Rocket Man' to join him in the demilitarised zone that separated the two countries – a meeting teed up by a presidential tweet which gave it the feel of online dating. The impromptu summit also had the chemistry of a romantic reunion. No matter that the dictator's crimes included murder, enslavement, rape, torture, forced abortions, knowingly causing mass starvation and carrying out executions with anti-aircraft guns and flame-throwers.[7]

In their aptly timed book *How Democracies Die*, the Harvard academics Steven Levitsky and Daniel Ziblatt developed four behavioural warning signs to help identify an authoritarian. First, when a politician rejects the democratic rules of the game. Second, when he 'denies the legitimacy of opponents'. Third, when he 'tolerates or encourages violence'. And fourth, when he 'indicates a willingness to curtail the civil liberties of opponents, including the media'.[8] Prior to 2016, Nixon was the only modern president to meet one of these criteria. Within his first 100 days, Trump had ticked off all four.

In another timely book from the burgeoning 'democracy in peril' canon, *Strongmen: How They Rise, Why They Succeed, How They Fail*, Ruth Ben-Ghiat outlined various authoritarian traits: the emphasis on restoring national greatness, the threats of violence, and how personal obsessions become policy fixations.[9] Again, Trump could have ticked off all those boxes with his Sharpie. After leaving office, he even called for the 'termination' of the Constitution.

———————

Knowing that he would be the new republic's first head of state, and having discarded the idea that the executive should be made up of a panel rather than a personage, the Founding Fathers prescribed the powers of the presidency with George Washington firmly in mind. That partly explains why the office was so ill defined and expansive, and why there was comparatively little discussion about the role during the constitutional convention, over which Washington presided. How to configure the legislative branch consumed much more time. When it came to the presidency, the most lengthy discussions focused on the design of the Electoral College, and on how to impeach a president. The question of presidential power was inadequately addressed.

As they mulled the separation of powers between the executive, the legislature and the judiciary, the framers believed that the general who had surrendered his sword at the end of the Revolutionary War would exercise the same self-restraint as president. As one of his biographers Garry Wills neatly put it, he 'gained power from his readiness to give it up'.[10] Put another way, Washington would be his own check and balance.

It helped also that Washington had no great ambition to be president. Before travelling from Mount Vernon to New York for his inauguration, the then 57-year-old spoke of his reluctance in taking on the role. 'My movements to the chair of government,' he wrote, 'will be accompanied with feelings not unlike those of a culprit going to the place of his execution.'[11]

The legislative branch was supposed to exercise more power than the executive branch, a hierarchy reflected in the order of the Constitution, in which Article 1 deals with Congress and Article 2 the presidency. Nonetheless, the framers granted Washington a panoply of prerogatives. As well as making the former general the commander-in-chief of the army and navy, he could veto legislation, appoint ministers, ambassadors and Supreme Court justices, pardon those found guilty by the federal judiciary and make treaties, so long as two-thirds of senators concurred. Alexander Hamilton suggested that Washington should be made head of state for life, although it was decided that the leader should serve four-year terms, though they did not stipulate how many.

The founders had the foresight to imagine a world without the father of the nation. The maxim 'in Washington we trust' only went so far. Checks and balances were inserted to produce what Richard Hofstadter has called 'a harmonious system of mutual frustration'. But even though Washington was not given constitutional carte blanche, a paradox of the new republic was that the new American head of state had considerably more power than the old British king.

This, it is worth pointing out, was not as anomalous as it seemed. As the historian Eric Nelson has argued in *The Royalist Revolution: Monarchy and the American Founding*, the War of Independence was primarily 'a revolution against a legislature, not against the king. It was, indeed, a revolution in favour of royal power.' The complaint of some revolutionaries was that the British parliament had usurped too many of the powers after the Glorious Revolution in the late 17th century, which deposed James II, and that King George should have overruled Westminster and governed the North American colonies directly. It was parliament that was tyrannical not the monarchy, which bolstered the argument that American liberties were better protected by a strong executive rather than popular assemblies.[12] It was possible to be a 'royalist patriot'. Hamilton fitted that description.

Partly because of America's early status anxiety, and a desire that the country's new leader should be on a par with the monarchs of Europe, it was agreed that Washington should have a grandiose title. 'His Elective Highness' and the more wordy 'His Highness the President of the United States of America, and Protector of their Liberties' were two early contenders. His Supremacy, His Mightiness and His Magistracy were also in the running. John Adams, who served as Washington's deputy, preferred, 'Your Majesty'. Washington, however, favoured nomenclature that sounded more republican than regal: the President of the United States of America.

Washington had no interest in occupying a palace – Mount Vernon was more than adequate. He did not request a salary, although Congress insisted on paying him the princely annual sum of $25,000. In another sign of his modesty, when Washington discussed the design of the new national capital with the French architect Pierre Charles L'Enfant, he favoured a system of broad avenues but rejected the European penchant for monuments to individuals. Nonetheless, the presidency came with monarchical trappings. His inaugural celebrations in April 1789 featured what looked like a royal barge which carried him across the Hudson River to Lower Manhattan, where he stepped ashore onto a crimson carpet under a crimson canopy. There was a 13-gun salute, a small armada of ships in the harbour and a procession led by a troop of horses, two companies of Grenadiers and a company of Scottish Highlanders. A male voice choir even sang 'God Save the King', albeit with the insertion of Washington's name.[13]

Inevitably perhaps, there were complaints that George III had merely been superseded by George I. Jefferson likened the presidency to 'a bad edition of a Polish king'. Yet Washington used his powers sparingly. During his eight years in office, he issued only eight presidential proclamations. He was also respectful of Congress, regularly signing into law legislation which he opposed. Only twice did he wield his presidential veto.[14] Though he presided over the Senate on a few occasions – the Constitution does not forbid it – he found its deliberations tedious. In steering clear of Congress thereafter, he established a clearer demarcation between the executive and legislative branches.

Always he was mindful of being a role model: that he was personally drafting a code of conduct for future presidents. 'I walk on untrodden ground,' he said. 'There is scarcely any part of my conduct which may not hereafter be drawn into precedent.' From the moment he took his oath of office, he also understood that the founding was a joint enterprise, and that he was a first amongst equals. And just as he surrendered his sword after vanquishing the British, Washington gave up the presidency after two four-year terms. Though not originally a constitutional requirement, this became an unwritten convention.

America, then, had what the historian Arthur M. Schlesinger Jr described in the early 1970s as an 'imperial presidency', a term ordinarily associated solely with the excesses of Richard Nixon but which was intended to be more all-encompassing – he used it to describe a strong presidency, albeit with supposedly equally strong accountability. From the outset, however, the office was open to abuse. As Levitsky and Ziblatt have pointed out, 'The Constitution is virtually silent on the president's authority to act unilaterally, via decrees or executive orders, and it does not define the limits of executive power during crises.'[15] In defining presidential power, the constitutional scholars Aziz Huq and Tom Ginsburg have spoken of the 'thin tissue of convention'. Joseph Ellis notes: 'One of the beauties of inherently ambiguous definition of executive power in the Constitution was that it could expand or contract like an accordion.'[16] But that presented the opportunity for an American form of czarism as well – an opening for a leader like Donald Trump.

Once Washington had stepped down, his successors frequently tried to push presidential powers to the limit. John Adams, who succeeded Washington, attempted to ban the opposition. Exploiting tensions with France, the notoriously thin-skinned New Englander pressed Congress to pass the 1798 Alien and Sedition Acts, which had the draconian effect of criminalising criticism of the president. This led to America's first authoritarian crackdown, which included the prosecution for sedition of a Vermont congressman, Matthew Lyon, who had criticised Adams for his 'unbounded thirst for ridiculous pomp, foolish adulation and selfish avarice', and a Pennsylvania newspaper editor who had labelled him 'a power-mad despot'.[17]

Next came Thomas Jefferson, whose famed aversion to centralised government seemed to vanish when he was at the centre of government. Though the Constitution stipulated that the presidency did not have 'the sole prerogative of making war and peace', Jefferson dispatched a naval squadron to the Mediterranean to fight pirates in the Barbary War without the approval of Congress, which he wilfully misled. Likewise, he circumvented Capitol Hill in 1807 when the British warship HMS *Leopard* fired on the USS *Chesapeake* as it was leaving port in Norfolk, Virginia, which prompted him to unilaterally close American waters to British vessels.

Jefferson knew that the boldest move of his eight-year tenure, the Louisiana Purchase from France, was constitutionally dubious but pressed ahead regardless. Doubling the size of the United States, a land grab central to Jefferson's vision of America as an 'empire of liberty', was too enticing an opportunity to let the Constitution stand in his way. In fairness, he did propose amending the Constitution, and agonised over wielding a measure of federal power that made so hypocritical his criticisms that the Federalists, his great rivals, had acted like monarchists. Yet that would have been a lengthy process at a time when Napoleon was already showing signs of seller's remorse. Instead, he embarked on what Joseph Ellis has called 'the most aggressive executive action ever by an American president'.[18]

The Jefferson presidency was therefore at odds with the Jeffersonian idea of the presidency. As he conceded after leaving office, 'A strict observance of the written laws is doubtless one of the high duties of a good citizen, but it is not the highest. The laws of necessity, of self-preservation, of saving our country when in danger, are of higher obligation.'[19] Extraordinary times justified extraordinary measures, Jefferson was essentially saying, the rationale deployed by many of his successors similarly accused of executive overreach.

The first truly wartime president, James Madison, who served as commander-in-chief during the War of 1812, was more circumspect. As the chief architect of the Constitution, and the author of the Bill of Rights, he was reluctant to violate either its letter or spirit. Madison, however, came to be regarded as a weak president, partly because of his determination to work within constitutional confines. So again, an ominous idea took hold, that presidents risked being derided as bantams if they used their powers sparingly.

Andrew Jackson was not only the first populist president, but the first brazen authoritarian. The former general rejected the orthodoxy that the legislative branch was superior to the executive. To hammer home the point, he vetoed a dozen bills passed by Congress, a greater number than all his presidential forerunners. Vengeful and mean-spirited, Jackson bludgeoned his opponents, tried to censor northern abolitionists and was notorious for sacking cabinet members. His 'You're fired' approach to presidential staffing meant that he racked up four secretaries of state and five treasury secretaries, more even than Donald Trump.

During his eight years in office, Jackson pushed for only one major bill, the 1830 Indian Removal Act, which allowed him to carry out the forced eviction of Native Americans from their traditional territory with genocidal fury. 'The Trail of Tears', it was called by the Cherokee people. Ethnic cleansing by presidential fiat. Compounding one moral atrocity with another, Jackson wanted the vacated land to be used for slave plantations.

The age of Jackson may have been a phase of democratic expansion, but Jackson himself displayed some ugly anti-democratic tendencies. Opponents called him 'King Andrew I'. A 'democratic autocrat' is how a 19th-century biographer described him.[20] 'To detractors, he appears an incipient tyrant,' Professor Daniel Feller, the editor of the Andrew Jackson Papers, has noted, 'the closest we have yet come to an American Caesar.'[21]

More surprising in the rogues gallery of presidential authoritarians is the presence of heroes of the American story. No president, for instance, expanded the powers and prerogatives of the executive branch as quickly or as dramatically as Abraham Lincoln. To save the union, he was prepared to break the Constitution. After the first shots of the Civil War were fired at Fort Sumter, he ordered the mobilisation of a 75,000-strong militia force, blockaded southern ports and began assembling an army of volunteers, even though the Founding Fathers had specifically stated that it was the job of Congress to declare war and raise an army rather than the president. However well intentioned, the very act of waging civil war was unconstitutional, since

Lincoln was trying to coerce Confederates into rejoining a union they had decided to leave.

His early decision to suspend the writ of habeas corpus, the legal procedure barring the government from holding an individual indefinitely without showing due cause, was constitutionally dubious, to say the least. Lincoln claimed this legal guarantee could be lawfully suspended in 'cases of rebellion or invasion'. Yet these were powers laid down in Article 1 of the Constitution, thus implying they belonged to Congress not the president.

As the war intensified, Lincoln expanded the areas where the writ of habeas corpus was suspended. Ultimately, in September 1862, his Secretary of War, Edwin Stanton, issued a nationwide decree, which banned any 'act, speech, or writing, in discouraging volunteer enlistments, or in any way giving aid and comfort to the enemy, or in any other disloyal practice'. As well as being called 'the Great Emancipator', then, Lincoln was also dubbed 'the Great Suspender'.

Negating habeas corpus paved the way for the arrest of as many as 15,000 Americans, some of whom were apprehended simply for singing Confederate songs. Rather than the courts, they were tried before military commissions, and, if found guilty, served as political prisoners. Over the course of the Civil War, Lincoln also shut down more than 300 critical newspapers, most of them sympathetic to the Confederacy, an act of mass censorship which trashed the First Amendment. Together these measures amounted to 'the most extreme suppression of free speech to occur at any time in U.S. history', according to the Harvard law professor Noah Feldman, who describes Lincoln as 'a kind of dictator who could suspend constitutional rights at will, based on a claim of necessity'.[22]

Even his most celebrated wartime move, the issuance of the Emancipation Proclamation in January 1863, was unconstitutional. A president alone did not have the power to abolish enslavement. Lincoln himself publicly acknowledged that freeing the enslaved required a constitutional amendment, but he opted for the Jeffersonian defence that extraordinary times called for extraordinary presidential power. As he remarked in 1863, 'Certain proceedings are constitutional when, in cases of rebellion or invasion, the public safety requires them, which would not be constitutional when, in absence of rebellion or invasion, the public safety does not require them.'[23]

History has absolved Lincoln of blame. No president stands so tall. As part of his sanctification, he is venerated for remaining true to the idea of America if not the exact letter of the US Constitution. After all, he saved the union, and then, as his thinking and war aims evolved, brought about the abolition of slavery. Nonetheless, the leader widely regarded as America's greatest-ever president, whose memorial shares pride of place with Washington's on the National Mall, repeatedly violated his sworn oath to defend the Constitution. The Civil War turned him into what Feldman has called 'a constitutional dictator'.

Given this often-forgotten history, it was intriguing to witness the sense of horror when, at the height of the George Floyd protests in 2020, troops from the DC National Guard lined up in battle formation on the steps of the Lincoln Memorial wearing flak jackets, face masks and wraparound sunglasses. Soldiers who looked more like storm troopers were defiling Lincoln's shrine. Yet this ominous show of force, and the suspension of norms that it represented, was less historically incongruous than at first glance it seemed. When it came to iron-fist rule, Lincoln, after all, was no saint.

The back half of the 19th century saw a run of weak incumbents, which, from Andrew Johnson to William McKinley, even trivia hounds might be hard-pressed to name and place in order. Yet the emergence at the turn of the new century of the United States as a truly global power necessitated the resurgence of a powerful presidency. The Spanish-American War in 1898, where US forces intervened in the Cuban war of independence against Spanish colonial rule, highlighted the president's role both as commander-in-chief and the shaper of foreign policy. Fuelled by the jingoism of the popular press, the view took hold that a strong America required a strong American president.

McKinley, who was seen as a puppet of his political cronies, was not the man to meet this moment. His assassination in 1901, however, paved the way for Vice-President Theodore Roosevelt to take charge, a buccaneering New Yorker, viewed as a 'madman' within McKinley's inner circle, who relished an expanded and more aggressive role. Placing himself at the head of a great power rising, Roosevelt regularly circumvented Congress in pursuit of a more dynamic foreign policy, and added his signature to more than a thousand executive orders to pursue his progressive domestic agenda.

During his eight years in office, he came to believe that all executive actions were permissible unless deemed impermissible by law, an 'Unless I can't, I will' approach to presidential power. 'There was a great clamour that I was usurping legislative power,' he later reflected. 'I did not usurp power, but I did greatly expand the use of executive power.'[24] By making the White House rather than Congress the vital centre of Washington power, 'TR' created the modern-day presidency.

This maximalist view of presidential power took hold. Woodrow Wilson, who is usually cast as a paragon of progressive virtue, frequently bordered on the despotic. When confronted in 1917 with the twin threats of a belligerent Imperial Germany and the Bolshevik Revolution, he abandoned much of the high-mindedness that was supposedly his touchstone, and mounted a crackdown on German-Americans and radicals in the labour movement using tactics more reminiscent of a police state. German-Americans were imprisoned in internment camps – anti-German hysteria even extended to renaming the frankfurter the hot dog. Labour leaders were placed under surveillance. Industrial rebellions, which were spreading across the midwest, were ruthlessly crushed. Brutal counterinsurgency techniques, used by the military during the war in the Philippines, were deployed against American workers.

The passage of the 1917 Espionage Act allowed for the suppression of anti-war newspapers and the arrest of dissenters who resisted the draft. The 1918 Sedition Act curbed the right of free speech, and made it an offence to use 'disloyal, profane, scurrilous or abusive language' against the government, the American flag or the military. To flush out anarchists and communists, the Wilson administration created the General Intelligence Division, the first non-military intelligence agency, and appointed as its head a former clerk at the Library of Congress named J. Edgar Hoover. Mass arrests and mass deportations soon followed.

The period between 1917 and 1921 therefore became a dark interlude, as Adam Hochschild has recently chronicled in *American Midnight: The Great War, a Violent Peace and Democracy's Forgotten Crisis,* in which he shone a spotlight on the 'mass imprisonments, torture, vigilante violence, censorship [and] killings of Black Americans', and argued, 'A war supposedly fought to make the world safe for democracy became the excuse for a war against democracy at home.'[25]

When tensions rose during the Great Depression in the early 1930s, and impoverished veterans descended on Washington with their families – a group dubbed 'The Bonus Army' because of the payments they were demanding from the government – President Herbert Hoover ordered the most savage of crackdowns. In a military operation mounted in July 1932, and masterminded by General Douglas MacArthur, the administration deployed infantrymen wielding bayonets, four troops of cavalry, five tanks, tear gas and even a machine-gun squadron to clear away the protesters' encampments. 'When it was all over,' wrote the historian Howard Zinn of this often-neglected episode, 'two veterans had been shot to death, an eleven-week-old baby had died, an eight-year-old boy was partially blinded by gas, two police had fractured skulls, and a thousand veterans were injured by gas.'[26]

The ongoing economic crisis became the predicate for an extra-constitutional power grab by Hoover's successor, Franklin Delano Roosevelt, who, like Woodrow Wilson, is traditionally cast as a progressive hero. Though his first inaugural is best remembered for its opening paragraph, in which he told his fellow Americans that 'the only thing we have to fear is fear itself', the passage that generated more comment at the time was his call for a strong presidency operating at the limits of the Constitution. Though FDR vowed to work 'within my constitutional authority' and to abide by 'the normal balance of executive and legislative authority', he also warned of a 'temporary departure from that normal balance of public procedure,' a forbiddingly ambiguous phrase. What he wanted from Congress was 'broad executive power to wage a war against the emergency, as great as the power that would be given to me if we were in fact invaded by a foreign foe.'[27]

Over the course of his 12 years in office, he greatly enlarged the job spec of the presidency, becoming, in the words of his biographer William E. Leuchtenburg, not just a chief executive but also a 'chief legislator'. But in addition to all the New Deal legislation he pushed Congress to enact, Roosevelt issued more than 3522 executive orders in 4,422 days in office – or 300 a year – which was a record. Never before had the White House been staffed by so many advisors. His fireside chats gave him a degree of ubiquity in the lives of Americans that was also without precedent.

When the Supreme Court challenged his authority, ruling that nearly a dozen of the newly created New Deal agencies were unconstitutional, FDR tried to engineer a power grab. His controversial court-packing plan, which would have created as many as six additional justices, was intended to alter its political complexion and make it more malleable. Yet, in a rare reversal, the court-packing plan died in the Senate, where even usually pliant Democratic allies complained that one arm of the government, the executive, should not have the power to alter another branch of the government, the judiciary. The senior Democrat, James A. Reed, a one-time senator for Missouri, spoke for many when he called Roosevelt's court packing scheme 'a step towards making himself dictator in fact.'[28]

So appalled was the essayist H. L. Mencken that he drafted a satirical 'Constitution for the New Deal', which decreed, 'All governmental power of whatever sort shall be vested in the President of the United States.'[29] Yet in the era of Hitler and Mussolini, it was partly the fear of America succumbing to the European-style dictatorship that prompted FDR to seek dictator-like powers. Huey Long, he feared, could mount a challenge from the left, while the then army chief, General Douglas MacArthur, posed a threat from the right. 'If I fail,' Roosevelt confided, 'I shall be the last one.'[30]

Faced with the prospect of America being drawn into a second world war, FDR sought to accrue even greater powers. Three months before Hitler invaded Poland in 1939, the president altered the military chain of authority, so that the secretaries of navy and war came under his personal direction. In another break with tradition, he issued an executive order declaring what he called 'a limited national emergency'. Following the Japanese attack on Pearl Harbor, he urged Congress to pass the 1941 War Powers Act, which made the executive branch the strongest it had been in the nation's history by granting it the authority to carry out more surveillance on US citizens. A second War Powers Act, passed the following year, established two new agencies, the Office of Price Administration and the National War Labor Board, which gave Roosevelt unparalleled control over the economy.

On 19 February 1942, Roosevelt's personal day of infamy, he also added his signature to Executive Order 9066, which authorised the internment of every single Japanese-American on the West Coast. More than 125,000 Japanese-Americans, two-thirds of whom had been born on American soil, were rounded up and interned until the end of the war in what amounted to concentration camps. In its legal challenge, the American Civil Liberties Union grimly noted, 'Enforcing this on the Japanese alone approximates to the totalitarian theory of justice practised by the Nazis in their treatment of the Jews.'[31]

By then, Roosevelt had become the only president to dispense with the two-term tradition established by Washington, racking up victories in the 1932, 1936, 1940 and 1944 elections. Like his court-packing scheme, however, this came to be seen as a worrying departure from democratic norms. Two years after his death, a bipartisan coalition in Congress passed the 22nd Amendment, which established the two-term limit.

After Roosevelt's death in April 1945, Harry S. Truman inherited a vastly expanded presidency, and was determined to institutionalise its power through organisational reforms, such as the creation of a National Security Council at the White House. The threat of war with the Soviet Union became his pretext, since the president was now expected not only to be a national figurehead but also an international colossus: the leader of the free world.

Like Roosevelt, Truman used his existing presidential prerogatives to the full, and wanted to extend them further by dispensing with the two-thirds rule required for the Senate approval of international treaties. Truman was the only president ever to use the most awesome power at his disposal, by ordering atomic strikes on Hiroshima and Nagasaki, not that this violated the Constitution. He also sent US forces into Korea without congressional approval, which did. Through an executive order, he nationalised the country's steel mills when a strike threatened to shut them down – a decision overturned by the Supreme Court. As Arthur M. Schlesinger complained in *The Imperial Presidency*, 'The chronic international crisis known as the Cold War at last gave presidents the opportunity for sustained exercise of almost royal prerogatives.'[32]

Richard Nixon, the only incumbent ever to resign from office, came close to breaking the presidency. Most infamously, he was complicit in the cover-up of the break-in at the Democratic National Headquarters in the Watergate complex, the scandal which led to his downfall. By ordering the secret bombing of Cambodia without congressional approval, and sending troops into the country without the necessary authorisation, he also violated the Constitution. As part of an illegal domestic spying operation, he even ordered wiretaps on journalists whose coverage displeased him without seeking warrants from the courts. His 'enemies list', including reporters, businessmen, labour leaders, politicians and the Hollywood actor Paul Newman, was the stuff of tinpot totalitarianism.

Before Nixon's resignation, Congress moved to rein in his imperial presidency by passing the 1973 War Powers Act – which Nixon tried to veto. This required the president to notify lawmakers about troop deployments and to seek congressional approval for those lasting longer than 60 days.

After his departure, the view took hold that the Constitution worked. The threat alone of impeachment was sufficient to force his resignation. Thus, the country's democratic seawalls had held firm.

Yet the Nixon years established dangerous precedents. In the midst of the Watergate scandal, the Office of Legal Counsel in the Nixon Justice Department decreed that 'the indictment or criminal prosecution of a sitting President would impermissibly undermine the capacity of the executive branch to perform its constitutionally assigned functions', a precedent which stands to this day even though it has no grounding in the Constitution or Supreme Court opinions. By stating that '[t]he spectacle of an indicted president still trying to serve as Chief Executive boggles the imagination', the Justice Department created the impression that a president floated above the law, and that he could avoid the gravitational pull of codes and statutes.

Worse was to come. Less than a month after Nixon left office, his arms held grotesquely aloft in his trademark victory salute as he made his exit, Gerald Ford issued a presidential pardon which protected his predecessor from prosecution. 'Our long national nightmare is over,' Ford claimed, in a televised address from the Oval Office, 'Our Constitution works; our great Republic is a government of laws and not of men. Here the people rule.' But for all the lofty words, and for all the good intentions – Ford thought the pardon would help unify the nation – the decision reinforced the sense that presidents operated above the law. Certainly, Nixon appeared to think that himself. 'When the president does it, that means that it is not illegal,' he told the British journalist David Frost, in the most shocking exchange of their 1977 television interviews.

During his two years in office, Ford signalled he would conduct a less monarchical presidency. He dropped the playing of 'Hail to the Chief' whenever he entered the room, and replaced it with his old college football team's fight song. After beating Ford in 1976, Jimmy Carter also dispensed with some ceremonial trappings, as well as decommissioning the presidential yacht and reducing the size of his fleet of limousines – the elongated length of a presidential motorcade had long been a symbol of executive power.

Quickly the perception took hold, however, that Carter had allowed the presidency to become too feeble – although the Georgian's problem was arguably that he was too honest, given his inclination for

delivering unsparing speeches calling attention to the country's problems. 'We have not an imperial presidency,' complained Gerald Ford
in 1980, 'but an imperilled presidency.' By electing Ronald Reagan,
the American people indicated its desire for a stronger, more charismatic leader.

Delighted to be playing what his biographer Lou Cannon called
the 'role of a lifetime', Reagan not only set out to 'Make America great
again', his campaign slogan in 1980, but the presidency itself. He reinstated 'Hail to the Chief' and summoned again the US Army Herald
Trumpets, with their heraldic symbols and ceremonial tabards. The
backdrops for his speeches, such as the Brandenburg Gate in Berlin,
brought movie-style set decoration to politics. His administration
also revived some old Nixonian tricks such as keeping clandestine
operations secret from Congress – most notoriously, the illegal sale
of arms to Iran in order to fund the right-wing Nicaraguan rebel
group, the Contras.

Tellingly, however, Reagan was pretty much given a pass at the
time, while retrospectively the Iran-Contra scandal has done little to
taint his reputation or dull the cult of Reaganism. Americans could
live with a president who violated the rules, especially if he embodied
positiveness and national strength.

After Reagan, presidential power ebbed and flowed. George H. W.
Bush struggled with the performative requirements of the job, even
though, as a commander-in-chief and diplomat, he was among the
most accomplished of post-war presidents – as his leadership during
the first Gulf War and at the end of the Cold War demonstrated.
As Carter discovered, modesty and self-effacement were hardly
vote-winning virtues.

Bill Clinton, who understood the need for showmanship, was
determined to modernise the presidency by bringing it into closer
alignment with popular culture and by making it less stuffy and
emotionally aloof. Yet missteps, such as revealing on MTV that he
preferred briefs rather than boxers, diminished the standing of the
office. 'The Incredible Shrinking President,' blasted *Time* magazine's
famed cover in June 1993, featuring giant letters and a diminutive

Bill Clinton. Clinton even had to plead for meaningfulness after the Republican rout in 1994. 'I am still relevant,' he said at a primetime press conference in April 1995 that only one US network bothered to cover. 'The Constitution gives me relevance.'

Far from being imperial, the office now looked impotent, according to Gary Rose, a professor of government who in the late 1990s published a study on the waning power of the White House, *The American Presidency Under Siege*. The resurgence of Congress; the hounding of the modern-day media; the influence of unelected lobbyists. All had chipped away its prestige. Victory in the Cold War meant that it was no longer as necessary for Americans to rally around the 'leader of the free world'. In a further sign of diminution, Clinton became the first president since Andrew Johnson to be impeached, following his affair with Monica Lewinsky.

Under George W. Bush, the presidency started sliding into even deeper recession. During his first eight months in office, he was criticised for being a 'do-nothing' president who spent too much time on the golf course and clearing brush at his Texas ranch. The very fact that he was reading a book called *The Pet Goat* to a classroom of second-graders in Saratoga, Florida, on the most fateful morning of his presidency seemed to affirm his inconsequentiality. Yet after the attacks of September 11th, crisis underscored the centrality of the presidency.

National security again provided the pretext for George W. Bush – and significantly, his deputy, Vice-President Dick Cheney – to greatly expand executive power in ways that were constitutionally dubious. The denial of the writ of habeas corpus to terror suspects rounded up in Afghanistan. The torturing of prisoners. The warrantless surveillance programs conducted by the National Security Agency. The use of 'signing statements' – Bush issued more than a thousand of them – to assert a unilateral right to decide which laws he should enforce and which laws he could ignore. Just as the Cold War granted the presidency almost royal prerogatives, so, too, did an open-ended 'War on Terror'.

His successor, Barack Obama, a one-time constitutional law professor, was more respectful towards the Constitution. But even this liberal-minded president backed the NSA's spying program, persisted with the use of signing statements (albeit not so prolifically as Bush), and followed the usual presidential practice of launching military action without congressional approval. 'Shoot first, ask Congress later,' was his approach to military strikes against ISIS. When his administration brokered a historic nuclear 'executive agreement' with Iran, he deliberately did not label it a treaty so that he could avoid ratification in the Senate.[33] Because of his reliance on executive orders to circumvent Republican obstructionism on Capitol Hill, Obama was also pilloried for abusing the power of his office, although in actual fact he issued them at a slower rate than all of his predecessors going back to Grover Cleveland in the late 19th century.

An oft-heard criticism of both Obama and Bush was of executive overreach. But in these highly polarised times, a powerful executive is one of the few things that Democrats and Republicans agree on, so long as it is their party wielding that power.

Despite this long history of presidents using their powers to the full, and frequently crossing the line into either a constitutional grey zone or outright illegality, the trope persists that Donald Trump is completely without precedent. Yet this is only partially true. For sure, no modern-day president had trashed so many behavioural norms. No president had resisted so strongly the peaceful transfer of power. No president had ever before mounted a coup in the manner of January 6th. Yet in pushing the bounds of authority Trump was following in well-trodden footsteps.

Often it is said that what differentiates Trump is his rejection of democracy. Certainly, that sets him apart from figures such as Lincoln, FDR and Woodrow Wilson, who played fast and loose with the Constitution but who regarded the electoral process as sacrosanct, and were motivated by something larger than ego and self-glory. Yet Nixon was a democratic cheat, whose authoritarian paranoia reached the point where he even sought to corrupt a presidential election in 1972 that he was certain to win in a blow-out. Nixon also became so erratic in his final days – delivering drunken, self-pitying, Lear-like rants – that the Pentagon put in place safeguards to make sure any order to launch a nuclear warhead would not be acted on. After January 6th, General Mark Milley, who later described Trump as a 'wannabe dictator', also made sure the departing president could not push the button on Armageddon.

Nor can Trump be regarded as unique for combining the demagogic and authoritarian strains. His great presidential hero, Andrew Jackson, had already blazed that trail – and, it should not be forgotten, parlayed his claim of having an election stolen away from him into victory four years later.

From a historical viewpoint, what makes Trump markedly different, certainly from post-Civil War presidents, is the failure of his party to rein him in. When FDR tried to pack the Supreme Court, senior Democratic lawmakers blocked his path. When Grover Cleveland intimated that he would seek a third nonconsecutive term in the White House, he could not win the backing of his sceptical party. In Nixon's final days, a delegation of senior Republicans, including Barry Goldwater, made the journey from Capitol Hill to the White House to tell him to quit.

In the aftermath of January 6th, no senior Republican took an equivalent drive down Pennsylvania Avenue. The day after Trump had urged the mob to lynch his vice president, Mike Pence held a make-up session with him in the West Wing, having by that time already forestalled any serious discussion amongst Cabinet members of invoking the 25th Amendment, which allows for the removal of a president. Mitch McConnell, in full pearl-clutching mode, delivered a stern speech at the end of Trump's second impeachment trial stating, 'There is no question that President Trump is practically and morally responsible for provoking the events of that day.' But moments earlier, he had voted for his acquittal, and weeks later he indicated his willingness to vote for Trump if in 2024 he became the party's presidential nominee. With Trump, criticism from the likes of McConnell was frequently followed by capitulation.

Though the storming of the Capitol has not been followed by an equivalent of the Khrushchev epiphany in 1956, when the then Soviet leader stood before his party Congress to denounce Stalin's cult of personality, its aftermath did witness a Kremlin-like purge. Liz Cheney, the only Republican in a leadership position to persist in her criticism, was first ousted as House Republican whip. Then, when she sought re-election in Wyoming, she was 'primaried' by a Big Lie true believer. Of the ten House Republicans who voted for his second impeachment, four retired rather than run for re-election, and another four lost primaries to opponents backed by Trump.

A considerable number of Republicans have acquiesced to Trumpism out of fear. Strongmen have a tendency of making those around them seem weak. Few have exhibited the political courage of Mitt Romney, who became the first senator in history to vote to convict a president from his own party during Trump's first impeachment trial. Yet a frightening number of Republicans also appear to be untroubled by his fascistic tendencies.

Hardline conservatives have continued to nurture closer ties with figures on the European far right. The Hungarian prime minister Viktor Orbán, who John McCain once labelled 'a neo-fascist dictator', was feted at the 2022 CPAC conference in Texas.[34] Tucker Carlson took his Fox News show on the road to Budapest, to showcase Orbán's achievements. Ted Cruz addressed via video link a gathering of the Spanish far-right party Vox, and spoke of their 'shared values'. Leading conservatives celebrated the election in 2022 of Giorgia Meloni, Italy's most far-right leader since Mussolini. 'Buona Fortuna!' tweeted Mike Pompeo, Trump's one-time secretary of state.

It is precisely this authoritarian strain within the modern-day GOP, and within the conservative movement more broadly, that makes Trump so dangerous and historically different. His Republican allies have facilitated and often encouraged his lawlessness, which marks a break from the past.

Yet it is also important to acknowledge an essential continuity, for when it comes to authoritarianism in America Trump walked through a half-open door. He did not create a constituency yearning for an American strongman. Already it was in existence. At her husband's first inauguration in 1933, Eleanor Roosevelt noticed that the line of his speech that got the loudest cheer was his call for a strong executive that would test the bounds of the Constitution.[35] She herself, a fierce civil libertarian, suggested he should become a 'benevolent dictator'. Some of the country's leading newspapers went further. 'For Dictatorship if Necessary' was the supportive head-line the following morning in the *New York Herald Tribune*.[36] Even the liberal columnist Walter Lippmann lent support. 'The situation is critical, Franklin,' he wrote. 'You may have no alternative but to assume dictatorial powers.'[37]

Despite being pilloried by critics for his autocratic tendencies, and despite the furore surrounding his failed court-packing plan, FDR kept on winning election after election – in 1936, then again in 1940 and 1944. The 22nd Amendment would not have been required had American voters themselves not repeatedly endorsed a domi-nant presidency.

Later in the century, Lyndon Johnson won a landslide re-election victory in 1964, despite being accused by his Republican opponent, Barry Goldwater, of overreaching his powers. As Johnson memora-bly remarked, 'Most Americans are not ready to trade the American eagle in for a plucked banty rooster.'[38] After ditching the playing of 'Hail to the Chief', Jimmy Carter had to bring it back for special occasions, after complaints 'that I had gone too far in cutting back the pomp and the ceremony'.[39] Carter was forced to concede that Americans preferred a self-confident to a self-conscious presidency.

There has also been a tendency to forgive, as well as forget, the transgressions of iron-fist presidents. Despite his atrocities, the face of Andrew Jackson continues to adorn the 20-dollar bill. In polls of historians conducted between 1949 and 2005, he was ranked 'great' or 'near great' more than a dozen times.[40] Only in the last decade have Democrats started to change the name of their annual Jefferson-Jackson dinners, a staple of the political calendar, as they distanced themselves from his baleful legacy.

None of Lincoln's illegalities have dislodged him from his histori-cal throne of grace. FDR continues to be lionised, the internment of Japanese-Americans remembered but largely excused. Even Nixon's reputation has been rehabilitated, as his death rites in 1994 served to show. His coffin was carried by military pallbearers. There was a 21-gun salute. A band played 'Hail to the Chief'. His funeral in California was attended by the full complement of living presidents: Ford, Carter, Reagan, Bush and Clinton. Up until Trump, Nixon had been America's biggest political villain, yet he was given an affectionate and respectful national send-off, a posthumous version of his pardon.

Polls suggest there is surprisingly strong public support for presidents who trample on the Constitution. Back in the mid-1990s, one in 16 Americans thought that a military dictatorship would be a 'good' or 'very good' thing. By 2014, it had risen to one in six.[41] For millennials, faith in democracy has also waned. Polling suggested that only 19 per cent thought military rule would be illegitimate.[42] Survey data gathered between 2016 and 2017 found that almost a third of citizens believed that following the 'will of the people' was more important than abiding by constitutional principles that underpin the rule of law. Almost a third – 31 per cent – thought that having a strong leader who didn't bother with Congress was a good way of governing. Overall, almost a fifth of Americans were 'highly disposed towards authoritarianism'. Matthew C. MacWilliams, the academic who gathered much of the data, concluded, 'Trump support is firmly rooted in American authoritarianism.'[43]

Millions of voters supported Donald Trump, not despite his authoritarianism but rather because of it. It was central to his appeal. When he floated the idea during the 2020 campaign of 'negotiating' a third term in office, liberal critics may have been appalled but not his MAGA brethren.

In the presidential election, a greater number of Americans voted for him in 2020 than four years earlier. More than 74 million voters, either explicitly or tacitly, clicked on the terms and conditions of his unorthodox and imperious presidency, an 18 per cent increase on his vote four years previously. He won 25 states. A shift of less than 43,000 votes in three states – Arizona, Georgia and Wisconsin – would have thrown the election into the House of Representatives. Given that the Republicans dominated a greater number of state congressional delegations, Trump would have emerged the victor.

Even after January 6th, Trump remained the undisputed leader of the American conservative movement and the frontrunner for the Republican presidential nomination in 2024. The effortless ease with which he dismissed his challengers in the Iowa caucus and the New Hampshire primary confirmed his supremacy.

His brand of authoritarianism, which had now become his hallmark, remained popular too. Half of Republicans preferred 'strong, unelected leaders' over 'weak, elected ones', suggested an Axios-Ipsos poll conducted in September 2022.[44] So even though a second Trump presidency would likely be even more lawless than the first, by the midpoint of 2024 it had become frighteningly plausible.

If the evidence of Trump's authoritarianism was so overwhelming, why did we in the media not do more to call it out? Confessedly, it is a scratch I keep on itching. A problem for news organisations was that we were covering an abnormal presidency while trying to abide ourselves by normal rules of journalistic engagement. Likening a sitting president to a pre-war European dictator or a Latin American potentate violated *our* behaviourial norms. It crossed a line. Trump's attacks on the media, moreover, made impartiality even more of an imperative. Nor did we want to follow him into the gutter, which is precisely where he wanted us to descend. The problem was that in trying to remain normal, we normalised him.

Though we regularly used language such as 'jaw-dropping', 'unprecedented' and 'unorthodox', mainstream correspondents were reluctant to reach for stronger speech, such as fascist or, its diluted derivative, 'fascistic'. Many of us were squeamish even about using the word 'lie' to describe his thousands of falsehoods, because it implied we could read his mind, and be certain of intent. Similarly, we were hesitant about labelling him 'racist', despite decades of incriminating evidence. Though frequently we reported on his admiration for authoritarians, we were not ready to lump Trump fully in with them.

Institutional timidity also kicked in. The BBC complaints unit, a body independent of its news division, found against me when I described the ten out of ten score that Trump awarded himself for his handling of the Covid-19 pandemic as being amongst his 'ridiculous boasts'. However, to say that it wasn't ridiculous was ridiculous. The complaints unit also ruled I had overstepped the mark in speaking of Trump's 'narcissistic hunger for adoration' and 'mind-bending truth-twisting'. But, again, both were incontrovertible. Additionally, it found that I had broken the BBC's impartiality rules because my coverage of Trump was 'not offset by the limited, and relatively restrained, criticism of the Democrats, Joe Biden and Congress', in the words of the ruling. This was false equivalence gone mad, 'both siderism' taken to the point of absurdity. In order to speak of Trump's 'ridiculous boasts' was I expected now to concoct equally ridiculous boasts from Biden, and to cite evidence that did not exist? Evidently, our definition of impartiality has become so warped that we could no longer draw attention to Trump's flaws without suggesting a parity of wrongdoing from Biden.[45]

Fearful of being seen as elitist and anti-populist, especially in the aftermath of Brexit, even as august a news organisation as the BBC was sometimes hesitant about telling the full truth. This I say out of a sense of dismay rather than bitterness. I am reluctant to levy criticism against an organisation I love. But it meant we reported Trump as a rogue president rather than an aspiring autocrat or, as he later became, a fully-fledged authoritarian.

Another analytical shortcoming of the media as a whole was our failure to properly excavate the past. All too often we recycled the idle cliche that Donald Trump was 'a president like no other'. All too often we disregarded, or failed to explore, the history that contradicted that storyline. This failing exposed a larger problem, a form of exculpatory bias which was not liberal or conservative, but rather Whiggish. It was a 'better America bias': a presumption of progress predicated on the idea that US history was principally a parable of self-improvement and advancement. Though we were prone to excessive negativity about the present, we were guilty of excessive positivity about the past.

5

1776 and all that …

The simplest and most rousing depiction of the American story I have ever seen came at Walt Disney's Magic Kingdom during my first trip to the United States in the summer of 1984. It was a film entitled *American Journeys*, which was shown at an attraction called the 'Circle-Vision 360°', a ring-shaped auditorium in which the audience was encircled by nine giant screens. The presentation opened in the manner of a Gary Cooper epic, with shots of a covered wagon blazing a trail through a giant desert landscape. From the Wild West, we were transported over the Rockies, through the plains, from sea to shining sea, and then on to New York harbour, the starting point for so many American stories. Our itinerary took in fishing villages in New England, a hoedown in the Appalachian Mountains, a rodeo out west, the flight deck of a nuclear-powered aircraft carrier, the launch pad of the Space Shuttle, and the giant sculptures of Mount Rushmore. It ended at a Statue of Liberty illuminated by exploding fireworks – the rockets' red glare.

The orchestral soundtrack was rich and majestic – what sounded like a movie score by John Williams, interwoven with the tone poems of Aaron Copland. The commentary was delivered in a sonorous voice, with echoes of the Almighty. 'All Americans have shared a common dream. And the dream was that there was something here, in this vast unspoilt land, for each of us.' If that did not pluck sufficiently hard at the patriotic heartstrings, there were more tugs to come: 'Those first American journeys took many years and many lives, but the journey and the dream live on.'

This cinematic expedition doubled as a potted national story. Low points, such as the Civil War, were dealt with in the blink of an eye. 'The dream would not be without sacrifice,' admitted the commentator, without unpacking that troubling thought. Enslavement was never mentioned. True to the Hollywood formula, this was history with a happy ending. There was a happy beginning and middle as well.

Originally, the presentation at the Circle-Vision 360°, *America the Beautiful*, had served as Cold War propaganda. With its 'voice of God' commentary translated into Russian, it had been screened at the American National Exhibition in Moscow in 1959, the expo at which the then Vice-President Richard Nixon clashed with Nikita Khrushchev in their famed 'Kitchen Debate' over the competing merits of capitalism and communism.

An updated version of the film came out in the summer of 1984, on the eve of the Los Angeles Olympics, so I inadvertently became one of the first visitors to watch it. In an attempt by Disney to move with the times, and to make the American story more racially representative, the producers had added a scene from a jazz club on Bourbon Street in New Orleans, featuring an ensemble of African-American musicians. In the telling of an upbeat story, Black entertainers and sports stars were always useful supporting actors and character witnesses. Still there was no mention of how African-Americans had been denied access to the American dream for so much of the country's history. On the contrary. At one point, an actor playing Abraham Lincoln intoned, 'Most governments have been based on the denial of civil rights. Ours began by affirming those rights.'

Overall, then, the presentation continued to reflect the master narrative of the Cold War years: a story of unrivalled national success, shared values, common purpose and continual progress that, if not unanimously embraced, was widely agreed upon at the time.

My 16-year-old self was completely taken in by this blurring of history with folklore. Nor did it strike me as perverse that this historical presentation was housed in 'Tomorrowland'. One of the attractions of America was its focus on the future, which then seemed founded on an assuredness about the past. History served as glorious prelude. Of the here and now, it didn't ask too many troubling questions. A sucker back then for this kind of sentimentalism, I loved this Mickey Mouse version of American history.

Forty years on, things are very different, for the battlefields of yesteryear have become combat zones of the modern day. Rarely in American history has so much thought been given to history. Not only are we preoccupied with the political geography of America, but also its politicised historiography. Contemporary debates have become impossible to separate from days of old. Modern-day identity politics is a battle over who exactly comprises 'We the People', and the implications for equality and inclusivity of a phrase that has come to be regarded as so promissory.

The fight over gun control is a clash over the meaning of the Second Amendment. How to interpret the sweeping provisions of the 14th Amendment, with its guarantee of 'due process of law', 'equal protection' and birthright citizenship, is central to an array of contested areas: immigration, affirmative action, and, more recently, on whether its prohibition on former office holders 'who engaged in insurrection or rebellion' from occupying office again might apply to Donald Trump – the legal basis of attempts ahead of the 2024 election to exclude him from primary ballots in Colorado and Maine.

The past permeates almost every aspect of national life. No country in the world lives and contests its history with such passion and ferocity. The banners often held aloft by women in their 60s and 70s at pro-choice rallies speak of the ceaseless conflict: 'I can't believe I'm still protesting this shit.' History is no longer an anchor, but rather the storm seas that never calm. They could get even rougher as the country nears its semiquincentennial, its 250th birthday.

America has become so polarised, partly because of the splintering of its collective historical myths – one of the main functions of legends, after all, is to paper over cracks. How old fashioned it therefore feels to recall the lyrics from Bill Clinton's Fleetwood Mac theme tune during the 1992 campaign, 'Don't stop thinking about tomorrow', and the final line of its chorus, 'Yesterday's gone, yesterday's gone.' If only.

In a sign of the times, one of Joe Biden's first acts as president was to banish from the White House website the 1776 Report, his predecessor's pet historical project. He also disbanded the commission which produced it. Trump had wanted the 45-page report to push back against 'a radicalised view of American history [that] lacks perspective, obscures virtues, twists motives, ignores or distorts facts, and magnifies flaws', and to produce a 'pro-American' history curriculum promoting 'patriotic education'.[1] Following the president's instructions to the letter, the panel, which did not include a single credentialled historian, gave America a clean bill of historical health, especially on the question of race.

Far from being 'a uniquely American evil', enslavement was a global phenomenon foisted on the new republic. The report, which was published on the Martin Luther King public holiday in 2021, also absolved the Founding Fathers of any blame for owning enslaved people. Put simply, America was 'the most just and glorious country in all of human history'. End of story. George Orwell's famous line felt too strong: 'Totalitarianism demands … the continuous alteration of the past, and in the long run probably demands a disbelief in the very existence of objective truth.' But substitute the word 'totalitarianism' with 'Trumpism' and it rings truer. Trump, after all, had commissioned a work of fake history.

The 1776 Report was intended also as a rebuttal to the 1619 Project at the *New York Times*, which made no bones about its historiographical intent. 'It aims to reframe the country's history by placing the consequences of slavery and the contributions of black Americans at the very center of our national narrative,' its authors wrote when it was first published in 2019, on the 400th anniversary of the first ship carrying enslaved Africans arriving in what was then the English colony of Virginia.[2]

Since then, the fight over the teaching of history in schools has been conducted with almost the same intensity as battles over abortion and guns. Critical race theory (CRT), the concept that America's institutions were riddled from the start with systematic racism, has become the focus of fierce, sometimes even violent, contestation. Conservative-minded parents fear their children are being indoctrinated to hate America, and taught that they should feel shame and guilt for sins committed before they were born. Liberal-minded parents believe that schools should teach an unadulterated version of history, showing how the country has regularly fallen short of its professed ideals. How to interpret the past is where white identity politics and minority identity politics now face off.

School meetings have therefore turned into shouting matches, frequently requiring the presence of police. Many schools now hold meetings online, lest parents come face to face. Some school board officials have even received death threats. 'Brenda, I am going to gut you like the fat fucking pig you are when I find you,' read one of the threatening letters to a school board member, Brenda Sheridan, in Loudoun County, Virginia, an affluent suburb on the outskirts of Washington DC, who was being bullied into resigning her position.[3]

In 24 states, lawmakers have attempted to bring in educational gag orders, in an attempt to dictate how topics such as racism, sexism and American history are taught. Since September 2020, more than 200 local, state and federal government bodies have introduced more than 600 anti-CRT bills, resolutions and executive orders.[4] The Florida Governor Ron DeSantis has placed himself at the forefront of the 'war on woke', by passing the Stop Woke (Wrong to our Kids and Employees) Act. It bans the teaching in schools of any materials which would cause children to 'feel guilt, anguish or any other form of psychological distress' – a move, essentially, to shield white children from learning about Black history.[5] As a result, a school in Miami-Dade County even removed from its elementary library Amanda Gorman's Inaugural poem, 'The Hill We Climb'. Elsewhere, classics such as Toni Morrison's *Beloved*, Margaret Atwood's *The Handmaid's Tale* and Anne Frank's diary have been censored.

In these contemporary history wars, statues have become lightning rods. Neo-Nazis and torch-wielding white nationalists descended on Charlottesville, Virginia, in August 2017 for their Unite the Right rally, because the city had announced plans to remove a statue erected in 1924 of the Confederate general Robert E. Lee. In the George Floyd summer of 2020, demonstrators were more determined to tear down the monuments of white supremacy than to press for police-reform legislation.

Most of these memorials had been put up during the Jim Crow era to remind Blacks of their second-class citizenship. They were as much totems of the segregated south as 'whites only' water fountains. So down came statues of the Confederate president Jefferson Davis, his top generals, such as Lee, and slavery advocates, such as John C. Calhoun. When demonstrators tried to demolish a statue of his presidential soulmate, Andrew Jackson, in Lafayette Park opposite the White House, Trump called for them to be punished with the maximum sentences available under federal law, up to 10 years in prison.

History has not only become a driver of popular protest but of populist politics. Nostalgic nationalism explained much of the appeal of Donald Trump's slogan 'Make America Great Again', the genius of which lay in its lack of historical specificity. Without Trump offering up much of a timeline – when pressed by the editorial board of the *New York Times*, he pointed to the industrial expansion at the turn of the 20th century and the late-1940s and 1950s – voters were left to conjure their own halcyon days. The Tea Party movement and January 6th insurrectionists, as we have seen, drew inspiration from the revolutionary era. As the president of the American Historical Association, Jacqueline Jones, put it when she addressed the organisation's annual conference a year after the revolt, 'Scholarship had spilled out of the Ivy Tower and onto the streets.'[6]

Contemporary political ideology has become more historical. Originalism, the idea that 21st-century jurisprudence should reflect the original intentions of the 18th-century framers, is one of the few core conservative ideas to have survived the Trump years intact. Conversely, presentism, the notion that figures from the past can legitimately be judged by modern-day mores and values, has become a driving idea on the left. This thinking led a San Francisco education board in 2021 to vote in favour of renaming 44 schools, including those honouring Washington and Lincoln – a decision it later reversed – and New York councillors to vote unanimously to banish a statue of Jefferson from City Hall, because he enslaved more than 600 African-Americans.

History tests are being applied to contentious issues. In overturning *Roe v. Wade*, the Supreme Court ruled that the right to abortion was not 'deeply rooted in the nation's history', an argument predicated on the idea that rights not laid down in the Constitution were only valid if they were grounded in tradition. In his majority ruling, Samuel Alito used the word 'history' no less than 67 times. When, the following day, Clarence Thomas authored the majority opinion in a case overturning New York's conceal-gun carry laws, he invoked 'history' 95 times. In both cases, professional historians felt the need to submit amicus briefs – an advisory to the court – partly because these judgements had become a battle over how to interpret the past. Indeed, so pervasive has originalist thinking become that the conservative jurists on the Supreme Court now act more like amateur historians than professional jurists: adjudicators of historical events, rather than arbiters of constitutional law, self-styled sleuths of American antiquity. The former Supreme Court Justice Stephen Breyer has labelled the practice 'law office history'.[7] However, it was more metaphysical than that, for right-wing jurists claimed to be speaking for the dead.

Political discourse is now routinely infused with parables from the past. When the Black Mississippi congressman Bennie Thompson opened the January 6th committee hearings, he started with a history lesson. As well as making the obligatory reference to 1814, when the British had ransacked the Capitol, he spoke also of 1862, 'when American citizens had taken up arms against this country'. In that first full year of the Civil War, he pointed out, Congress had changed the oath of office lawmakers were required to recite, so that they now vowed to defend the Constitution 'against all enemies – foreign *and domestic*'.

In her opening statement, the Republican congresswoman Liz Cheney urged viewers to consider the meaning of the painting in the Capitol Rotunda, depicting George Washington surrendering his sword at the conclusion of the Revolutionary War. 'With this noble act, Washington set the indispensable example of the peaceful transfer of power,' explained Cheney. 'The sacred obligation to defend this peaceful transfer of power has been honoured by every American president. Except one.' Viewers watching the cable news networks, which carried the two-hour presentation in full, could have been forgiven for thinking they were watching the History Channel. But history and news had folded in on each other.

When the January 6th Committee published its final report in December 2022, its foreword, written by the departing House Speaker Nancy Pelosi, was entitled 'The Last Best Hope of Earth', words appropriated from Lincoln. In her own introductory remarks, Liz Cheney recalled how her great-great-grandfather, Samuel Fletcher Cheney, had answered the call to join the Union Army.[8] Personal narratives, usually paying tribute to the sacrifice or success of a politician's parents, have long been a rhetorical go-to. But now we have entered the realm of Ancestry.com.

When it comes to political stage management, historical backdrops are in vogue. For his first campaign speech of 2024, Joe Biden travelled to Valley Forge in Pennsylvania, where George Washington's army had endured bitter coldness, disease and food shortages as it regrouped during the winter of 1777–8. There, he accused Trump of 'trying to rewrite the facts' of January 6th, and of 'trying to steal history the same way he tried to steal the election'. He also reminded voters of Washington's selflessness in not seeking to serve as president for the rest of his life. 'America made a vow,' said Biden. 'Never again would we bow down to a king.'

Needless to say, the past is increasingly viewed through a partisan looking glass, another reminder of how historical consciousness is shaped by political consciousness, and how feelings outrank facts. Polling conducted by the American Historical Association has shown that Democrats believe that people of colour and women do not receive sufficient attention. Republicans think that the military, religious groups and the Founding Fathers have been neglected. At the root of these conflicting views lies a fundamental divide. Republicans overwhelmingly believe that American history should be celebrated, while Democrats think that history has to be reckoned with and atoned for.

Conservatives accuse liberals of promoting what they call a 'woke' interpretation, heavy on self-flagellation and light on self-congratulation. Liberals have spurned conservative versions of the past, such as the 1939 epic *Gone with the Wind*, which perpetuated the myth of the 'happy slave'. From their history books, documentaries and films, Americans are increasingly looking for bias confirmation, rather than elucidation. In Barack Obama's first inaugural address, he urged his fellow Americans 'to choose our better history', which spoke of how bifurcated it has become.

So the righting of historical wrongs is a driver on the left. The defence of a glorious past is a nostrum on the right. Do you want to defend the civil-liberties revolution of the 1770s or the civil-rights revolution of the 1960s? Are you 1776 or 1619? Increasingly, the debate is being conducted in a crassly binary form.

The history of American history is worth revisiting if only to demonstrate that the Disneyfication of the national story long predated Walt Disney. America's earliest chroniclers accentuated the positive, serving as cheerleaders as much as historians. Early accounts glorified the American Revolution, celebrated the genius of the Founding Fathers, granted the US Constitution a sacred status and promoted the exceptionalist idea that the United States was unique and superior to other countries. Typical of this self-congratulatory genre was Benson Lossing's *A Primary History of the United States for Schools and Families*, published in 1857, which gushed: 'Every one born in this free and beautiful country, should be proud of it, thankful for

God for it, and willing to do everything that is right to keep it free and good.'[9]

The chief proponent of this bullish approach was George Bancroft, a scholar, diplomat and one-time secretary of the US Navy, whose ten-volume history of the United States enjoyed in the homes of the 19th century upwardly mobile the same kind of shelf life that the Encyclopaedia Britannica came to have in the mid-20th century. Writing in purple and patriotic prose, this Harvard academic asserted in his *History of the United States, from the Discovery of the American Continent* that the fledging republic had already become a modern-day Shangri-La. '[O]ur constitution engages the fond admiration of the people ... Prosperity follows the execution of even justice, invention is quickened by the freedom of competition, and labor rewarded with sure and unexampled returns,' he wrote, inter-weaving early iterations of what would later be called the American Dream and American exceptionalism: 'A favoring Providence, calling our institutions into being, has conducted the country to its present happiness and glory.'[10]

Even the Civil War did not shake his faith in America. Indeed, when Bancroft published an updated edition of his masterwork in 1882, he saw no need to amend or temper the optimism of the original. 'The foregoing words, written near a half century ago, are suffered to remain,' he explained, 'because the intervening years have justified their expression of confidence in the progress of our republic. The seed of disunion has perished; and universal freedom, reciprocal benefits, and cherished traditions bind its many states in the closest union.'[11]

George Bancroft was essentially an American version of the great British historian Thomas Macaulay, a proponent of what came to be known as the Whig interpretation of the past. Macaulay's declaration that 'the history of England is emphatically the history of progress', found an echo in how Americans told their story. Divisions were therefore glossed over. Some historians even avoided the phrase 'Civil War', preferring to label the conflict the 'War for Southern Independence'. Rather than acknowledge that enslavement lay at the heart of the conflict, many historians promoted the ideology of the 'Lost Cause': the idea that the Confederates were noble warriors in a battle waged to defend states' rights against an overbearing central government. In the late 19th century, William Wirt Henry, the president of the American Historical Association, even spoke of the 'great benefits slavery conferred on the slaves', because it raised them from 'a state of barbarism' to 'a state of civilisation'.[12]

In *The Republic*, Plato spoke of the noble lie, the promulgation of myths by a self-selecting elite to nurture social harmony. That pretty much summed up the American historiographical tradition during the first century of the country's existence.

Not until the early 20th century, with the emergence of the 'Progressive school' of American historians, did Bancroft and his 'drum and trumpet history' encounter serious intellectual pushback. Where Bancroft saw unity, progressives eyed class conflict and division: southern slaveholders against northern industrialists, Jeffersonians against Hamiltonians, labour versus capital, Republicans versus Democrats. Charles Beard, a history professor at Columbia, became the movement's leading light, and a hugely controversial figure because of his radical reinterpretation of the American Revolution. In his signature work, *An Economic Interpretation of the Constitution of the United States*, which was published in 1913, he posited that the Founding Fathers were self-interested property owners driven primarily by the personal profit motive, rather than anything more idealistic, universal or grandiose. The Constitution, he correctly argued, was specifically designed to thwart majority rule.

This sacrilegious thinking met an immediate backlash. Progressive historians, such as Beard and David Saville Muzzey, the author of a popular school textbook, *An American History*, were pilloried for producing what one critic called a 'perversion, distortion and pollution' of the national story. In another foretaste of the modern-day culture wars, some municipalities banned Muzzey's books. As the country descended into the Great Depression, Progressive historians were maligned as communist propagandists.[13]

Though the Progressive school dominated academic historiography from 1910 until the outbreak of World War II, they did not prevail for long. The post-war years saw the emergence of the 'consensus school' of historians, who downplayed conflict and emphasised shared experiences and collective endeavours. For them, the overriding lesson of history was that Americans were united around cherished ideals: personal freedom, democratic government, the primacy of capitalism, the ownership of property and the sense of opportunity – the character traits thought to give the United States an ideological edge over the Soviets.

Richard Hofstadter, whose breakthrough book, *The American Political Tradition, and the Men Who Made It*, was published in 1948, is seen as one of its pioneers. But Hofstadter, who argued that history should not be used as an ideological weapon that set American against American, was primarily a myth-buster, hacking away at the Mount Rushmore-style idolisation of figures such as Lincoln and Jefferson. 'The mythology that has grown up around Thomas Jefferson,' he wrote, 'is as massive and imposing as any in American history' – especially the falsehood that he was 'a militant, crusading democrat'.[14]

Whatever the school of historiographical thought, the American story had for the most part been a story of white men told by white men. In the 1960s and 1970s, however, a monocultural history started giving way to a multicultural reinterpretation. Responding to the demands of the civil rights movement inevitably meant revisiting the legacy of enslavement and origins of segregation. Critical race theory first emerged in the 1970s. The feminist movement sought to rescue women from historical invisibility.

As a result, history became more hyphenated. African-American studies and women's studies finally received more attention. More women and people of colour came into the historical profession. In 1974, Congress passed the Ethnic Heritage Studies Program Act, 'to encourage greater understanding of the ethnic background and roots of all American citizens'. Two years later, as part of America's bicentennial celebrations, Gerald Ford recognised Black History Month 'to seize the opportunity to honor the too-often neglected accomplishments of Black Americans in every area of endeavor throughout our history'. In 1979, the American Historical Association finally appointed a person of colour as its president. For the first 95 years of its existence, all of its presidents had been white men. Even as late as the 1960s, the organisation's then head, Carl Bridenbaugh, argued that history could only be explained by Brahmins, after complaining that 'many of the younger practitioners of our craft ... are products of lower middle-class or foreign origins, and their emotions not infrequently get in the way of historical reconstruction'.[15]

At the same time, the crisis of national confidence brought on by Vietnam prompted a wider reckoning about past triumphs. In 1980, the left-wing academic Howard Zinn published his landmark study, *A People's History of the United States*, a revisionist work which challenged 'the fundamental nationalist glorification of country', and sought to tell the American story from the perspective of the losers, rather than the winners. 'I prefer to tell the story of the discovery of America from the viewpoint of the Arawaks,' wrote Zinn, by way of introduction, 'of the Constitution from the standpoint of the slaves, of Andrew Jackson as seen by the Cherokees ...' His book became an unexpected bestseller.[16]

Swathes of the American populace, excluded for so long from the national story, were finally getting their historical due. After Black History month came Italian-American History Month and LGBT History Month and Native-American Heritage Month. The trend was towards separate stories, rather than an overarching national narrative. This fracturing sparked a conservative backlash, and the history wars of the 1990s.

An irony of this battle was that it stemmed from a good-faith attempt to reaffirm some sort of historical consensus around a national story. In September 1989, two months before the fall of the Berlin Wall, George H. W. Bush convened a summit of state governors in Charlottesville, Virginia, to agree on national standards in education. As part of that initiative, a panel was appointed to draw up criteria for the teaching of history. Their report was released just before the 1994 congressional midterm elections, as that year's Republican Revolution was reaching its crescendo. In such a feverishly partisan climate, it instantly became embroiled in politics.

On the eve of the report's publication, Lynne Cheney – the former head of the National Endowment for the Humanities, the wife of Dick Cheney, and the mother of Liz Cheney – launched a pre-emptive strike. In the opinion pages of the *Wall Street Journal*, under the catchy headline 'The End of History', she complained that the panel 'tend to save their unqualified admiration for people, places and events that are politically correct'. Heroes, such as Washington, made 'only a fleeting appearance'. Harriet Tubman, by contrast, merited six mentions.[17] The right-wing shock jock Rush Limbaugh immediately took up the cause, lambasting the historians for framing the American past as 'inherently evil'. The guidelines should be 'flushed down the sewer of multiculturalism'.[18]

'Knowledge of history is the precondition of political intelligence', the guidelines had noted, a statement that was incontestable. But, just as Richard Hofstadter feared, the past was being wielded as a cudgel. Gone was the opportunity to forge any historical consensus.

Observing the history wars of the Trump and Biden years is like watching a replay of the battle that played in the 1990s, albeit with opposing armies more ruthless in pursuit of victory. In April 2021, the Department of Education called for the history curriculum to reflect the 'unbearable human cost of systemic racism' and the 'consequence of slavery', all of which Mitch McConnell called 'divisive nonsense'. Like history itself, the history wars were repeating themselves, this time both as tragedy and farce.

———

If the Circle-Vision 360° at Disneyland was the most uncomplicated depiction of American history I had seen, the Broadway musical *Hamilton* was by far the most scintillating. How could one not be inspired by this tale of immigrant success: the 'bastard son of a whore' who rose to become 'a hero and a scholar', the father of the US financial system and chief architect of national government? How could one not be thrilled by the verbal gymnastics of Lin-Manuel Miranda's hip-hop libretto, with its syncopated retelling of America's founding?

What a masterstroke to have Washington sing as a duet with Hamilton, his speechwriter, the final address he made as president – although Lin-Manuel Miranda left out his warning about the polarising effect of party politics and risk it brought of 'riot and insurrection'. What an audacious idea to cast the musical with Black actors, especially during the Obama presidency. Rendered in such a current way, the show brought together the past and the present as if they were in a more perfect union. I was an instant fan. When I celebrated my 50th birthday by taking our children to see it on Broadway, I remember thinking life could not get much better.

Partly because of its association with Obama, *Hamilton* was criticised for being too woke. More problematic was how the musical is too Whig. *Hamilton* glosses over enslavement, and the slave-holding of the Founding Fathers. Its hero did little to advance the abolitionist cause, and married into the Schuyler family, a major New York slaveholder. Hamilton is also miscast as a champion of democracy, rather than as someone who warned of its excesses and believed in the ascendancy of elites. King George III is demonised, even though Hamilton himself was an Anglophile who favoured a monarch-like presidency.

Hamilton is a Broadway show. Primarily for our entertainment does it exist. As theatre, it is fully deserving of its rave reviews. Yet for a production that notes at one point how 'history has its eyes on you', and which was inspired by Ron Chernow's 2004 biography, *Alexander Hamilton*, it plays fast and loose with the historical record. Very much in keeping with the tradition of *American Journeys*, it is fitting that *Hamilton* has ended up on the streaming channel Disney+.

How, then, should the American story be told? If one were to produce a modern-day Circle-Vision 360° that offered a truly panoramic picture, what would be its master narrative? Firstly, the format might be altered, away from a Hollywood-style presentation to more of a 'journey of discovery' documentary along the lines of the popular TV show *Who Do You Think You Are?* That programme relies, after all, on unexpected twists and surprises, many of which challenge long-held preconceptions and involve venturing down unexpected and personally confronting paths.

Some myth-busting, another genre popular on the streaming channels, would help. Christopher Columbus, who island-hopped around the Caribbean, never made land on the North American continent. Plymouth Rock was not where the Pilgrim Fathers first came ashore, and nor was Plymouth Plantation the first white English settlement. Jamestown in Virginia had been founded 13 years before.

Rather than focus predominantly on the colonies established by the British, the influence of the Spanish and the French should receive greater acknowledgement. America's oldest European-established, continuously occupied community is St Augustine, Florida, which was founded by the Spanish in 1565, 50 years before English settlers established Jamestown. Spain controlled Florida and New Mexico, and in 1716 formally established a new colony on the Gulf Coast, Texas. New Spain encompassed more than half of the land mass of what is now the continental United States. The main coin circulating in the British colonies was the Spanish dollar, which is where the modern-day currency gets its name. The French not only settled Louisiana, which was named after the Sun King, Louis XIV, but founded Detroit and St Louis.[19]

The retelling of the *Mayflower* voyage in 1620 as an origin story has also promoted the belief that American history starts at the moment of European settlement, a whitewashing of the Native-American story, and a denial of thousands of years of heritage involving the original custodians of the land. It is also mistaken to view the arrival of the *Mayflower* as the first interaction between white settlers and Indigenous Americans. Contact with Europeans had been going on for at least a century, partly because slave traders kidnapped Native Americans. By the time the Pilgrims came ashore, a few members of the Wampanoag tribe had already mastered English.

The story of Thanksgiving is a feel-good myth: a happy tale of Pilgrims cordially breaking bread with Native Americans, which has been packaged up over the years as an act of convivial coexistence. Some of the inaccuracies are harmless enough. It is thought, for example, that venison was served, not turkey and pumpkin pie. (This modern-day menu was invented by a 19th-century magazine publisher, who read about that first feast and lobbied Lincoln to turn Thanksgiving into a national holiday.) Yet it is the larger fiction that is more damaging. Thanksgiving has nourished the false idea that Indigenous Americans gladly greeted white European settlers and lived with them harmoniously, a comforting narrative of colonial validation and contrived acceptance.

In fact, the Pilgrim Fathers asserted the dominance of the white race with murderous force. During these early years, in a cycle of reprisal killings, there were massacres on both sides. But the savagery of the white settlers was grotesque. Wigwams were set ablaze, and the women and children who fled the flames put to the sword. When, in 1675, a group of Indigenous Americans banded together to fight the settlers, the dead body of their leader Metacomet – who the English nicknamed 'King Philip' – was treated like a trophy. His head was decapitated and displayed on a pike at the entrance of Plymouth Plantation, where it remained for 20 years. British redcoats used germ warfare against the Native Americans, by handing them blankets infected with smallpox. Their commander, Sir Jeffery Amherst, spoke of trying to use 'every other method that can serve to extirpate this execrable race'.[20]

That Native Americans fought back so fiercely, and maintained a campaign of resistance for so long, suggests that they should truly be regarded as America's first revolutionaries. After all, as Jill Lepore has noted, 'They revolted again and again and again.'[21] It speaks of contemporary America's problem of historical overload that the grievances of Native Americans do not get more of an airing, as issues confronting First Nations peoples do in Canada. In the United States, they tend to be crowded out by other pending historical problems.

The Thanksgiving holiday also has an ignoble history. The feast was seized upon in the late 17th century by New Englanders worried that their cultural influence in the new colonies was being diminished. Thereafter, as the historian David Silverman has shown in his book *This Land Is Their Land: The Wampanoag Indians, Plymouth Colony and the Troubled History of Thanksgiving*, this mythic event came to be repurposed whenever white Protestants felt their hegemony being threatened. This was especially true in the 19th century, when waves of Catholic and Jewish European immigrants challenged the primacy of white Protestantism. Thus, the Pilgrim Fathers were co-opted to assert the dominance of WASP (white, Anglo-Saxon and Protestant) culture.

A more honest recounting would tell a more nuanced story of the American Revolution. What made the triumph of Washington's ragtag army all the more remarkable was that somewhere between a fifth and a third of white colonialists remained faithful to the crown. King George III could also rely on the backing of enslaved people and Native Americans.

Misplaced, then, is the idea that independence enjoyed universal support. Frequently glossed over is the proclamation made in 1775 by Lord Dunmore, the British governor of Virginia, known as his 'Offer of Emancipation', that slaves owned by rebels in the colony would be granted freedom if they fought alongside the British Red Coats. Revisionists, like Jill Lepore, have argued that it was this calculated promise of emancipation, more so than the Boston Massacre, when in 1770 British soldiers fired on a patriot mob, or the Tea Party, that stiffened the resistance of southern colonies to British rule.[22]

The achievements of the Founding Fathers have to be weighed against their failures, which are commonly overlooked. On the positive side of the ledger, as the historian Joseph Ellis has noted, are a series of firsts: the 'first successful war for colonial independence', which led to the foundation of 'the first nation-sized Republic', which created 'the first wholly secular state' and established a multi-pronged form of government and political parties engaged in peaceful debate. Yet the framers also compounded the original sin of slavery and created a flawed model of pseudo-democracy. As Ellis notes: 'The triumph was also a tragedy of monumental proportions ... the ingredients for an epic historical narrative that defies all moralistic categories, a storyline rooted in the coexistence of grace and sin, grandeur and failure, brilliance and blindness.'[23]

The myth of the melting pot, founded on immigrants first being welcomed and then speedily assimilated, does not withstand scrutiny. 'May America be an asylum to the persecuted of the earth,' toasted George Washington after the last British ships had left New York harbour at the conclusion of the Revolutionary War. But it was more of a rhetorical flourish than a multicultural mission statement. From the beginning, America adopted a defensive stance towards immigration. As early as 1790, Congress passed the Naturalisation Act, which stipulated that only free whites of 'good moral character' who had lived in America for at least two years could become citizens. By the 1850s, the Know Nothing party – or the Native American Party, as it was originally known – had become a third force in politics by capitalising on Protestant disquiet about the influx of Irish and German Catholics, and fears fuelled by the revolutions of 1848 in Europe. In the 1870s, the rise of nativist malice during the 'Yellow Peril' scare led to the enactment of legislation limiting the number of Asian immigrants. The 1924 Immigration Act, which was passed amid a panic over the danger posed to America by European radicalism, introduced quotas based on national origin that favoured northern and western Europeans over those from the south and east.

Only in 1965, the year that the United States became a truly multiethnic democracy, did the US government embrace the concept of a multiethnic immigration policy. Again, the architect was Lyndon Johnson, who ended racial quotas by signing the Immigration and Nationality Act, in a ceremony conducted with the Statue of Liberty as a backdrop. And again, the white backlash was quick in coming.

Always it is worth remembering how many new immigrants returned home, rather than making their homes in America: of how a mass influx was followed by a mass exodus. Of the 55 million Eastern Europeans who migrated to America between 1846 and 1940, the historian Tara Zahra estimates that between 30 and 40 per cent returned home, after becoming disillusioned with life in America or feeling homesick – what she calls 'the Great Departure'.[24]

Tensions between immigrant groups have been a recurring problem. At the outbreak of the First World War, Woodrow Wilson's reluctance to embroil the United States in the conflict partly grew from the fear of exposing ethnic divisions, and in particular the rivalries between Anglophiles and the Irish and Germans. 'We definitely have to be neutral,' Wilson warned in 1914, 'since otherwise our mixed populations would wage war on each other.'[25]

The notion of the 'American dream', the belief that hard work will be rewarded with economic abundance and social upward mobility, can also be hallucinatory. The US capitalist system has long been geared towards those at the top of the ladder – the slave owners, the robber barons, the 'one per cent' – rather than strivers trying to make an ascent. Though colonial America was more economically egalitarian than other countries at the time, there was a steep rise in income equality from the beginning of the 19th century, with the fracturing taking place along familiar lines: urban versus rural, north versus south, white versus non-white.

America witnessed a 'great levelling' between 1910 and 1970, partly, as the economists Jeffrey G. Williamson and Peter Lindert have pointed out, because the First World War destroyed so much private wealth and government intervened more aggressively to curb capitalist excess. But the wealth gap opened up again in the 1970s, and since then income polarisation has gone hand in hand with political polarisation. Between 1989 and 2016, the year that Trump won election, the wealth gap between the richest and poorest families more than doubled.[26]

The very term 'American Dream' has also been misappropriated. First coined in the 1930s by the historian James Truslow Adams in his book *The Epic of America* – his publisher rejected his preferred title 'The American Dream' – the phrase was originally intended to describe a new national credo which rejected the materialism of the Gilded Age, and the greed of the super-wealthy robber barons. Adams was trying to advance a more egalitarian ethos, the 'dream of a land in which life should be better and richer and fuller for everyone'. As the historian Sarah Churchwell has pointed out, 'The American dream – far from validating a simple desire for personal advancement – once gave voice to principled appeals for a more generous way of life.'[27] It was only in the post-war years that the phrase came to be associated primarily with consumerism, materialism and financial self-centredness.

From the Salem witch trials to the rise of QAnon, from P. T. Barnum to Donald J. Trump, America has always been prone to fantasy, post-truthism, conspiratorialism, information manipulation and alternative facts. The Pilgrim Fathers made land believing that Satan would conspire against them. During the revolution, George III was cast as the anti-Christ. Hamilton, the father of the country's financial system, was seen as the frontman for a cabal of Jewish financiers. The Confederates believed the north was conniving against them. Henry Ford's newspaper, the *Dearborn Independent*, published the horribly anti-Semitic *The Protocols of the Elders of Zion*.[28] In the 1970s, it was claimed that the moon landing had been faked – a drama produced by Walt Disney, scripted by Arthur C. Clarke and directed by Stanley Kubrick. The '90s were awash with conspiracies that Bill and Hillary Clinton had murdered their friend and aide, Vince Foster, who had taken his own life in 1993.

An 'American tradition' is how the historian Robert A. Goldberg described this strain of thinking in his 2001 study, *Enemies Within: The Culture of Conspiracy in Modern America*, which originated with the messianism of the first Anglo-Saxon settlers, and was fuelled thereafter by suspicion towards other racial, religious and ethnic groups. Conspiratorialism became a byproduct of exceptionalism and pluralism.[29] The author Kurt Andersen identified the same essential continuity in *Fantasyland: How America Went*

Haywire, a 500 Year History: 'Mix epic individualism with extreme religion; mix show business with everything else; let all that steep and simmer for a few centuries; run it through the anything-goes 1960s, and the Internet age; the result is the America we inhabit today, where reality and fantasy are weirdly and dangerously blurred and commingled.'[30] It brings to mind the poet Robert Penn Warren's warning that 'a crazy man is a large-scale menace only in a crazy society'.[31]

If we are to persist with a 'great man' view of the past, with its focus on the likes of Washington and Lincoln, it needs to run in tandem with the 'great women' view, what is sometimes called the missing half of American history. Most high schoolers graduate with an understanding of what happened at Seneca Falls in 1848, the year that marked the launch of the women's rights movement, but it pales alongside other milestones. Doubtless they have heard of Rosa Parks, but not perhaps the names of Virginia Durr, a driving force behind the abolition of the poll tax, the freedom rider Diane Nash, a co-founder of the Student Non-Violent Coordinating Committee who was just as brave as John Lewis. It is with good reason that the 2016 movie about three African-American NASA mathematicians – Katherine Johnson, Dorothy Vaughan and Mary Jackson – whose role was never properly recognised was titled *Hidden Figures*. Indeed, a study by the National Women's History Museum found that less than a quarter of the historical figures taught in schools are women.[32]

Another way of diluting the great man theory of history would be to promote the great movement theory, with an emphasis on the struggle for Black equality, the feminist revolution, and other social and scientific missions, such as the moonshot. That, arguably, is where American greatness is the easiest to locate.

Placing a new emphasis on communitarianism, as opposed to individualism, would help give a more complete picture, as Anne-Marie Slaughter, the first woman to serve as the director of policy and planning at the State Department, has argued. Rather than thinking in terms of 'rugged individualism', the term coined by Herbert

Hoover to describe the creed of self-reliance and independence from an overbearing government, she has suggested that 'rugged interdependence' provides a more helpful frame.

After immersing herself in the stories of the wives who accompanied their husbands on the wagon trains heading west, she was struck by how they came to rely on other families who joined them on the journey and who helped them form settlements at the end. So a story that had once been told through the looking glass of individualism actually had a strongly collective bent.

The same 'stories of solidarity and reliance on strangers' were evident, too, with the Underground Railway, and the Great Migration, when some six million African-Americans left the American south in search of a more equitable life in the north. For Slaughter then, 'rugged interdependence' becomes 'an invitation to look back at any part of American history and make room for many more voices, to open up to the traits and traditions of many different groups of Americans who have not been able to tell their stories or who have been silenced or ignored when they tried'.[33]

Rather than seeing government as the problem not the solution, the core idea of Reaganism, we should never forget its role in the building of America. 'The Southwestern states could never have been settled at their present human density without immense expenditure of government funds on water engineering,' the cultural commentator Robert Hughes once wrote. 'They are less the John Wayne than the Welfare Queen of American development.'[34]

The telling of the American story might benefit from the French custom of numbering republics. Under this schema, the years following the Civil War, when the 13th, 14th and 15th Amendments ended slavery and expanded democracy, would become known as 'The Second Republic'. The Third Republic might begin with female suffrage, the fourth with Roosevelt's New Deal, which dramatically expanded the federal government. The Fifth Republic would be dated from what is often referred to as 'the Second Reconstruction', which culminated with the passage of the 1964 Civil Rights Act and the 1965 Voting Rights Act. It would challenge the nostrum that the Founding

Fathers were saintly and infallible, and also potentially elevate the role played by founding mothers, such as the women's rights activist Susan B. Anthony, Eleanor Roosevelt and the heroines of the civil rights movement, like Rosa Parks.

America's historiographical isolationism also needs to end. Rather, there should be a greater acknowledgement of how other countries have shaped its history. The Haitian slave revolt that started in 1791, for instance, had a dramatic impact on American thinking, heightening fears amongst southern slaveholders that the same fate could befall them. It also opened the door on the Louisiana Purchase, since Napoleon no longer viewed his continental landholding as so useful after losing control of one of his prized Caribbean colonial assets.

Just as historical amnesia has been a recurring problem, so, too, is historical illiteracy. Surveys have shown that half of Americans think that the Civil War predated the War of Independence. Two-thirds have little sense of the term 'Reconstruction'. A study in 2023 revealed that US history scores among eighth graders had plummeted to their lowest-ever scores. Just 13 per cent of pupils were at or above the 'proficient level'.[35] Donald Trump illustrated this deficiency himself when he spoke during his presidency as if the Black abolitionist Frederick Douglass was still alive, and expressed surprise at learning Lincoln was a Republican.[36] The more history becomes a driver of politics, the more historically unlettered America seems to get. The past is not merely being forgotten or misremembered. Commonly, it never gets taught.

Whatever the frame, complexity is the key to unlocking the past, for it is the very contradictions of the American story that help us make more sense of it. Too often we are asked to make a binary choice between a 'feel good' and a 'feel guilty' history. By way of remedy, the Harvard scholar Jill Lepore, the author of the widely acclaimed 2018 overview, *These Truths: A History of the United States*, has spoken of the need for a 'both/and' version of history. David W. Blight, another historian I greatly admire, put it well when he noted, 'We need to teach the history of slavery and racism every day, but not through a forest of white guilt, or by thrusting the idea of "white privilege" onto working class people who have had very little privilege.'[37] Though the fashion is for cancellation, the aim of history should be contextualisation. 'Washington can't be cancelled,' wrote his biographer, Alexis Coe, on President's Day in 2022. 'If you erase Washington, you erase America.'[38]

But just imagine if Disney used its Circle-Vision 360° to present a more honest retelling of the national story. There would be a rush for the doors. Protests would be mounted outside the gates. Governor Ron DeSantis would likely shut it down. History is an argument without end, the Dutch historian Pieter Geyl once dryly noted, a comment that is especially apposite in early 21st-century America.

6

America's constant curse

On the night that George Floyd's murderer was convicted, a victory parade unfolded on the streets of Minneapolis that served both as a celebration and catharsis. It began outside the federal courthouse, where the trial of the former police officer Derek Chauvin had just concluded, a building so heavily fortified for the duration of the proceedings that its perimeter looked more like a federal penitentiary. Then it powered through the streets of downtown, where protesters wielded their Black Lives Matter banners as if they were carnival revellers. This was not, though, a moment of unalloyed joy. When the march briefly came to a halt, a young protest leader shouted into a microphone how the verdict brought only 'a little bit of justice', but at least Chauvin was now behind bars.

Police killings we had watched many times before. The advent of smart phones, combined with the multiplier effect of the internet, had created an online archive of police brutality. In July of 2016, the city of Minneapolis, and the wider world, had already viewed the killing of Philando Castile, a 32-year-old African-American shot dead by a police officer who had pulled his Oldsmobile to the side of the road, while his four-year-old daughter looked on from the back seat and his girlfriend live-streamed his dying moments on Facebook. Even as the Chauvin trial reached its climax, we had covered another fatal police shooting, of a 20-year-old Black man, Daunte Wright, in a suburb, Brooklyn Center, little more than 10 miles from the court-house. This time a female officer had pulled her pistol, mistaking it for a Taser.

Yet the murder of George Floyd was especially appalling. Police shootings normally occurred in a split-second, often because an officer had panicked or made a fatal, momentary misjudgement. Chauvin, by contrast, had knelt on George Floyd's neck for more than nine minutes, and listened to him exclaim 'I can't breathe' more than 20 times. As each cry became more desperate than the last, onlookers pleaded with Chauvin to stop pressing down on Floyd's neck, which only seemed to make him more bloody-minded and unbending.

The timing of George Floyd's murder was strangely synchronous. Just 12 hours before, another video had gone viral that was filmed in New York's Central Park. It showed a white woman, Amy Cooper, making a 911 call to summon the NYPD so that officers could apprehend a Black man, Christian Cooper, who had politely requested that she leash her pet cocker spaniel in an area of park-land favoured by bird-watchers, where dogs were prohibited from roaming free. Before placing the call to the police, she had warned Cooper, a mild-mannered comic-book writer, that she was 'going to tell them there's an African-American man threatening my life', a warning which exposed how the scales of justice were tilted so heavily in favour of whites.

Race, then, was already dominating the national conversation when the video of George Floyd's murder first started being replayed. Instantly, it was likened to the most jolting imagery from the civil rights era, the footage which emerged from Birmingham and Selma, and the black-and-white photographs of the murdered Black school-boy Emmett Till's open casket. No wonder that there was such jubilation when Chauvin was convicted in a unanimous jury verdict.

In the midst of this street party, however, came distressing news. Reports started filtering through from Columbus, Ohio, first in scraps of information then minutes later in a fuller telling, of yet another police shooting. An officer had shot dead a 16-year-old

African-American, Ma'Khia Bryant. Body-camera footage revealed that the killing was not as clearcut as the murder of George Floyd. Armed with a knife, the teenager had lunged at another girl in the moment of her death. A grand jury later deemed the shooting to be a justifiable homicide. Yet once again, the first instinct of a white officer had been to discharge his firearm and use lethal force.

Though the timing was horrendous, the news from Columbus should hardly have come as a shock. America's racial history is littered with these kinds of instantaneous reversals: Lincoln being assassinated just days after the guns fell silent at the end of the Civil War; the NAACP campaigner Medgar Evers being gunned down by a white supremacist on the same night that Kennedy delivered a long overdue speech to the nation in which he described civil rights as a moral issue 'as old as the scriptures' and 'as clear as the American Constitution'; the Watts riots coming immediately after the passage of the Voting Rights Act; the Supreme Court taking up the *Shelby* case just three days after Barack Obama won re-election. More so than in any other area of national life, there was something tragically recurring about Black American history.

The words were beautiful, the sentiment irresistible, the promise seemingly radical:

> We hold these truths to be self-evident, that all men are created equal, that they are endowed by their Creator with certain unalienable Rights, that among these are Life, Liberty and the Pursuit of Happiness.

Yet the superlative passage from Thomas Jefferson's Declaration of Independence was never intended as a statement of racial justice. Jefferson's definition of men did not include people of colour or, needless to say, women. To the country's Founding Fathers, the notion of equality was outside their realm of thinking. Enslaved Blacks were primarily regarded as property, rather than people, a unit of labour rather than flesh and blood.

The original draft of the Declaration of Independence had included an acid-worded indictment of King George III for imposing slavery, which Jefferson described as an 'execrable commerce', an 'assemblage of horrors', and a 'cruel war against human nature itself'. Yet when the Second Continental Congress reviewed the draft, it struck out this 138-word passage. Delegates from South Carolina and Georgia led the opposition, but Jefferson, who was only 33 at the time, was taken aback by how quickly 'our Northern brethren' capitulated. In order to forge the union, the question of enslavement became a taboo. The whitewashing of history therefore began with the country's founding statement.

Enslavement, as the ambivalence of these northern delegates attested, was not solely a southern problem. The entire US economy had become reliant on it. Back then, Newport, Rhode Island, was the most profitable slave-trading port in North America. Only Charleston in South Carolina had more enslaved people than New York City. By 1787, only Massachusetts and Vermont (which had not yet been admitted to the union) had outlawed this cruel trade. It was not until 1804, more than a quarter of a century after the Declaration of Independence, that New Jersey became the last northern state to abolish it.

Though the north was the home to a nascent abolitionist movement, the north-south divide on enslavement had just as much to do with meteorology as morality. 'The real obstacle to slavery in New England was economic, not ethical,' wrote the historian David Reynolds. 'The climate was too harsh for big commercial crops like tobacco and rice; this almost meant that New Englanders lacked both the need and the means to invest in slavery on a large scale.'[1]

At the constitutional convention in Philadelphia, at least 19 out of the 55 framers were slaveholders. Never would they have emerged with a draft constitution had they not compromised over enslavement. So even though the words 'slave' or 'slavery' do not appear in the final document, they provided the subtext for the newly minted constitution. The doyen of US historians, Edmund Morgan, called it 'the great paradox of American history' that the 'rise of liberty and equality in this country was accompanied by the rise of slavery'.[2] Nowhere was it better exemplified than in Virginia, which was the cradle of enlightened ideas about liberty but also the largest slave-holding colony.

The architecture of US democracy was heavily shaped by the subjugation of Blacks and the codification of white supremacy. During the debate in Philadelphia over how many seats each state should be apportioned in the House of Representatives, pro-slavery southerners argued that enslaved people should be counted as a full person to boost the political clout of their region – though obviously they would never be allowed to vote – while some northerners argued they should not be taken into consideration at all. From this dispute emerged the notorious three-fifths compromise.

This boosted the strength of southern states in Congress and also, crucially, in the Electoral College. Indeed, the method of electing the president marked a double victory for what came to be known as the slave states. First, it prevented the south from being overwhelmed in presidential elections by the more populous north. Second, each state was given the same number of presidential electors as members of its congressional delegation, an arithmetic which favoured the southern states because of the three-fifths compromise. After the 1800 election Jefferson was even described as 'the Negro president', because he would not have won had it not been for the three-fifths rule artificially inflating the influence of the south.

When the framers debated the vexed question of the Atlantic slave trade, there were even some slaveholders who believed that human trafficking should be made illegal, partly because they recognised its cruelty, but also because plantations were already sufficiently well stocked. Yet southern delegates raised objections, and another compromise was hammered out. Congress would not be allowed to ban the international slave trade until at least 20 years after the Constitution was ratified, which ended up being in 1808. This allowed enslavement to become even more entrenched, and thus exacerbated the very problem which the constitutional convention had been so reluctant to confront.

In another sop to the south, the Constitution included the fugitive slave clause, which required the return of slaves who escaped. The federal government was also given the power to suppress domestic rebellions, a section drafted with slave revolts in mind. The Constitution therefore ended up being a pro-slavery document, what the abolitionist crusader William Lloyd Garrison later called 'a covenant with death' and 'an agreement with Hell'. The cancer was present from the outset. Thereafter, compromise followed compromise, spreading the disease to more parts of the body.

The Louisiana Purchase presented an early opportunity to drastically weaken the institution of slavery, by making abolition a prerequisite of new states entering the union. Yet Jefferson feared that such a controversial precondition of entry would imperil the new republic, especially without his preferred plan in place to repatriate freed slaves to Africa or the West Indies and to compensate slaveholders, both of which were impractical and prohibitively expensive. Rather than threatening slavery, then, westward expansion embedded it even further. Again, Jefferson thought compromise was a price worth paying for national unity – 'Justice is on one scale and self-preservation the other,' as he put it. To press the issue risked civil war.

When in 1819 Missouri became the first territory to petition for statehood, the slavery question became more pressing. But, again, Congress came up with a north-south accommodation, the Missouri Compromise of 1820, which preserved the delicate balance between slave states and free. Under this arrangement, Missouri entered the union as a slave state, while Maine was admitted as a free state. Crucially, it also mandated that slavery would be prohibited in all new states north of a line of latitude drawn at 36 degrees 30 minutes, Missouri's southern border – except for Missouri itself.

By agreeing on the Missouri Compromise, the United States survived its most serious sectional crisis yet. But only just. As John Quincy Adams opined, 'The present is a mere preamble – a title page to a great, tragic volume.' So worried was Jefferson, who was now living out his retirement at Monticello, that he admitted to losing sleep: 'This momentous question, like a fire bell in the night, awakened and filled me with terror. I considered it at once as the knell of the Union.'[3]

Later that decade came another fire bell, this time with the nullification crisis brought on by Congress's decision to impose heavy tariffs on British imports. Southern plantation owners feared that Westminster would retaliate by levying tariffs on cotton, the crop upon which the institution of slavery was based. So the South Carolinian slave owner John C. Calhoun, who served as vice president both to John Quincy Adams and Andrew Jackson, declared that his state had 'interposed her state sovereignty' and 'nullified' the hated tariff. In response, President Jackson, who was determined to assert federal authority against what he viewed as a treasonous state challenge, threatened to march on Columbia, South Carolina's state capital.

With the country at risk of civil war, Congress produced yet another compromise, this time agreeing to reduce tariffs in order to dampen sectional tensions. 'We want to see no sacked cities, no desolated fields, no smoking ruins, no streams of American blood shed by American arms,' explained Senator Henry Clay of Kentucky, the main architect of this detente. But it was a delicate peace.

Victory in the Mexican-American war fought from 1846 to 1848 brought with it a familiar problem: of whether enslavement should be lawful in the newly acquired western territories. The result was the Compromise of 1850, a series of laws, again negotiated by Henry 'The Great Compromiser' Clay. It allowed California to enter as a free state, clarified the borders of Texas, fudged what should happen in New Mexico and Utah by making them territorial governments, abolished the slave trade in the District of Columbia and enacted a more punitive fugitive slave act. With something for everyone – the north got another free state in California, while the south got a tough new fugitive slave act – President Millard Fillmore, in a spectacular feat of wishful thinking, declared it 'the final settlement'. His successor, President Franklin Pierce, adopted the same hubristic tone, proclaiming during his 1853 inaugural address, 'We have been carried in safety through a perilous crisis.'[4]

All of these accommodations were labelled 'compromises', a term which implied a certain equanimity and suggested a positive outcome. But truly they were appeasements of the south. Whatever the terminology, these trade-offs merely postponed the inevitable. Slavery was the problem that refused to go away, the dilemma that defied peaceful resolution.

The territory of Nebraska, a land mass covering modern-day Nebraska and also the Dakotas, Montana and Kansas, became the next area of contention. This time, Senator Stephen Douglas of Illinois, a diminutive Democrat nicknamed 'The Little Giant' who brokered the Compromise of 1850, proposed legislation allowing western states to make up their own minds on the slavery question without interference from the federal government. But the problem with this form of self-determination, which Douglas labelled 'popular sovereignty', was that it opened the way for enslavement anywhere outside the south. The main effect, then, of what became the 1854 Kansas-Nebraska Act, was to repeal the Missouri Compromise, which for three decades had been the loose knot which tied together the union. Kansas immediately became a battleground, with the south hoping it would become the 16th slave state and the north determined to keep it free.

'Bleeding Kansas' was the name given to the series of fatal clashes from 1854 to 1859, a mini-Civil War fought between pro-slavery and anti-slavery gangs and militias in which dozens of people died. Congress also became a combat zone. It was after Charles Sumner compared the pro-slavery forces in Kansas to a rapist attacking a virgin that Preston Brooks tried to kill him with his cane on the floor of the Senate.

Civil war now seemed unavoidable. In Kansas, a bloody dress rehearsal was already underway. Public opinion was becoming more polarised. Harriet Beecher Stowe's 1852 novel, *Uncle Tom's Cabin*, which introduced the horrors of enslavement to a mass readership, became a bestseller, and provided fresh impetus for the northern abolitionist movement. Tensions were further inflamed when the Supreme Court handed down its *Dred Scott* judgement in 1857. In perhaps its worst-ever decision, the Court ruled that the framers of the Constitution regarded enslaved people as property, and that Blacks, in the words of Chief Justice Roger Taney, were therefore 'beings of an inferior order, and altogether unfit to associate with the white race either in social or political relations, and so far inferior that they had no rights which the white man was bound to respect'. Taney, a former Maryland slaveholder, then went on to declare that the Missouri Compromise and the Compromise of 1850 were unconstitutional, which meant the federal government could no longer limit the expansion of slavery into western territories. The compromise that had kept the union together no longer had any legal standing.

For the first half of the 19th century, tensions over slavery had been mirrored within the two major parties, the Democrats and Whigs. Both needed the support of the south, as well as the north, to win the presidency. Both had northern and southern wings, with all the obfuscations on slavery that required. The creation of the Republican Party in the mid-1850s, an exclusively northern party which did not need to curry favour with the south, upended this political dynamic. Its leader, Abraham Lincoln, achieved national prominence when he took on Stephen Douglas in the 1858 Illinois Senate race – their series of seven face-to-face debates became the stuff of legend. Even though Lincoln ended up losing, he won plaudits for his honest elucidation of the slavery problem. 'A house divided against itself cannot stand,' he had prophesied in Springfield, Illinois, as he launched his Senate campaign. 'I believe this government cannot endure, permanently, half slave and half free.'

Louder and louder became the drumbeat of war. The following year, the abolitionist John Brown, a leader of the anti-slavery forces in 'Bleeding Kansas', launched his attack on the federal arsenal at Harpers Ferry. The raid was intended to spark a wider slave rebellion but petered out within 36 hours and was thought initially to have done irreparable harm to the anti-slavery cause. However, Brown displayed such stoicism at his execution – 'I, John Brown, am now quite certain that the crimes of this guilty land will never be purged away; but with blood,' declared the note handed to a guard who led him to the scaffold – that northerners recast him as a martyr. Ralph Waldo Emerson, the country's leading intellectual, described this revolutionary as a 'new saint', who had made 'the gallows glorious like the cross'. Later, Union soldiers would sing, 'John Brown's body lies a-mouldering in the grave, but his soul goes marching on,' as they headed into battle. Brown's lionisation heightened paranoia in the south over the danger of slave rebellions and the inevitability of civil war.

Bleeding Kansas. *Uncle Tom's Cabin. Dred Scott.* Harpers Ferry. The valorisation of John Brown. The strain on the existing party system was now overwhelming, and the Democratic Party, which could no longer paper over its cracks, split along regional lines. Ahead of the 1860 presidential election, northern Democrats nominated Senator Stephen Douglas, who campaigned on popular sovereignty, while the southern Democrats backed the pro-slavery candidate, John C. Breckinridge of Kentucky, who later served as a Confederate officer. This schism within the Democrats created an opening. Though Abraham Lincoln, the Republican candidate, received just 39 per cent of the vote, it was enough in a four-way contest to secure him an Electoral College victory. Vowing to preserve the union – Lincoln had not pledged yet to free the enslaved – he won the presidency without a single southern electoral vote.

Weeks later, believing that Lincoln would move swiftly to abolish slavery, South Carolina seceded from the Union, the first of 11 southern states to do so. In February 1861, the Confederate State of America came into existence. By mid-April, following the militia attack on Union forces at Fort Sumter in Charleston harbour, the country was in a state of civil war. Over the next five years, more than 750,000 Americans were killed fighting their compatriots. Places on the map that many hitherto had not heard of – Antietam, Shiloh, Manassas and Gettysburg – became landmarks to fratricide and dissolution. More people were slain in the two-day Battle of Shiloh in

April 1862, in south-western Tennessee, than lost their lives in all of America's previous conflicts.

Not even the defeat of the Confederacy, following the deadliest conflict in American history, resolved the race question. Nor did the 13th, 14th or 15th Amendments. The era of Reconstruction, the 12-year occupation of the south which resulted in gains for freed Blacks, proved fitfully short-lived. Another squalid compromise brought it to an end.

This time the bone of contention was which candidate won the 1876 presidential election – the Republican Rutherford B. Hayes or his Democratic opponent, Samuel Tilden. In dispute were the results in South Carolina, Florida and Louisiana, where a white supremacist terror campaign had intimidated many Blacks from voting (had it not been for the suppression of Black votes, Hayes would have won convincingly). Under what was dubbed at the time the Bargain of 1877, Hayes was handed victory. But only in return for an agreement that federal troops, whose presence in the five military districts that the Confederacy had been carved into during Reconstruction had been so crucial in the mass registration of Black voters, would no longer enforce civil rights. Southerners labelled it 'Redemption'.

Later, this pact came to be known as the Compromise of 1877, but it was yet another act of appeasement. Preserving the Union meant relegating Blacks to second-class citizenship, and returning them to a form of bondage. Just as enslavement had been the price for creating a semblance of national unity after the American War of Independence, segregation became the price of preserving a semblance of national unity after the American Civil War and up until the mid-1960s.

All this is why the storm over critical race theory is so excessive. At the heart of CRT is the simple proposition that racial discrimination was implanted in legal and social institutions from the founding. It is a statement of the historically obvious, and one widely accepted by historians since the early 1970s, when Edmund Morgan spoke of the American paradox. 'We must face the shameful fact: historically America has been a racist nation,' wrote another leading scholar, Arthur M. Schlesinger Jr, in *The Disuniting of America: Reflections on a Multicultural Society*, a book published at the start of the 1990s which railed against political correctness, 'the cult of ethnicity' and identity politics. 'We white Americans have been racist in our laws, in our institutions, in our customs, in our conditioned reflexes, in our souls. The curse of racism has been the great failure of the American experiment, the glaring contradiction of American ideals and the still crippling disease of American life.'[5] More than three decades on, that appraisal still rings true.

From the three-fifths compromise to the make-up of the Electoral College, from the resistance to a powerful central government to the malapportionment of the Senate, the American system was designed to be a bulwark against racial change. When in the early 19th century a change to the Senate's procedural rules allowed for unlimited debate, it meant that an organised minority wielded even more of a veto power, because of its ability to filibuster legislation. Thereafter, southern segregationists used the filibuster to such devastating effect in thwarting civil rights bills by preventing them ever coming to a vote that the veteran congressional correspondent William S. White aptly described the Senate as 'the only place in the country where the South did not lose the civil war'.[6] The accusation of systemic racism, then, is irrefutable. As Ta-Nehisi Coates has written, 'For African-Americans, unfreedom is the historical norm.'[7]

Beginning with George Washington, slave-holding Virginians won eight of the first nine presidential elections. Hardly an auspicious start. History has perennially excused the father of the nation on the question of slavery, a judgement based partly on the provision made in his will for the liberation of what he called 'a species of property which I possess, very repugnantly to my own feelings'. However, although he was the only presidential slaveholder to free his slaves, his benevolence has been exaggerated. Washington postdated this liberation until after the death of his wife, Martha (although he allowed his valet, William 'Billy' Lee, to go free, and the country's first First

Lady released the others a year later). At the time of his death, more than 300 enslaved people worked his Mount Vernon estate.[8]

His genius as a general and his statesmanship as president have eclipsed his cruelty as a slaveowner. Indeed, frequently he is referred to as 'a gentleman farmer', a label that conceals a multitude of sins. One of the richest men in the country, his wealth derived from chattel slavery. Even his dentures were crafted from teeth extracted from the mouths of his enslaved labourers.[9]

His response to the plight of Ona Judge, a slave seamstress working for Martha Washington, who escaped after 22 years of servitude, was indicative. Washington, who had just ended his second term as president, dispatched a slave catcher to retrieve her. After hunting her down in New Hampshire, the slave catcher warned Washington that New Englanders favoured her freedom. But the now former president ordered that Ona Judge be brought back to Mount Vernon, believing her emancipation would set a 'dangerous precedent'.[10] For the most part, Washington treated enslavement as unmentionable. 'I do not like to think, much less talk about it,' he admitted in 1794, which not only typified his approach but that of the new republic.[11]

On slavery, Thomas Jefferson, who owned more than 600 enslaved Blacks over the course of his lifetime, was a clump of contradictions. More so than most of his fellow Virginians, he recognised the barbarism of slavery, describing it as 'a moral depravity' and 'hideous blot'. Knowing that the trade violated the enlightened spirit of the revolution, he also pushed in Virginia for a ban on the importation of slaves.

Yet he was thoroughly convinced of the biological inferiority of Blacks, which he set out in *Notes on the State of Virginia*, a work which read in parts like a flowery scientific treatise justifying white supremacy. In it, Jefferson claimed whites were more beautiful, intelligent and less prone to perspiration. Blacks were at least as brave as whites, and arguably more adventurous. 'But this may proceed from a lack of forethought, which prevents their seeing a danger until it is present.'[12] Jefferson's racism, of course, did not dampen his libido.

Sally Hemings, an enslaved woman at Monticello, gave birth to at least six of his offspring.

Throughout his career in public life, Jefferson looked upon enslavement as an intractable dilemma, which he likened to holding 'a wolf by the ears, and we can neither hold him, nor safely let him go'. This explained what the historian David Brion Davis has called his 'immense silence' on the issue from the mid-1790s onwards, and his failure as president to challenge the status quo.[13]

The dualism of Jefferson's position was inked into the pages of his *Autobiography*, which he wrote aged 77, six years before his death. 'Nothing is more certainly written in the book of fate, than that these people are to be free,' he wrote, adding, 'Nor is it less certain that the two races, equally free, cannot live in the same government. Nature, habit, opinion have drawn indelible lines of distinction between them.' In a revealing illustration of deliberate historical erasure, the first 18 words of that passage were chiselled into the Jefferson Memorial in Washington. The last 28 words, about the impossibility of biracial co-existence because of the inferiority of Blacks were junked.

Even if Jefferson and Washington had wanted to do significantly more to end slavery, which is highly contestable, they feared it would break the Union. So just as we talk of the Compromise of 1820, the Compromise of 1850 and the Compromise of 1877, we should also speak of the Compromise of George Washington and the Compromise of Thomas Jefferson.

What differentiated Lincoln was his refusal to accommodate the south, and the absence of the usual political constraints which gave him licence to do so. Not needing Dixie votes, he did not have the same compulsion to compromise. Even so, the Great Emancipator's legacy is profoundly ambiguous.

Although he abhorred the brutality of slavery, he was not an abolitionist per se, and never claimed to be one. It is more accurate to describe him as being anti-slavery, a subtle but important distinction, because his efforts were focused initially upon stopping its expansion, rather than bringing about its end. 'I have no purpose, directly or indirectly, to interfere with the institution of slavery in the States where it exists,' he promised during his first inaugural address, which reflected his desire at the outset of his presidency to defend a white Union, rather than to free the enslaved. 'If I could save the Union without freeing any slave, I would do it,' he wrote to Horace Greeley, the publisher of the *New-York Daily Tribune*, in the summer of 1862, in a letter which revealed his pragmatism on the issue, 'and if I could save it by freeing all the slaves, I would do it.'[14]

Like Washington and Jefferson – and most other white politicians of his age – he was convinced of the inferiority of the Black race, and rejected out of hand any semblance of 'social and political equality'. As the historian Eric Foner has noted, Lincoln did not see Blacks as being 'an intrinsic part of American society', and for much of his career favoured their recolonisation.[15]

So 'Honest Abe' did not always answer the call of his better angels. While some of his speeches scaled rhetorical heights not even Jefferson could reach, he continued to publicly use the word 'n***er' until after the start of the Civil War. Though we celebrate his eloquence during his debates with Stephen Douglas, we tend to overlook how he twice used the n-word in their first encounter, and again thereafter. 'When the question is between the white man and the n***er,' he explained during a speech in 1860, 'they go in for the white man; when it is between the n***er and the crocodile, they take sides with the n***er.' As the Harvard historian Henry Louis Gates, who published an eye-opening anthology of Lincoln's thoughts on race and slavery, has pointed out, most Lincoln scholars find this racist language 'so surprising and embarrassing that they consistently avoid discussing it.'[16]

The issuance in 1863 of the Emancipation Proclamation reflected an evolution of his thinking on race. No longer did he talk of recolonisation, compensation for slaveholders, or of only the gradual repeal of slavery. Nonetheless, the proclamation was primarily motivated by his wartime determination to cripple the south by swelling the ranks of the Union army, through the enlistment of Blacks fleeing the plantations as it marched into Dixie. It was applicable, moreover, only in

Confederate states, and left slavery intact in four Union states where it was still legal.

In the American imagination, he continues to be regarded as the great hero of the story. The Lincoln Memorial has become the country's most holy anti-racism shrine. It was the site of King's 'I Have a Dream' speech and the stage for the opera singer Marian Anderson's performance of 'My Country, 'Tis of Thee' in 1939, a strongly patriotic song sometimes called 'America', after the Daughters of the American Revolution barred her from singing at Constitution Hall.

When Barack Obama launched his presidential bid, he did so in Springfield, Illinois, Lincoln's home. On winning the presidency, he followed the route of the pre-inaugural train journey that Lincoln had completed in 1861, and was sworn in with his hand pressed on the Lincoln Bible (an artefact also used in 2017 by Donald Trump). The 'New Birth of Freedom', a line borrowed from the Gettysburg address, provided the theme for his inaugural address. America's first Black occupant of the White House clearly wanted to convey the impression that the Great Emancipator was his presidential soulmate. As Henry Louis Gates has noted, African-Americans 'have done more perhaps than even white Americans have to confect an image of Lincoln as the American philosopher king and patron saint of race relations'.[17] But Lincoln is a vexing figure. For the presidents who followed, Lincolnesque ambivalence became a recurring motif.

Franklin Delano Roosevelt is a case in point. Because the New Deal lifted so many Americans out of poverty, and demonstrated how government could be a force for good, he continues to be garlanded by liberal America. His record on race relations, however, is hardly deserving of accolades. At the 1932 Democratic convention, it is often forgotten, FDR was the candidate of the southern and the western factions of his party, even though he was the governor of New York, and only managed to seal the presidential nomination by making the segregationist Texas senator, John Nance Garner, his running mate (Garner memorably said the vice presidency was 'not worth a bucket of warm piss').[18]

After his election, the New Deal did little to challenge the southern white power structure. Fearing it would split the Democratic Party and stymie his legislative program, Roosevelt did not back an anti-lynching law, even though there had been some 3,500 attacks since the turn of the century.[19] Similarly, he did nothing to promote Black voting rights, nor object when the Federal Housing Administration codified housing segregation throughout the land. Partly as a result of his soft-pedalling on civil rights, some of his staunchest support came from race-baiting segregationists, such as Governor Theodore Bilbo of Mississippi.

The New Deal years were not without significant racial progress. FDR appointed the first Black federal judge, and brought together a group of African-American advisors dubbed his 'Black cabinet'. After the civil rights leader A. Philip Randolph called in 1941 for a March on Washington – the forefather of the 1963 event – Roosevelt signed an executive order promising an end to discriminatory hiring in military and defence factories. However, the order left Jim Crow in place. As the historian Tony Badger has observed, 'One of the reasons why white southern politicians, normally conservative and anti-federal government, could be so enthusiastic about the New Deal was that it appeared to leave segregation untouched.'[20]

For all his shortcomings on civil rights, FDR's economic program was enough to win him the support of the growing number of Blacks living in northern cities who could vote. This brought about an historic realignment. Blacks ended their traditional allegiance to the Republicans, the party of Lincoln, and switched to the Democratic Party, despite it being the home of so many southern segregationists. Thus, the Roosevelt coalition came into being – an improbable amalgam of southern racists, northern progressives, blue-collar whites, African-Americans and bowtied intellectuals. Pushing civil rights risked splintering this election-winning coalition. Preserving the Roosevelt coalition necessitated a Roosevelt compromise on race.

Harry Truman, whose grandparents were slaveholders who had fought for the Confederacy, was politically braver than his predecessor.

Shocked by the treatment of Black soldiers returning from the war – 'My very stomach turned over when I learned that Negro soldiers, just back from overseas, were being dumped out of army trucks in Mississippi and beaten,' he opined – in 1948 he sent to Congress the strongest civil rights program ever to emerge from the White House. It called for a federal anti-lynching law, an expansion of voting rights, a fair employment practices commission to end workplace discrimination, and an end to segregation on trains, buses and airplanes that crossed state borders. Truman knew that his program would be thwarted in the Senate, the graveyard of civil rights reforms. So he signed executive orders desegregating the military and eliminating discrimination in federal hiring practices.

Though Truman was far from saintly – in private, he referred to African-Americans as 'n***ers' – he pushed for a strong civil rights plank at the 1948 Democratic convention, which sparked a walkout of southern Democrats and prompted Strom Thurmond, the then Governor of South Carolina, to run as a Dixiecrat. Truman knew he risked destroying the Roosevelt coalition, and thus losing the election, but believed he had to take a principled stand.

So began the slow break-up of what was then known as the solid Democratic south, a process that would unfold over the next 40 years. Thurmond and his States' Rights Party ended up winning four Deep South states – Mississippi, Alabama, Louisiana and South Carolina. Never again in a presidential election would the Democrats sweep the states of the Old Confederacy, as they had done since 1932. Still, Truman emerged the victor.

Ambivalent about racism, Dwight D. Eisenhower thought nothing of including among the four great Americans whose portraits hung in the Oval Office a painting of the Confederate general Robert E. Lee, or getting a belly laugh from racist jokes. 'I do not believe we can cure all the evil in men's hearts by law,' he once said, discounting the value of legislation – although in his second term, the Eisenhower Justice Department, at the instigation of its reform-minded Attorney General Herbert Brownell, pushed for piecemeal improvements on voting rights.

A stickler for the chain of command, the former Supreme Allied Commander did believe, however, that orders should be obeyed, and was therefore prepared to enforce the rulings of federal courts, even when he did not agree with them. So when in 1957 whites in Little Rock refused to desegregate the city's Central High School, and to defy the Supreme Court's *Brown* decision, he dispatched the 101st Airborne Division, the famed 'Screaming Eagles', to make sure the 'Little Rock Nine' could attend class. This decision he took with enormous reluctance, and afterwards defended in purely legalistic rather than moral terms. America needed to show a watching world, he said, that it was not subject to mob rule. Eisenhower rued the day, moreover, that he appointed as chief justice the former Republican Governor of California, Earl Warren, an architect of the *Brown* decision. He called it the 'biggest damned-fool mistake I ever made'.

The Kennedy presidency was an historic opportunity missed. By the end of the 1950s, federal judges were now repeatedly ruling against segregation. Ugly racial episodes, such as Little Rock, hardened public opinion against the south. Northern businesses were reluctant to invest in recalcitrant Dixie states. Many segregationists realised that Jim Crow's days were numbered. Yet so determined was Kennedy not to reopen the cleavage between the northern and southern wings of his party that he refused to press early in his presidency for meaningful civil rights legislation. Consequently, white supremacists, such as George Wallace, were emboldened to believe they could prolong the life of Jim Crow, while Black activists became convinced that they needed to mount more militant protest campaigns and to push for further reforms. At the beginning of the decade, equality was the watchword. By 1963, Black protesters were demanding affirmative action and reparations, policies which white America was not so willing to countenance.

Through his caution and inaction, Kennedy therefore squandered this chance to bring about a more peaceful transition towards a more racially equitable America. Only late in his presidency, when the Black revolt threatened to overwhelm his presidency, did he alter course, and propose far-reaching legislation that would bring segregation to an end. By then, however, white extremists such as Wallace had grown in stature, and militant Blacks, such as Malcolm X, had come to the fore. The moment had slipped away.

No modern president did more for African-Americans than Lyndon Johnson, the legislative mastermind behind the 1964 Civil Rights Act and the author of the 1965 Voting Rights Act. Yet the southerner who after Selma movingly recited the words 'We shall overcome' was also prone to racism. Johnson frequently referred to the 1957 Civil Rights Act, which as Senate majority leader he helped steer through Congress, as the 'n***er bill'. When he appointed the first Black Supreme Court justice, he explained his decision to pick Thurgood Marshall, the NAACP lawyer who led the charge for the *Brown* decision, in the basest of terms: 'When I appoint a n***er to the bench, I want everyone to know he's a n***er.'

And so it continued. Richard Nixon started his career as an ally of the civil rights movement. In the 1950s, he had been a member of the NAACP and also befriended Martin Luther King, who he initially hoped would endorse him ahead of the 1960 election. But his early forays into the south that year – his reception in Atlanta was likened to the hysteria surrounding the premiere of *Gone with the Wind* – persuaded him that the Republicans could make deeper inroads into Dixie. Up against Kennedy, he pursued an embryonic version of the southern strategy that meant downplaying civil rights, a decision which probably cost him the election.

In 1968, though, his appeals for 'law and order' – which became code for associating Black advance with Black lawlessness – resonated more strongly with his 'silent majority'. As a Nixon advert put it: 'The first civil right of every American is to be free from domestic violence.' It showed how racially neutral language could be deployed to exploit racial anxieties. This was delineating. As the historian Michelle Alexander later reflected, 'In the 1968 election, race eclipsed class as the organising principle of American politics.'[21]

As president, Nixon accelerated the desegregation of southern schools, actually implemented affirmative action, and focused on economic gains for Black Americans. But his achievements in this field were often overshadowed by his harsh rhetoric against busing. As Leonard Garment, one of his White House aides, once put it, his civil rights policies were 'for the most part operationally progressive but obscured by clouds of retrogressive rhetoric'.[22]

To become the governor of Georgia, Jimmy Carter had hidden from view his liberalism on race, and cynically sought endorsements from prominent white supremacists. But during his inaugural address at the State Capitol in Atlanta in 1971, he came out of the civil rights closet. 'I say to you quite frankly that the time for racial discrimination is over,' he said, which prompted a walkout from some of the segregationist diehards in the Democratic Party.

As president, he appointed high-profile African-Americans to prominent positions – the Georgia Congressman Andrew Young, an acolyte of Martin Luther King, became ambassador to the United Nations – granted more federal support for Black colleges, and supported affirmative action at a time when the policy was coming under assault from conservatives and the federal courts. Perhaps his most significant contribution, though, came in the foreign realm, with his championing of human rights in other countries. His biographer Jonathan Alter claims he 'globalised the American civil rights struggle'.[23]

For all his charm and sunniness, Ronald Reagan's record was execrable. In the 1960s, he had opposed the 1964 Civil Rights Act, 1965 Voting Rights Act and the 1968 Fair Housing Act, placing himself firmly on the wrong side of history. When in the early '70s he heard that African delegates had apparently danced in the aisles of the United Nations following a vote to recognise the People's Republic of China, he vented in a telephone call to President Nixon about 'those monkeys from those African countries – damn them, they're still uncomfortable wearing shoes!'[24]

Reagan launched his 1980 campaign with a speech defending states' rights at the Neshoba County Fair in Mississippi, close to where three civil rights workers had been murdered in the 1960s – a bullhorn more than a dog whistle. His demonisation of Black 'welfare queens' played on longstanding racial stereotypes about laziness and dependency. As president, he opposed sanctions against South Africa, and used the US veto at the United Nations in defence of the apartheid regime.[25] His 'War on Drugs' penalised Black drug use far more severely than white drug use. Federal penalties for the use of crack cocaine were 100 times more severe than the punishment for the use of powder cocaine, the party drug of prosperous whites. Like Washington, FDR and JFK, however, Reagan has been granted absolution. Even Barack Obama happily joined in his veneration when he ran for president in 2008, citing his spirit of optimism, the most uncontested part of his legacy, and ignoring his record on race.

Like Reagan, George H. W. Bush also ended up taking the low road to the White House, by allowing one of his political action committees to run the race-baiting Willie Horton ad (running for the Senate in Texas in the mid-'60s, he had also opposed the Civil Rights Act). It was the southern strategy on steroids, and showed how even moderates relied on race-baiting.

So determined was Bill Clinton to avoid being 'Willie Hortoned' that he made great play during the 1992 New Hampshire primary campaign of flying back to Arkansas for the execution of Ricky Ray Rector, a Black man who had murdered a police officer in the early 1980s – the state's first capital punishment in a decade. No matter that Rector, who had been lobotomised, was in such a confused mental state that he famously asked for the pecan pie from his final meal to be saved for when he returned from the execution chamber, or that the night before his execution he had told his lawyer that he was 'gonna vote Clinton'.

To hammer home his centrist 'New Democrat' credentials, months later Clinton mounted a full-frontal attack on a little-known Black rapper Sister Souljah, who in an interview had suggested, 'If Black people kill Black people every day, why not have a week and kill white people?' 'If you took the words "white" and "black" and you reversed them,' he said, in a clear pitch to white voters, 'you might think David Duke was giving that speech.' A politician famed for feeling people's pain was semaphoring that he also felt their prejudice.

After his victory in 1992, Clinton revelled in his reputation as America's 'first Black president', a moniker bestowed upon him by the author Toni Morrison. But as the Nobel laureate once confirmed to me, the term came not in recognition of his positive contribution to race relations, as was commonly supposed, but rather because she thought he was treated during his impeachment like a Black perp.

Having spoken during his second inaugural address of racial division as 'America's constant curse', Clinton acknowledged the need for symbolic gestures such as apologising to families affected by the infamous Tuskegee syphilis experiment, which for decades used Black men to study the full progression of a disease that caused blindness and early death without offering treatment. Packed with Black appointees, his administration and ambassador corps were the most multiracial the country had seen. Yet his crime policies fuelled the dramatic rise in Black mass incarceration, and his political project was centred upon trying to stop the drift of conservative Democrats to the Republicans, especially in the south.

George W. Bush, by appointing top-tier figures such as Colin Powell and Condoleezza Rice, helped normalise the sight of Blacks at the highest level of government, which in turn helped smooth the path for Barack Obama. His appeal to Black church-goers was part of an attempt to create a Republican multi-racial coalition of the faithful. His support for AIDS relief in Africa, which helped save 25 million lives, is arguably his chief foreign-policy success.

Like his father, however, he played the race card to reach the White House. On the opening day of his South Carolina campaign, he appeared at Bob Jones University, where inter-racial dating was still banned, and said later in the campaign that it was for South Carolinians to decide whether or not to fly the Confederate flag. His campaign even spread rumours that John McCain, his main Republican rival, had fathered a Black love child – an especially cruel lie given that the McCains had adopted a Bangladeshi refugee.

The pattern, then, is one of ceaseless compromise and cynicism, intermittently offset by moments of enlightenment and panicky reform. The politics of race, and specifically the need to hold together election-winning coalitions, routinely trumped the morality of racial justice. In their period of domination from the New Deal onwards, Democrats did not want to splinter the Roosevelt coalition, which from 1932 to 1968 helped win the party seven out of nine presidential elections. In their period of domination from the civil rights era onwards, in which they won five out of six presidential elections, Republicans realised that the road to the White House went through the white south.

Preserving a fragile unity, whether at the national or party level, was always the enemy of equality. Political exigencies almost always held sway, whether it was FDR's need to hold the Democratic Party together, Kennedy's fear of powerful southern Democrats on Capitol Hill, Reagan's determination to conquer the south, or Clinton's desire to reclaim the region for the Democrats. Politics were only overridden, as in 1963, when the fear of widespread Black disorder jolted Kennedy into action, or, as in 1965 after Selma, the horror of brute force southern racism created a groundswell of support for reform.

So although a Black man was finally elected as president in 2008, Barack Obama had been set up to fail by his 43 predecessors.

Rightly it is often said that Obama's election as president was more significant in advancing racial equality than his presidency. For a nation whose unity had relied for most of its first 200 years on the subjugation of Black Americans, first through a compromise allowing for enslavement, and then through a compromise validating segregation, it was immense. No history that he would go on to make was ever likely to match the enormousness of this singular achievement. But Obama himself had downplayed the racial dimension of his candidacy. To win over white voters, he did not present his campaign as an extension of the freedom struggle or portray himself as the heir of the civil rights movement.[26] His bestselling autobiography, *Dreams from My Father: A Story of Race and Inheritance*, was a rumination on his family's history, not his country's baleful racial past.

Though many white liberals saw a vote for Obama as a means of righting a historical wrong, and of expiating personal racial guilt, the young senator himself went out of his way not to frame the election in recriminatory terms. Obama wanted white Americans to feel good about their country, rather than feel guilty. To become a history-defying victor, he became a history-downplaying candidate, which meant avoiding the divisive legacy of enslavement, segregation and the unfinished business of the civil rights era.

Lincoln was the forefather he latched onto, a rare figure of transcendence in modern-day America, and a ghostly wingman who helped Obama position himself firmly in the historical mainstream. Passages of his launch speech in Springfield felt like historical muzak, with middle-of-the road mentions of 'the genius of our founders', the 'band of patriots [who] brought an Empire to its knees', the construction of the transcontinental railroads, the New Deal, the moon landing and 'a King's call to let justice roll down like water', which was about as innocuous a reference to the freedom struggle as was possible to get.

Only when he travelled to Selma in the spring of 2007, to deliver a sermon marking the commemoration of Bloody Sunday, did he link himself directly to the civil rights movement, partly to counter early criticism from some in the Black community that although he could claim an African heritage and an American heritage he was not sufficiently African-American. Or, put another way, he was not Black enough. Obama even claimed that Bloody Sunday had inspired his parents to procreate: 'So don't tell me I don't have a claim on Selma. Don't tell me I'm not coming home to Selma, Alabama.' Immediately, though, the fact-checkers were onto him. Selma unfolded in 1965, the year Obama celebrated his fourth birthday.

Botching the timeline of the civil rights era probably reinforced his early inclination to give it a wide berth. Yet Obama's strategy of avoidance became politically unsustainable early in 2008 when the fiery sermons of his Black pastor, Jeremiah Wright, first surfaced, with their 'God damn America's and denunciations of American history. The senator's emergency response came with what was dubbed his 'race speech', which implied it focused on his Blackness. But it was primarily a meditation on his mixed heritage: how he was 'the son of a Black man from Kenya and a white woman from Kansas', the 'grandson of a white man who had served in Patton's army during World War II', and the 'husband of a Black American who carries within her the blood of slaves and slaveowners'.

Obviously, the setting, the National Constitution Center in Philadelphia, across the way from Independence Hall, was intentionally symbolic. For it was in that hallowed sarcophagus that the framers had produced a document 'stained by this nation's original sin of slavery'. In full professorial mode – that term back then was a compliment – Obama told of how the Founding Fathers had allowed the slave trade to continue for a further 20 years in an attempt to break the stalemate at the constitutional convention, and paraphrased William Faulkner's dog-eared dictum: 'The past is never dead. It's not even past.'

Yet even as he acknowledged 'the brutal legacy of slavery and segregation', he lambasted Wright for expressing 'a profoundly distorted view of this country – a view that sees white racism as endemic, and that elevates what is wrong with America above all that we know is right with America'. Black anger was real and understandable, said Obama, but he also acknowledged 'a similar anger exists within segments of the white community. Most working- and middle-class white Americans don't feel that they have been particularly privileged by their race.' Still, even with his presidential ambitions on the line, he stated that he could not disown his friend Jeremiah Wright, any more than he could disown his white grandmother, 'who on more than one occasion has uttered racial and ethnic stereotypes that made me cringe'. Both were key figures in the Obama story. Both were representative characters in the American story.

What made the speech so politically compelling, then, was its equipoise: his attempt to reconcile two very different Americas, and to revive the consensual tradition of national storytelling. In so doing, he was attempting the same balancing act that he had pulled off so masterfully during his breakthrough speech at the 2004 Democratic convention, with its ringing assertion, 'There is not a liberal America, there is not a conservative America; there is a United States of America.' With race, however, this needle was harder to thread.

In surveying the country's troubled past, Obama seemed to be presenting himself as a dispassionate arbiter. He did not stand before the American people as a politician who could necessarily solve what he called the country's 'racial stalemate'. Indeed, he seemed to mock 'wide-eyed liberals' who thought an Obama presidency would 'produce racial reconciliation on the cheap'. Clearly, though, he hoped he could be a president who could engineer some kind of ceasefire. His candidacy was in many ways an invitation for Americans to close the door on the past.

His Father's Day speech at a Black church in Chicago in June 2008, just months after his Philadelphia address, encapsulated this even-handed approach. Its message was that Black men needed to be better fathers. Here, in his scolding of absentee Black dads, there were even discernible echoes of Bill Clinton's Sister Souljah moment, for the primary audience seemed to be white voters, rather than his mainly Black congregation. For the remainder of the campaign, he returned to his strategy of avoidance. When, in a strange cosmic fluke, he delivered his remarks accepting the Democratic presidential nomination on the 45th anniversary of MLK's 'I Have a Dream' speech, he referred only to 'the young preacher from Georgia' and decided, as he confided in his memoir, 'not to draw too much attention to the fact'.[27]

The approach throughout was to de-emphasise his race. 'The thing is a Black man can't be president in America, given the racial aversion and history that's still out there,' one of Obama's pollsters, Cornell Belcher, told the Black journalist, Gwen Ifill. 'However, an extraordinary, gifted, and talented young man who happens to be Black can be president.'[28] Later, Obama summarised the approach of his campaign high command, which he himself endorsed. 'To them, the immediate formula for racial progress was simple – we needed to win.'[29]

It *was* indeed a winning strategy, which was repurposed during his eight years in the White House. Not wanting his presidency to be defined by his pigmentation, he deliberately avoided the subject. There was no presidential equivalent of his Philadelphia race speech. On the first Father's Day of his presidency, he spoke again about the problems of absentee fatherhood.[30] For the most part, he used race-neutral language. On the rare occasions when he failed to bite his tongue, as in June 2009, when he complained that the Cambridge police had 'acted stupidly' by arresting the Black Harvard academic Henry Louis Gates for trying to enter his own home in a leafy suburb of Boston, he ran into trouble. The famed 'Beer Summit', which brought Gates together with the white officer who carried out the arrest, looked clumsy and contrived. But the thinking behind it was obvious: sharing a beer in the garden of the White House was an act of neutralisation and normalisation.

Unfortunately, the lesson that Obama drew from this ill-judged episode was that any intervention on race was likely to backfire. As he reflected in his memoir: 'The Gates affair caused a huge drop in my support among white voters, bigger than would come from any single event during the eight years of my presidency.'[31] Thereafter during his first term, the most gifted American orator of the modern era, and a figure uniquely well placed to speak on this most vexatious of issues, decided to remain mute. The Obama compromise.

The problem for Obama, and for the country more broadly, was that his victory had created soaring expectations among Black Americans, and created a false sense of racial progress among whites. A Black man in the White House offered proof that the country no longer had a serious race problem. After watching Obama take states like Virginia, Ohio and North Carolina, Ta-Nehisi Coates later noted, 'Anyone could easily conclude that racism, as a national force, had been defeated.'[32] African-Americans naturally thought that a Black man in the White House might finally confront the country's race problem. Supportive whites were seduced by the wishful thinking that the simple act of electing him was problem solved. Others who were less sympathetic thought that America no longer had to obsess so much about race. This was the tension at the heart of his presidency that he never managed to resolve.

Not long into his presidency, a number of influential Black writ-ers challenged the soothing narrative of racial progress that Obama had come to embody. In her 2010 bestseller, *The New Jim Crow: Mass Incarceration in the Age of Colorblindness*, Michelle Alexander argued, 'We have not ended racial caste in America; we have merely redesigned it.' The mass incarceration brought about by the 'war on drugs' – which meant that the penal population jumped from around 300,000 to two million in less than 30 years – had 'emerged as a stun-ningly comprehensive and well-disguised system of racialised social control that functions in a manner strikingly similar to Jim Crow'.[33]

Perhaps even more influential were the essays of Ta-Nehisi Coates, a writer likened to James Baldwin, who lyrically articu-lated the sense of false hope. 'Obama has pitched his presidency as a monument to moderation,' he wrote in one of his seminal essays in *The Atlantic*, noting the homage paid to conservative ideas and Ronald Reagan. 'Despite his sloganeering for change and progress, Obama is a conservative revolutionary, and nowhere is his conserva-tive character revealed more than in the very sphere where he holds singular gravity – race.'[34] In another essay, Coates wrote, 'Part of Obama's genius is a remarkable ability to soothe race consciousness among whites.'[35]

However, as Coates knew all too well, Obama's election had also heightened race consciousness among a sizeable demographic repulsed by the sight of a Black man as the nation's figurehead. There was fury on the right. A ferocious white backlash. Tea Party activ-ists brandished signs claiming Obama would institute 'white slavery'. Social media was awash with chimpanzee memes, and watermelon at the White House jokes. Newt Gingrich called Obama the 'food-stamp president'. Rush Limbaugh labelled him 'Barack the Magic Negro', the title of a song he broadcast repeatedly on his show. The 'racialisation' of politics became even more pronounced. Issues such as healthcare not directly related to race took on a racial cast once Obama advocated for them.

In a rare deviation from his strategy of avoidance, Obama's stron-gest and most heartfelt comments on race came in March 2012, after the killing of the African-American teenager Trayvon Martin, who was shot dead by a Florida neighbourhood watch coordinator, George Zimmerman. 'If I had a son, he'd look like Trayvon,' he said in the Rose Garden, after being criticised by Black leaders for failing to speak out. But his comments came only at the end of an appearance to announce his nominee for the presidency of the World Bank, and in response to a shouted question from a reporter at the end of that event as he was leaving the podium. He had not stepped into the Rose Garden to deliver a prepared statement on Trayvon Martin. Nor had his White House communications team previewed it beforehand or attempted to stage-manage a more meaningful event. Relegating these remarks only heightened the sense that the conversation on race, which so many of his supporters yearned for him to lead, was being treated like a non-essential dialogue, an afterword here, a stray thought there.

When a jury acquitted Zimmerman the following year, having decided that he acted in self-defence, it spotlighted the powerlessness of a Black president to effect meaningful racial change. The Black Lives Matter movement came into being, a protest group given fresh momentum after the police shooting of another African-American, Michael Brown, in Ferguson, Missouri. Anger at police brutality and racial injustice fuelled this nationwide movement, but as the Princeton Professor Keeanga-Yamahtta Taylor later reflected, 'Perhaps the most consequential factor, though, was the deep disappointment that came with the shortcomings or failure of the Obama administration to address the crises afflicting Black communities.'[36]

If not a truly transformational president, Obama, I hoped, could at least be a transitional figure by helping to smooth the path towards America becoming a majority-minority nation. Never was I more optimistic about that than in the penultimate summer of his presidency, a season that began in the valley but ended on the mountain. The low point came in Charleston, South Carolina, with an appalling act of racist violence: the massacre of nine Black parishioners at the Emanuel African Methodist Episcopal Church in Charleston. Quickly it emerged that the 21-year-old Dylann Roof, who carried out the attack, was a white supremacist who had set out to ignite a race war. In the lead-up to the attack, he had even photographed himself draped in the Stars and Bars of the Confederate army. Rather than worsening race relations, however, the killings seemed to bring about a fleeting moment of racial healing, which was crystallised when Obama led the mourning at the funeral of Clementa C. Pinckney, the pastor at that Charleston church. To the delight of the mainly Black congregation, Obama broke into song, a surprise rendition of 'Amazing Grace'. In that electrifying moment, he appeared to fully embrace for the first time the mantle of Black president.

Weeks later, on a suffocatingly hot day in Columbia, South Carolina, I watched the Confederate colours being lowered for the last time outside the grounds of the State House, the response from South Carolinian lawmakers to Dylann Roof's brandishing of this fabric of hate. Watching amidst a crowd of African-Americans who raised up their hallelujahs and punched the air in delight, it was tempting to look upon this ceremony as the final surrender of the Civil War, a 21st-century Appomattox. Yet already we were in the midst of a racial reversal. For the day before Roof had walked into 'Old Emanuel', his guns at the ready, Donald Trump had announced he was running for president with a flagrantly racist rant against Mexican immigrants.

As the 2016 campaign progressed, I fell into the analytical trap of looking upon Trump's success in the Republican primaries as white America's last hurrah. Clearly not all of his supporters were racist, but a good many doubtless were. Even though I almost embedded myself in the Rust Belt, his heartland, I was convinced he would lose the general election, partly because of his nativism.

I also made the mistake of framing the 2016 election as a battle between Donald Trump and Hillary Clinton, the outsider against the establishment insider. What I had not fully appreciated was the extent to which the contest was just as much an epochal struggle between a white nationalist and the country's most successful-ever Black politician. As the untitled leader of the Birther Movement, Trump had made his political name by questioning whether the US president was even a US citizen. So de-legitimising of the Obama presidency was this conspiracy theory that its millions of adherents could take solace in the belief that America had not truly elected a Black man as its head of state, after all. Birtherism negated the very idea of a Black presidency. A Trump victory would also negate the idea of a Black presidency.

The decency displayed afterwards by the Obamas made this transition more agonising to watch. Those welcoming hugs and polite kisses at the front porch of the White House on the morning of Trump's swearing in. The handshake at the conclusion of the new president's hellfire inaugural address, when Obama told his successor that he had done a 'good job', a nicety that Trump would have taken at face value as a genuine compliment. It brought to mind the mantra spoken of by Michelle Obama that Black Americans had to be twice as good to get on.

Speaking in the Rose Garden on the morning after Trump's victory, Obama had also struck a philosophical tone. 'The path this country has taken has never been a straight line,' he said. 'We zig and zag and sometimes we move in ways that some people think is forward and others think is moving back, and that's okay.' But these were especially hard words to hear for people of colour, whose gains throughout history had so frequently been reversed and revoked.

How alluring it had been to interpret Obama's victory as the end of American history. A Black man occupied a White House built by enslaved people. Finally and belatedly, the original sin of slavery had been absolved. Grace had finally led America home. Amazing grace. But the Obama years showed that hope and history rarely rhyme. Ushering in a post-racial America was impossible, because there could never be a post-historical America.

On the day after the conviction of Derek Chauvin, and with the first anniversary of George Floyd's murder a matter of weeks away, a CNN reporter contacted me, keen to survey the changes the last 12 months had wrought. Maybe the reporter knew that I had once written a book about the civil rights struggle. Perhaps it was because I had covered the protests in New York. But the reporter on the other end of the phone was an African-American journalist, John Blake, who had grown up in a tough neighbourhood of Baltimore, and did not need any guidance from a white foreign correspondent on any of those fronts.

John quickly explained why he was keen to talk. An online search had revealed that I had been the first reporter to use the words 'racial reckoning' to describe the response to the video of George Floyd's suffocation. Was the phrase justified? he asked, in gentle reproach. Why had I chosen to use it?

The term had obvious alliterative attractiveness, and almost instantly became the cliche of the hour. I promised him, however, that I had not used it glibly. Truly I had regarded the Floyd murder as a milestone event, a view based as much on my understanding of the past as rose-tinted thinking about the present. The response to the killing was reminiscent of the public revulsion at the wielding of billy clubs in Selma or the sight of the police dogs lunging at protesters in Birmingham (in the most famous image, it has since emerged, the police officer was actually restraining his animal). On both occasions, acts of police brutality that were caught on camera pricked the conscience of white America, and became the catalyst for racial change. Tragically, violence against Blacks had so often been the necessary precipitant of reform.

This time I did not expect an equivalent legislative response, firstly because the landmark reforms of the 1960s required a level of bipartisanship unimaginable in modern-day Washington; and secondly, because there was not such an obvious form of legislative redress. Nonetheless, in the days following Floyd's murder, as the country witnessed its most widespread racial protests since the slaying of Dr King, there were signs of immediate and significant change.

Like the walls of Jericho, those monuments and statues came tumbling down. Public support for the Black Lives Matter movement reached an all-time high. Books on race and racism – such as Robin DiAngelo's *White Fragility: Why It's So Hard for White People to Talk About Racism*, Ibram X. Kendi's *How to Be an Antiracist*, and Layla F. Saad's *Me and White Supremacy* – leapt onto the bestseller lists, in much the same way that sales of works on the Taliban and al-Qaeda soared in the aftermath of 9/11. In what was described as a wake-up call for 'Corporate America', 145 S&P 500 companies added at least one Black person to their boards. Even Mississippi decided to remove the colours of the Confederacy from its flag, which was astonishing for a Deep South state which had been the spiritual home of Jim Crow.

The term 'systemic racism' entered the mainstream. Joe Biden used it in his 2022 convention speech, in remarks following his victory that November and, more pointedly, in his inaugural address.[37] In this season of elite introspection, a greater number of affluent whites reflected on their privilege, and the advantages which had flowed from it, whether it be receiving more pay for the same work, or not having to rehearse with their sons and daughters how to act if a police officer pulled them over on the highway.

Though on Capitol Hill bipartisan talks aimed at enacting police reform eventually broke down, some 30 states passed more than 140 pieces of legislation. They restricted the use of neck restraints, guaranteed more accountability and heightened the use of body cameras. Even Donald Trump, in the immediate aftermath of the killing, signed an executive order in a Rose Garden ceremony promising to establish a national database on police misconduct.

Obviously the response to the murder of George Floyd had been so profound because the reaction to the video of him being suffocated was so visceral. Yet also at play were larger historical forces. Here, for the demonstrators who took to the streets, was an opportunity to press for the kind of racial breakthrough the Obama presidency had failed to achieve. Here was the chance to engage in the sort of conversation about race that America's first Black president had sought to avoid. Here was a chance to push back against Donald Trump, a businessman with a hideous record of racism, and a president who often fired off racist tweets and made bigoted remarks. 'Tell me one country run by a Black person that isn't a shithole,' he once asked aides. 'They are complete fucking toilets.'[38] In 2019, Trump instructed four Democratic congresswomen of colour, three of whom were born in America, to 'go back and help fix the totally broken and crime infested places from which they came'. Textbook racism. The anger of Black activists came not just from the sight of a Black man being murdered in plain sight by a white police officer, but of also seeing a Black man superseded as president by a virulent white nationalist.

America had not witnessed such a spurt of racial progress since the aftermath of King's assassination. However, just as the verdict in the Chauvin case had delivered only a little bit of justice, the murder of George Floyd had brought about only a little bit of reckoning. Certainly, it was not commensurate with the magnitude of the problem. So it was easy to understand the tone of exasperation when CNN's John Blake came to write his article. 'White America has been telling itself that it is experiencing a racial awakening for decades,' he wrote. 'These awakenings are like the cicadas that emerge every 17 years.' As for the term 'racial reckoning', it was what he called a 'rhetorical decoy, a way to avoid facing the deepest problems about race in America instead of a call to confront them'.[39]

When I had first used the term, I remember ruling out immediately its alliterative alternatives. Even a murder as awful as George Floyd's would certainly not bring about 'racial reconciliation', still less a 'racial resolution'. As so often before, it was impossible to reach consensus on a 'racial remedy'. The debate, moreover, quickly became polarised. When young Black activists adopted the slogan 'Defund the Police', many whites who supported reform were confronted with a demand they could not accept.

Even the most liberal-minded, who thought of themselves as allies of the Black Lives Matter movement, were reproached. In a follow-up to her 2018 bestseller, *White Fragility*, Robin DiAngelo, who is white herself, introduced into the lexicon the term 'nice racism', an approach typified by the use of phrases such as 'I have lots of friends of colour', which allowed for progressive whites 'to enact racism while maintaining a positive self-image'. She was denying white liberals the chance of absolution on the cheap, and suggesting that no amount of self-recrimination, or even self-loathing, could exonerate them from being complicit in systemic racism. So not only was there the usual rift between nativists and supporters of the ongoing struggle for equality, a divide was opening up between anti-racists.

This new breach I saw for myself on the first anniversary of George Floyd's murder, when commemorations were held at the spot where he was killed – an area, now marked out by concrete bollards that looked like checkpoints, which had been designated a police-free autonomous 'occupied protest' zone. A young woman of colour was shouting into a microphone that it was impossible for white people to be anything other than racist, a blanket condemnation which illustrated how schismatic and isolating the debate had become. As so often in modern-day America, an event which had the power to draw people together had driven people further apart.

Rather than using the term 'racial reckoning', maybe I should have spoken of how America was trapped again in the familiar cycle of 'racial repetitiveness'. A shocking event had been followed immediately by calls for action. But the cures demanded were unpalatable even to those sympathetic to change. In the 1960s, it had been affirmative action and reparations. In 2020, it was the demand to 'Defund the Police' and calls to pull down statues of national heroes, such as Washington and Jefferson. This in turn hardened the positions of opponents of racial change and bolstered their most extreme spokespeople. In this instance it was Trump who seized upon the phrase 'Defund the Police', and the disorder on the streets, to boost his chances of winning a second term in the White House, just as Nixon had exploited the racial turbulence of 1968 to win the presidency.

Since Trump left office, we have witnessed yet more regression. From the '60s onwards, Blacks and other minorities have fought hard for affirmative action, believing it helped compensate for a starting position in the race of life that almost always placed them far behind white Americans. Although the Supreme Court in its 1978 *Bakke* decision had banned the use by universities of racial quotas in their admissions processes, the use of affirmative action to promote diversity was still deemed constitutional.

In the summer of 2023, however, the court overturned 45 years of precedent and ended race-conscious admissions processes at colleges and universities. 'While I am painfully aware of the social and economic ravages which have befallen my race and all who suffer discrimination,' declared Clarence Thomas, 'I hold our enduring hope that this country will live up to its principles that ... all men are created equal, are equal citizens, and must be treated equally before the law.' Justice Ketanji Brown Jackson, the court's first Black female justice, responded by saying, 'Deeming race irrelevant in law does not make it so in life.'

Affirmative action, and race-conscious admissions, involves intricate issues and subtle arguments, not least whether a Black candidate should be privileged over a white candidate from an unprivileged background. Since the term was first coined during the Kennedy administration, it has been a disputable idea. Still, the Supreme Court ruling fitted a historical pattern. Not for the first time, a right won became a right taken away. It exposed a divide on race that was America's constant curse.

7

In Guns We Trust

Drills were scheduled every few months or so, a classroom ritual which involved locking the door, pulling down the blinds, turning off the lights and crouching under desks. Our children had been conducting them since the age of three, treating them like a game of hide and seek in which they remained motionless and mute. As they moved from kindergarten into elementary school, teachers told them they were rehearsing for a hurricane. Yet the threat came, of course, from a hail of bullets.

Founded in the '60s by a bohemian educator who thought America would benefit from more poets, the school was decorated with lines of verse and posters encouraging the pupils to let their inner lights shine. Classrooms felt like blissful oases in the bustling melee of downtown Brooklyn, a refuge from an often-violent world outside. In the age of Columbine, Sandy Hook, Parkland and Uvalde, however, no school in America was a safe harbour. In the back of our minds – and too often in the forefront – was the unsettling thought that our son and daughter's classrooms could be targeted next. After all, the murder of schoolchildren had become as routine a part of national life as Friday night football or Little League baseball.

I realise that might read like hyperbole. Words of a journalist straining too hard to make his point. Yet each day in America, 12 children die from gun violence. On average, another 32 are shot or injured. In 2020, gun violence surpassed traffic accidents as the leading cause of death among American children. In 2021, 4,752 children were killed by gun-related injuries – a considerably higher death toll than the attacks of September 11th.[1] Since Columbine in 1999, it has been estimated that more than 356,000 students have experienced firsthand gun violence at school.[2]

Back in the 1990s, the Centers for Disease Control started tracking gun violence as if it was a communicable disease. Now this scourge has reached epidemic levels. On average there are almost two mass shootings a day – defined as when four or more people are shot or killed in a single incident. These figures have almost become an abstraction, statistics that have lost their impact through constant repetition. One of the most damning aspects of modern-day American life is that mass shootings no longer have the capacity to shock. In January 2023, when a six-year-old boy shot his first-grade teacher in the chest at a school in Virginia, his parents' attorney described it as an 'unimaginable tragedy'.[3] But these kinds of outrages had become quotidian.

Gun-toting killers have been able to run amok in every realm of American life. Hospitals, churches, synagogues, military bases, shopping malls, farmers' markets, Walmarts, outdoor music festivals, nightclubs, breweries, Sweet 16 parties. It is with good reason that one of the leading gun-control advocacy groups is called Everytown.

No day in the calendar is sacred. On the 4th of July in 2022, during a parade on Main Street in Highland Park, Illinois, a gunman killed seven people, having turned the rooftop of a cosmetic shop into a sniper's perch. On Christmas Day in 2008, a shooter walked into a family gathering in a suburb of Los Angeles wearing a Santa Claus outfit and killed nine people. In 2022, there were three mass shootings in the run-up to Thanksgiving – at a Walmart in Chesapeake, on campus at the University of Virginia, and at a gay nightclub in Colorado Springs – which left 14 empty chairs at tables on the country's most widely celebrated public holiday.[4] On Lunar New Year in 2023, a 72-year-old man killed 11 and wounded nine others at a celebratory dance in Monterey Park, California. Every town on every day.

Covering mass shootings is the most depressing aspect of being a US-based correspondent. When the first reports of another attack come through, newsrooms undertake a demoralising – and dehumanising – form of journalistic triage, deciding what weight to give the killings based on the number of fatalities, the ages, race, religions and sexualities of the victims, or the motive of the killer. Under this rubric, massacres such as Uvalde, Parkland and the Las Vegas shooting instantly became major news events, demanding blanket coverage. But what of shootings involving, say, five, six or seven victims? Given the preponderance of killings, the general arithmetic rule, I am ashamed to say, is that the death toll usually needs to reach double figures before a team is dispatched to the airport. Mass shootings therefore defy that old newsroom dictum: if it bleeds, it leads. There has been so much bloodshed that most killings and shootings do not make headline news.

Looking back at the complete list of mass shootings over the past five years, I am struck by how few I can actually remember and how few we even bothered to report. Of the shootings I boarded a plane to cover, it is hard to arrange in my mind the precise chronology. Was the anti-Semitic attack on the synagogue in Pittsburgh in 2018, where Holocaust survivors were among the victims, before or after the massacre in Las Vegas, America's deadliest shooting, when 58 concertgoers were slain by a gunman shooting from the 32nd floor of the Mandalay Bay hotel? Did the Sutherland Springs church shooting in Texas, in which 26 people were killed, predate the Pulse nightclub shooting in Orlando, where 49 people were murdered? Because mass shootings lend themselves to 'listicle journalism', the distillation of news into lists, Google is full of memory prompts. 'The ten most deadly mass shootings' – all but three of which have come in the past 20 years. 'A list of recent high profile shootings in the United States' – an inventory compiled by the Associated Press in 2023, which included the gunman in Cleveland, Texas, who killed five of his neighbours, including a nine-year-old-boy, 'after they asked him to stop firing rounds in his yard because a baby was trying to sleep'.[5]

There was something so unvarying about observing the rituals of mass shootings. The candlelit vigils. The invocations from Republicans of 'thoughts and prayers' for the victims. The demands from Democrats for tightened gun controls, which were well meaning but almost always meaningless. The confirmation, which almost invariably came, that the guns used in these massacres had been purchased legally. The debate about whether teachers should be armed. The stories about how bulletproof backpacks were doing a roaring trade.

Without fail, an anchor in London would ask whether the latest shootings would finally break the legislative deadlock. But that question could almost always be dealt with in a single word: 'No.' Rather than limiting access to guns, mass shootings were usually followed by a spike in sales, as the industry profited from a misplaced sense of paranoia that a crackdown might be in the offing. The awful inevitability of it all was monstrous. One knew that in a few months or a few weeks, or sometimes even a few days, you would be repeating the cycle again.

Nor was gun violence the kind of story that could be left behind in the grieving community. It was on our doorstep too. Though our Brooklyn neighbourhood, Dumbo, was a model of urban regeneration – the home of converted warehouses, high-end furniture stores and hipster ice-cream parlours – there were 77 shootings within a mile radius of our apartment building during the first seven years we were resident. Of those, 25 were fatal. Fortunately, we never heard the sound of gunfire, or saw the shedding of blood. Even so, a drive-by attack took place late one night outside the nearby Shake Shack, the fast-food joint where we used to get our burgers, while there was another shooting on the far corner of our block, just across the street from where I queued each morning for coffee.

Every town. Everyday. Everywhere.

––––––––––

No passage of mangled syntax and dodgy grammar has become so ferociously contested in contemporary America as the Second Amendment, the 27 words decided upon by the Senate as the Bill of

172

Rights went through its clunky ratification process: 'A well regulated militia, being necessary to the security of a free state, the right of the people to keep and bear arms, shall not be infringed.'

In the modern era, the gun lobby has seized upon them to enshrine a right to personal gun ownership. Yet individual gun rights are not part of America's constitutional DNA. Rather, the thinking behind the Second Amendment was to offer states the surety that they could keep their armed militias, and thus preserve their autonomy. First and foremost, it was a safeguard against a federal standing army, which in post-revolutionary America was seen as an instrument of monarchical power, and thus a tyrannical throwback to the days of British rule.[6]

Armed militias, the term used to describe the ad hoc armies of the 13 colonies made up of citizen soldiers, would become the watchmen of America's newly won freedoms and guard against an overbearing federal government. It hardly needed affirming since so many Americans back then owned a gun – though, fatefully, of course, it was – that these yeoman militiamen required firearms. Nonetheless, the words were chosen carefully. The phrase 'well regulated militia' made it clear that while the framers wanted to codify the right to bear arms for military purposes, it should not be open ended, unfettered and universally applicable. The phrase 'bear arms' is also instructive. Armies and militias 'bear arms', not individual hunters. As the writer Garry Wills once memorably put it, 'One does not bear arms against a rabbit.'[7]

Gun ownership was intended as a collective rather than individual right, the cornerstone of what is known as 'the militia theory' of the Second Amendment. This remained the prevailing interpretation for more than 200 years. No documentary evidence has been found showing that individual gun ownership was discussed at the Constitutional Convention. Likewise, as Michael Waldman sets out in his invaluable 'biography' of the Second Amendment, the subject did not arise when it was considered on the floor of the House of Representatives. Always, the debate about the right to bear arms, in as much as there was one, was conducted in reference to militias. One of the few areas of contention, for instance, was whether or not the amendment should refer to conscientious objectors.

The long-forgotten Third Amendment provides insights into the original intent of the Second: 'No Soldier shall, in time of peace be quartered in any house, without the consent of the Owner, nor in time of war, but in a manner to be prescribed by war.' Again, it referred to military service, and was designed to guard against the creation of a standing army. It was not that the Founding Fathers opposed individual gun rights per se. The essential point is that the Second Amendment did not address that question.

By the end of the 18th century, as the new republic continued to suppress the Native-American population and face threats from France and Britain, it became clear that the United States would indeed need a trained standing army. As a result, state militias receded in importance, and the Second Amendment was no longer so constitutionally relevant. For the simple reason it was immaterial to contemporary life, it became known as 'the lost amendment'.

Certainly, the Supreme Court was of the opinion that the Second Amendment pertained to militias, rather than firearms. Between 1876 and 1939 it ruled on four separate occasions that it did not provide a constitutional protection for individual gun ownership. In *United States v. Cruikshank*, a horrid ruling handed down in 1876 which had the effect of allowing groups such as the Ku Klux Klan to terrorise Blacks seeking the right to vote, the justices ruled that the Second Amendment 'has no other effect than to restrict the power of the National government'.

In 1939, the court's ruling in *United States v. Miller* was even more germane. Here the justices had to decide on the constitutionality of the 1934 National Firearms Act, the first major federal gun-control legislation, which was introduced by the Roosevelt administration in the aftermath of the Saint Valentine's Day massacre, a gangland hit in Chicago thought to have been ordered by Al Capone. The case centred upon a bank robber, Jack Miller, who was arrested in possession of a sawn-off shotgun, but then released after a judge ruled that the new firearms legislation violated his Second Amendment right.

But in a landmark ruling, the Supreme Court decided there was nothing to suggest that Miller's sawn-off shotgun had 'some reasonable relationship to the preservation or efficiency of a well regulated militia', and was not protected under the Second Amendment.

Thereafter, the Supreme Court did not adjudicate on its meaning for almost 70 years, and the question, in legal circles at least, was considered settled. A study of law review articles on the Second Amendment published between 1887 and 1960 found that every single one endorsed the militia interpretation. There was not a single dissenting view.[8]

Just as the meaning of the Second Amendment has been widely and wilfully misinterpreted, the long history of gun control in America often has been ignored. At the state level, restrictions on gun ownership were as old as the country itself. Within the city limits of Philadelphia, New York and Boston, it was illegal to discharge a firearm. In Boston, possessing a loaded gun in the home was also prohibited. Pennsylvania, in a move that would send shivers down the spines of contemporary gun enthusiasts, at one stage demanded that all the guns in the state be gathered up so they could be cleaned and inspected.[9] James Madison, the main author of the Second Amendment, introduced a gun-control measure while serving in the Virginia legislature designed to punish people 'who shall bear a gun out side of his enclosed ground unless whilst performing military duty' – a statement which reaffirmed that the Second Amendment applied to armed groups, not lone gunmen.[10]

Laws regulating concealed weapons, such a modern-day bone of contention, are in no way new. As the historian Jill Lepore has documented, they were pioneered at the start of the 19th century in Louisiana and Kentucky, and adopted thereafter by other states such as Ohio, Tennessee, Virginia, Ohio and Alabama.[11] Gunslinging Texas followed suit in 1893. As the state's then governor, Jim Hogg, insisted, 'The mission of the concealed deadly weapon is murder. To check it is the duty of every self-respecting, law-abiding man.' Even in Dodge City, which was supposedly the wildest of the Wild West, a billboard decreed: 'The Carrying of Firearms Strictly Prohibited.'[12]

Many of these restrictions were intentionally racist and introduced to control people of colour, more so than guns. Native Americans were prevented from purchasing firearms. So, too, in most states, were free Blacks. Florida passed a law in 1825 that allowed whites access to 'all Negro houses' to 'lawfully seize and take away all such arms and weapons, and ammunition'. After the Nat Turner rebellion in 1831, when enslaved rebels killed up to 65 whites in Southampton County, Virginia, southern states passed a swathe of gun laws to keep firearms out of the hands of Blacks. In the *Dred Scott* ruling, barring Blacks from citizenship was also a means of denying them access to guns – 'to keep and carry arms wherever they went', in the words of the ruling.

Central to the original mission of the Ku Klux Klan was the disarmament of Blacks. At its founding, this white supremacist terror group was also a gun-control organisation. It is no coincidence, as Richard Hofstadter once noted, that the south and south-west are the 'most gun-addicted sections of the United States'. Their rural character was a factor, but as Hofstadter observed, 'It also stems from another consideration: in the historic system of the South, having a gun was a white prerogative.'[13] Gun laws became integral to maintaining the racial hierarchy. White power came from the barrel of a gun.

As for a uniquely American gun culture, it is largely a fabrication. Indeed, in the 19th century, firearms giants such as Winchester and Colt proved just as efficient at manufacturing folk tales celebrating the gun as they were at mass producing firearms. As America moved from being an agrarian society to an urban nation, they needed to turn the gun from being an object of practical necessity into an object of desire: something that was synonymous with American identity. Their continued profits, especially when government demand for firearms fell off during peacetime, depended on it. So they came up with a love story in which the central character was the gun.

To pull off this trick, they needed to show that the 'Wild West' lived up to its name, and that gunfights at the OK Corral were almost a daily occurrence. The gun industry therefore homed in on gunslingers such as Wild Bill Hickok, Billy the Kid, Calamity Jane and Buffalo Bill, grossly exaggerating and romanticising their exploits in order to drive up sales. Buffalo Bill became the hero of more than 500 dime novels, some of which he penned himself, but many of which were written in New York. As the royalties from these bestsellers kept rolling in, even he became embarrassed by these flights of homicidal fancy. 'I am sorry to have to lie quite so outrageously in this yarn,' he wrote at one point to his publisher. 'My hero has killed more Indians on one war trail than I have killed all my life.'[14]

In the 20th century, dime novels were displaced in popular culture by movies, which starred the likes of Gary Cooper, John Wayne and Ronald Reagan, who as a politician traded in the same kind of simple, idealised Western narratives – right versus wrong, good versus evil, white versus non-white. More than 750 westerns were released in the 1950s alone, and though the medium changed, the message remained the same. Cowboys embodied all that was best in America: a sense of rugged individualism, self-reliance, adventure, bravery, masculinity and, most crucially, gun ownership. No matter that these American icons tended to lead humdrum lives, where they were overworked, underpaid and frequently inebriated; that farmers in the Wild West outnumbered them by 1,000 to one; and that at least a quarter of cowboys were Black or Mexican.[15] For millions of Americans, the Wild West became an imaginary realm central to their sense of what it was to be American. By the careful design of the firearms industry, it was a dominion awash with guns.

The history of the American gun industry, then, is the story of US capitalism writ large. As Pamela Haag notes in her excellent study, *The Gunning of America: Business and the Making of American Gun Culture,* 'Gun markets and demand could never be taken for granted. It was the gun business's business to create them.'[16] The pursuit of profits relied on the proliferation of deadly weapons and the propagation of gun-related myths.

To understand how the original meaning of the Second Amendment came to be subverted, and how the long tradition of gun control came to be traduced, it is necessary to briefly sketch out the history of the National Rifle Association, the NRA. Founded in 1871, its initial mission was to rectify a glaring national weakness: the fact that so many Americans were terrible marksmen. Two Union army veterans, Colonel William Conant Church and General George Wingate, had been alarmed at how few of their recruits could properly wield a gun. Studies of the Union Army's marksmanship revealed that it had taken a thousand rounds to hit their target. Fearing this deficiency would be laid bare if the US army had to wage war on European battlefields, the organisation sought 'to promote and encourage rifle shooting on a scientific basis'.[17] Even as late as the 1950s, the sign at its national headquarters spelt out its founding mission: 'Firearms Safety Education. Marksmanship Training. Shooting for Recreation.'

In its early decades, the NRA focused on securing federal funding for new rifle ranges to encourage recreational target shooting, and also in promoting wildlife conservation for members who loved to hunt. In the 1930s, it supported many of the gun controls introduced by the Roosevelt administration to limit the traffic of the machine-guns and sawn-off shotguns used by organised crime, a civic-minded approach which the NRA made much of thereafter – and which is commonly cited today as proof of its original good intentions. 'I do not believe in the general promiscuousness of toting guns,' stated the NRA's then president, Karl T. Frederick, an Olympic gold medal pistol shooter, when he testified before Congress. 'I think it should be sharply restricted and only under licences.'[18]

Yet the storyline is not as clearcut. Often it is mistakenly thought that the NRA's opposition to commonsense gun laws only began in the late '70s, when the conservative movement as a whole became more radicalised. But its strong-arm lobbying on Capitol Hill, and dogged defence of gun rights, started as early as the 1930s, when Congress first started to pass gun-control legislation. As that first bill made its way through Congress, the organisation successfully diluted it by opposing measures such as banning the sale of hand-guns interstate.

As the NRA continued to evolve after the war from being a sports body into a lobby group, its resistance to gun controls stiffened. Between 1955 and 1963, Congress considered 35 gun-control bills.[19] The NRA opposed every one. In the mid-1950s, it also homed in on the Second Amendment, and commissioned an historical investigation to ascertain the original intent of the Founding Fathers. An internal 1955 report concluded that 'the Second Amendment appears to apply to a collective, not an individual, right to bear arms'. However, the NRA buried its own finding and instead promoted what became known as the individual right interpretation in its official journal, the *American Rifleman*.[20] In the early 1960s, the masthead of this influential monthly newsletter was amended, so that it read: 'The strength of the NRA ... depends entirely upon the support of loyal Americans who believe in the right to "Keep and Bear Arms"'.[21]

The assassination of John F. Kennedy posed a dilemma for the organisation. Publicly, it had little choice but to support the renewed push on Capitol Hill for tightened gun controls, not least because Lee Harvey Oswald had ordered his gun from an ad in *American Rifleman*. Simultaneously, in mailings to its growing membership, it framed the modest proposals as 'anti-gun'. Its hope was that the Senate committee considering the bill, which was packed with senators from hunting states, would slow or even halt its advance. When the committee held hearings, the NRA's main talking point was that the Second Amendment guaranteed 'the right to keep and bear arms'. Another argument, that would find an echo in the modern day, was that 'guns don't kill people, people kill people'. Automobiles were responsible for thousands of deaths, but limiting their sale would be ludicrous.

When Franklin L. Orth, the chief spokesman for the organisation, appeared on Capitol Hill, he began by pointing out all the measures that the NRA opposed – police approval to buy a gun, the requirement of a license to purchase or possess a firearm, the registration of ownership – none of which the bill proposed. Here again was a preview of an NRA communications strategy that came to be refined over the years: to exaggerate the threat posed to gun rights by the federal government, and to keep its membership in a perpetual state of hyper-vigilance and fear.

As the legislative process dragged into 1964, an election year, it became clear that the bill would not make it out of a committee so heavily stacked with senators from rural states. Thus, even the assassination of a US president did not lead to a tightening of gun controls. As the journalist Richard Harris wrote in a 1968 *New Yorker* essay chronicling this legislative defeat, 'Nothing renders Congress less capable of action than the need for it.'[22] It was a perfect description of congressional inaction, even more resonant now than it was back then.

After the Watts riots in 1964, the Johnson administration renewed the push for gun controls, motivated by the fear that too many firearms were in the hands of Black hoodlums. Yet the NRA refused to budge, having seemingly decided that Blacks with guns were less of a concern than whites being unable to protect themselves against Blacks with guns. Editorials in the *American Rifleman* euphemistically urged 'law-abiding citizens' to buy more weapons, advice which could easily be construed as an invitation for white vigilantism. The NRA adopted its now well-honed technique of bombarding lawmakers with phone calls, telegrams and letters, and scaremongering. Legislation could ban the private ownership of all guns, it falsely claimed.

The assassination in 1968 of Robert Kennedy, which came so soon after the slaying of Martin Luther King, again intensified the gun debate. Concerned citizens inundated senators with letters and phone calls. There was a racial element too. The spate of urban riots had made law and order a front-burner issue. Militant groups such as the Black Panthers – whose full name was the Black Panther Party for Self-Defense – had started openly carrying firearms at demonstrations. In 1967, members of the group had marched on the California State Capitol in Sacramento brandishing Magnums, shotguns and pistols, to protest against a bill pushed by the then governor, Ronald Reagan, aimed at disarming them. Thus, a protest *against* gun control ended up fuelling demands *for* gun control. Indeed, much of the impetus for the federal 1968 Gun Control Act was to crack down on the import of cheap small calibre weapons, the so-called Saturday Night Specials, which were ending up in Black neighbourhoods.

Unable to block the passage of legislation, the NRA instead sought to weaken it. With the help of sympathetic senators such as Strom Thurmond, they gutted the 1968 Gun Control Act of two of its central provisions: the creation of a national gun registry and licences for all gun carriers. Gun-control advocates were exasperated, their lamentations eerily similar to those of Democratic lawmakers today.

'It is just tragic that in all of Western civilisation, the United States is the one country with an insane gun policy,' mourned the Democratic Senator Joseph Tydings of Maryland in 1968, who, two years later, lost his bid for re-election largely as a result of his support for gun control.[23] When Johnson signed the weakened bill into law, he took aim at the NRA. 'The voices that blocked these safeguards were not the voices of an aroused nation,' he complained. 'They were voices of a powerful lobby, a gun lobby.'[24]

Johnson was right. By the end of the 1960s, the NRA was widely seen as the country's most influential lobby group, more powerful even than the union organisation, the AFL-CIO. As one unnamed senator confided, 'I'd rather be a deer in hunting season than a politician who has run afoul of the NRA crowd.'[25]

For absolutists in the NRA, not even weakening legislation was enough. Libertarians on the more radical fringe of the organisation opposed any form of gun regulation. When in 1971 an NRA member was shot dead during a raid carried out by the Bureau of Alcohol, Tobacco and Firearms to seize an illegally held cache of firearms, it further inflamed the grassroots membership. Some hardliners even believed the federal government had carried out the assassinations of the Kennedy brothers and Martin Luther King as false-flag operations, a pretext for gun confiscation.

Now a schism had opened up between the 'Old Guard' executive leadership team and a militant rank and file. When in the late '70s the NRA announced it was moving its headquarters from Washington to Colorado Springs, it seemed to signal a shift away from frontline politics, where the organisation had enjoyed so much success, and a return to its roots as a sporting body. Diehards therefore plotted a rebellion, which came at the NRA's 1977 convention, with the famed 'Revolt in Cincinnati'.

The leader of this successful putsch, Harlon Carter – a Texan who, in his teenage years, the *New York Times* later reported, had been convicted of murder after shooting dead a knife-wielding Mexican immigrant who he believed had stolen his family's car – became the new executive director. As the one-time head of its lobbying arm, the inaptly named Institute for Legislative Action, Carter redoubled the NRA's influence campaign on Capitol Hill. Integral to this mission was cementing the idea that the Second Amendment enshrined individual gun rights.

To tilt the constitutional debate in its favour, the NRA sponsored law review articles which rejected the long-held militia argument – what Michael Waldman has called 'a fusillade of scholarship and pseudo-scholarship'.[26] Carter, a former head of the US Border Control, also placed a new sign at the NRA headquarters, with its selectively edited interpretation of the Second Amendment: 'The right of the people to bear arms shall not be infringed.' The words 'well regulated militia' had been redacted.

By the late 1970s, the conservative movement was shifting rightwards and the Republican Party was becoming more pro-gun, partly because of the heightened influence of the NRA. While, at the 1972 election, the GOP platform had supported gun control, in 1980 its platform stated: 'We believe the right of citizens to keep and bear arms must be preserved.' In that year's election, the NRA for the first time endorsed a presidential candidate: Ronald Reagan.

Gun violence frequently marred the Reagan years. The attempt on the president's life happened fewer than 100 days into his term of office. In the summer of 1984, the year of Reagan's 'Morning in America' re-election campaign, the country witnessed what was then the deadliest mass shooting carried out by a lone gunman in its history. Twenty-one people were killed at a McDonald's restaurant in a suburb of San Diego, a massacre that I vividly remember because

I was staying at the time in Orange County, a 90-minute drive up Interstate 405.

In response to the San Diego shooting, Reagan remained silent, and continued to oppose restrictions on handguns. The former movie star, who had saddled up in so many 1950s westerns, even considered abolishing the Bureau of Alcohol, Tobacco and Firearms, the federal agency responsible for regulating guns. Though he had cheated death in 1981 – on the day that he left hospital, the Secret Service had to strap a bulletproof vest to his torso to protect the long incision in his chest – he continued to insist that gun restrictions would not have shielded him from the bullets.[27] Appearing in person before the NRA convention in 1983, standing beneath a giant version of the organisation's logo, an American eagle gripping a firearm in its talons, Reagan vowed to 'never disarm any American who seeks to protect his or her family from fear and harm'.[28]

During Reagan's second term, the NRA scored its most significant legislative success to date. It came in 1986 with the passage of the Firearm Owners Protection Act, what it celebrated as 'the most sweeping rollback of gun control laws in history'.[29] The culmination of an 18-year effort to repeal parts of the 1968 Gun Control Act, the new law specifically prohibited the federal government from creating a database of gun ownership, which firearms enthusiasts had long suspected would be the first step towards confiscation. It also invoked 'the rights of citizens … to keep and bear arms under the Second Amendment', the first time legislation had affirmed the individualist interpretation.

For all its gains during the 1980s, the decade ended with a series of setbacks for the NRA, which altered the terms of the debate. In January 1989, just three days before Reagan left office, a gunman wielding a semi-automatic assault rifle killed five children at his former elementary school in Stockton, California, squeezing off more than 100 rounds in one minute before turning the weapon on himself. In response to this schoolyard massacre, California banned assault weapons, and louder became calls for a nationwide prohibition.

Gun-control advocates now had a persuasive new figurehead: Jim Brady, Ronald Reagan's former press secretary, who had been shot in the head during the 1981 assassination attempt. With his wife, Sarah, he formed the Brady campaign to lobby Congress for tighter restrictions on handguns and assault weapons, including a seven-day waiting period to allow for background checks before purchase. On the tenth anniversary of the Reagan assassination attempt, in a massive fillip for their campaign, the couple even managed to enlist an unlikely ally: none other than the Great Communicator himself, whose thinking on guns had evolved. In an editorial for the *New York Times*, Reagan explained how, despite a history of mental illness, John Hinckley Jr had purchased his Saturday Night Special from a pawn shop in Dallas unhindered. 'This nightmare might never have happened,' the former president wrote, 'if legislation that is before Congress now – the Brady bill – had been law back in 1981.'[30]

Later that same year, another highly respected conservative, the former Chief Justice Warren E. Burger, added his voice to those calling for controls. Alarmed that the NRA's individualist interpretation of the Second Amendment was gaining ground in scholarly legal circles, Burger went on the *MacNeil/Lehrer NewsHour* in December 1991 to deliver a rebuttal: 'The gun lobby's interpretation of the Second Amendment is one of the greatest pieces of fraud, I repeat the word fraud, on the American people by special interest groups that I have seen in my lifetime.'[31] It was a memeable moment long before memes had been invented.

By the early 1990s, presidential politics was shifting too. Both Reagan and Bush had been card-carrying members of the NRA. Bill Clinton, by contrast, favoured gun control. When, in October 1991, a gunman massacred 23 diners at a Luby's Cafeteria in Killeen, Texas – which now became America's deadliest mass shooting committed by a lone gunman – demands for action became even more insistent. During the 1992 campaign, the then governor of Arkansas backed the Brady bill, a bold commitment from a centrist determined to shore up the Democratic Party in the south. Such was the fear of gun owners that membership of the NRA grew by 600,000.[32]

As president, Clinton did not waver on gun control, even when congressional leaders in his own party pleaded with him to steer clear of the issue, and southern Democrats actively stood in his way. Back in the early 1990s, there were still enough moderate Republicans with suburban constituencies who favoured reform. That drumbeat got louder after yet another horrific massacre in July 1993, the 101 California Street shooting, when eight office workers were killed at a law firm in San Francisco by a gunman wielding a pair of semi-automatic pistols. With bipartisan support, Clinton signed the Brady Handgun Prevention Act into law in 1993, a rare profile of political courage from a pragmatist famed for calculation and often cravenness.

This same bipartisan coalition came together in 1994 to push for an even more stringent measure: a ban on assault weapons. To build public support, the Clinton administration countered the NRA's pro-gun narrative with an anti-crime narrative: that the police were being outgunned. It helped to have the backing of three former presidents, Ford, Carter and Reagan, who also cast gun control as a godsend for the country's beleaguered police. 'We urge you to listen to the American public and to the law enforcement community,' they wrote in a joint letter, 'and support a ban on the further manufacture of these weapons.' After the ban came into effect, the number of mass shootings fell sharply. While the ten-year ban was in place, the risk of a person being killed in a mass shooting is estimated to have dropped by 70 per cent.[33]

Clinton and the Democrats paid a heavy political price. The 1994 Republican Revolution came just eight weeks after the ban became law. Not only did the Democrats lose control of the House for the first time in 40 years, but also their majority of southern seats in the House and Senate for the first time since Reconstruction. Gun legislation was not solely to blame, but unquestionably it was a factor. 'The NRA is the reason the Republicans control the House,' opined Clinton, a self-serving assessment which minimised the effect of his personal unpopularity.[34] Nonetheless, the view took hold that gun control had cost his party dear. For decades thereafter, Democrats, almost as much as Republicans, became an impediment for mean-ingful gun control.

The '90s saw the emergence of a new CEO of the NRA, a one-time special education teacher, former George McGovern volunteer and protégé of Harlon Carter named Wayne LaPierre. Under his stew-ardship, the NRA became even more outspoken and extreme. In a fundraising letter, shortly after Clinton came to power, LaPierre labelled the new administration 'a gun-grabbing goon squad'. Following the enactment of the assault weapons ban, he warned, 'The final war has begun.' Then, in 1995, he penned his most inflammatory fundraising letter yet, which claimed that the ban on semi-automatic weapons 'gives jack-booted government thugs more power to take away our constitutional rights, break in our doors, seize our guns, destroy our property and even injure and kill us'. It gave a green light to 'federal agents wearing Nazi bucket helmets and black storm trooper uniforms to attack law-abiding citizens'. A storm of protest followed. Former President Bush resigned his lifetime membership. LaPierre was forced to go onto CNN's *Larry King Show* to apologise. That appearance, however, provoked another backlash, this time from NRA hardliners who thought he had nothing for which to apologise.

After the Oklahoma City bomb attack in 1995, LaPierre's broad-side read like a summons to domestic terrorists, such as Timothy McVeigh. However, in an early indication of how even the use of unhinged language was no longer disqualifying when it came to occupying senior leadership positions in the conservative movement, LaPierre not only survived but grew in prominence. As Republicans escalated the culture wars, the NRA became their staunchest ally. Gun control was portrayed as a conspiracy by sneering bicoastal elites, 'an expression of contempt for Middle America', as the NRA board member Grover Norquist later put it.[35]

Anticipating other trends that were reshaping modern-day conservatism, the NRA became more performative in its politics. Though the bespectacled LaPierre was known to friends as shy and bookish – and also a hapless marksman – he learnt the art of dema-goguery. In 1998, Charlton Heston, the actor who played Moses, El

Cid, Ben-Hur and, perhaps more aptly, the circus manager in Cecil B. DeMille's *The Greatest Show on Earth*, became the NRA's president. Ahead of the 2000 election, Heston delivered what was perhaps his most hammed-up line to date. Addressing that year's NRA convention, brandishing a firearm of 'wooden stock and blued steel', he summoned his most biblical voice and thundered, 'From my cold, dead hands.'

The 2000 contest underscored the muscle of an organisation which had long benefited from the high turnout of its members at presidential elections – thought to be around 95 per cent. Partly because of opposition from the NRA, Al Gore ended up losing what were then three fiercely contested swing states, West Virginia, Arkansas and Tennessee. Had Gore won his home state of Tennessee, the hanging chads in Florida would have been a complete irrelevance, and there might never have been a second Bush presidency.

With the Texan crowned the victor, the gun lobby once again had an ally in the West Wing. A senior NRA official boasted that, under a Bush presidency, 'We work out of their office.'[36] Sure enough, in 2002, in a major reversal of official government policy, the Bush Justice Department placed on the record its belief that the Second Amendment 'broadly protects the rights of individuals' to own firearms.[37]

In the 9/11 years, as the country constructed a massive new security apparatus to guard against international terrorism, nothing was done to tackle the scourge of domestic gun violence, even though mass shooters killed more Americans than Islamist terrorists. So allergic was the Bush administration to any tightening of gun controls that even suspects placed on terror watch and no-fly lists were able still to purchase firearms – a vulnerability exposed in 2016 by the mass shooting at the Pulse nightclub in Orlando, which was carried out by Omar Mateen, a homegrown domestic terrorist who had once been under surveillance. Yet Republicans, backed by the NRA, refused to close this loophole. After the attacks of September 11th, Americans, understandably, faced all manner of inconveniences as part of the national effort to thwart future terror attacks. Gun owners, however, remained untroubled.

In 2004, as the sunset clause on the assault weapons ban was about to expire, Bush indicated he was open for an extension. But his fellow Republicans, who controlled both houses of Congress, were vehemently opposed. Amongst Democrats, too, there was no groundswell for extending the ban. By now, the orthodoxy had taken hold that pushing for gun control was a certain vote loser. Afterwards, Congress handed the gun lobby another easy victory, when it passed a law granting firearms manufacturers and sellers an unprecedented degree of immunity from many civil lawsuits.

The expiration of the federal assault weapons ban created an opening in the market which gun manufacturers immediately filled. They did so by developing the AR-15, a civilian version of what had long been unfashionable military weapons. The marketing campaign wrote itself. Gun enthusiasts could possess versions of the very weapons, the M16 and M4, used by US forces in the fight against al-Qaeda. Not only did they cash in on the War on Terror, the triumph of gun manufacturers was to associate the AR-15 with a galvanising principle: the right to bear arms. The weapon that the gun-control activists most wanted to ban became a trophy that gun enthusiasts most wanted to own. 'People who never planned to buy one went out and got one,' noted Grover Norquist. 'It was an f-you to the left.'[38]

One gun company even put on sale a JR-15, a smaller junior version for children, which it marketed to parents with the slogan: 'Get 'em one just like yours.'[39] The AR-15 has become an emblem of political identity, and an object of idolatry. No matter that in ten of the deadliest mass shootings since 2012, the killer wielded this very weapon.

By the end of Bush's eight years in office, America's gun culture had become even more firmly entrenched. Nearly three-quarters of Americans now believed that the Second Amendment protected individual gun ownership, a view endorsed by the Democratic Party in its 2004 platform.

Ultimately, however, it was not the NRA that led the final push to get the Supreme Court to rule in favour of its revisionist interpretation of the Second Amendment, partly because it feared the consequences both of success and failure. Much of its fundraising was centred on the threat posed to the Second Amendment, a revenue stream which might dry up if the Supreme Court ruled in its favour. Conversely, failure would embolden gun-control advocates.

Rather than the NRA, then, it was a group of libertarian lawyers who decided to target a law in the District of Columbia which barred individuals from keeping a handgun in their homes unless they were stored, locked or unloaded. The case centred on Dick Heller, a security guard and self-styled Second Amendment champion whose house on Capitol Hill had been shot up in the 1970s. The capital's strict gun laws, bemoaned Heller, meant that criminals could access firearms, but not law-abiding citizens to use in self-defence.

Ahead of the *Heller* decision, 15 eminent historians tried to bring their expertise to bear by putting their names to an amicus curiae brief, in which they noted: 'As historians of the Revolutionary era we are confident at least of this: that the authors of the Second Amendment would be flabbergasted to learn that in endorsing the republican principle of a well-regulated militia, they were also precluding restrictions on such potentially dangerous property as firearms.' Yet Antonin Scalia, who wrote the 5–4 majority opinion, would have none of it. 'The Second Amendment protects an individual right to possess a firearm unconnected with service in a militia,' he wrote. It was the first time that any federal court had ruled that the Second Amendment enshrined an individual's right to own a gun.

Describing the ruling as 'a dramatic upheaval of the law', justice John Paul Stevens wrote in his dissenting opinion, 'The militias were – and still are – the protected party.' But in a further indication of how Democrats remained traumatised by the gun politics of the '90s, Senator Barack Obama, who was then campaigning for the presidency, issued a statement guardedly welcoming the ruling. It provided, he said, 'much-needed guidance to local jurisdictions around the country'. His squeamishness about taking on the gun lobby continued after the 2008 election. When he unveiled his top 13 priorities for his first year in office, gun control did not make the list.[40] Throughout his first term, he did nothing to curb gun rights.

Heller marked the culmination of a half-century campaign, in which the gun lobby succeeded in upending the terms of the gun debate. Over that period, the NRA pioneered a destructive brand of politics mimicked by the Republican Party. It was based on incendiary rhetoric, a theological absolutism, a binary and polarising framing of issues, the demonisation of the federal government, the need to keep its members in a perpetual state of fear and paranoia which involved the stoking of a conspiratorial mentality, the mischaracterisation of its opponent's position, and, finally, a deliberate distortion of history.

———

Often it is said that America made its choice about gun control in the aftermath of the Sandy Hook Elementary School massacre in 2012, when even the murder of 26 people, including 20 children aged between six and seven, failed to produce any change in gun laws. An attempt to reinstate the assault weapons ban could not even muster a majority in the Senate, where it was defeated by 60 votes to 40. The Obama administration's more modest attempt to expand background checks to most firearm sales was blocked by an anti-gun control coalition, which included four Democratic senators representing the rural states of Montana, Alaska, Arkansas and North Dakota. Two years later, when the president unveiled a series of executive actions on gun control which he knew would be instantly challenged in the courts, he wiped tears from his eyes as he recalled the schoolchildren gunned down at Sandy Hook, and the failure of Washington to take protective action.

But it was not America that made a choice. It was Congress. A clear majority of Americans wanted tighter gun controls. After Sandy Hook, more than 90 per cent favoured a law requiring background checks on all gun-show sales, while almost three-quarters, a record number, supported a ban on handguns.[41] Indeed, polling suggests that Americans have always backed stronger restrictions on the use of firearms. The earliest poll, a survey by Gallup in 1938, showed 79 per cent in favour of gun control. Between 1938 and 1972, as the historian Matthew J. Lacombe has shown, support for gun control never dipped below 66 per cent.[42]

The years since Sandy Hook have seen more than 3,500 mass shootings, but scarce little action to tighten gun restrictions. After the Las Vegas shooting, there was a piecemeal change, when the Trump Justice Department outlawed a device called a bump stock, which enabled semi-automatic weapons to be fired more quickly. But the Trump administration quickly shelved its proposal to ban stabilising braces, which helped snipers shoot more accurately, after the NRA signalled its displeasure.

Hopes for meaningful reform again flickered after the high-school shooting at Parkland, Florida in February 2018, when a 19-year-old gunman killed 19 people. In a White House meeting with lawmakers, which unusually was broadcast live on television, Trump indicated his openness to comprehensive gun-control legis-lation, and even hinted at reinstating the assault weapons ban. The following day, however, he met privately with lobbyists from the NRA, and instantly backed off.

Trump's speedy volte-face drove the 'monster under the bed' narrative that Republican presidents and lawmakers live in fear of the NRA. That, however, was only partly true. Most are motivated more by their love of guns, and their fetishisation of semi-automatic weapons such as the AR-15. The kind of Republican moderates who backed the 1994 assault weapons ban have been purged from the party, primaried out of existence. Now the Republican congressio-nal caucus is full of hardline conservatives who love the NRA, rather than fear it. Given the extent of this political symbiosis, it is hard any more to distinguish the NRA from the GOP and vice versa.

Likewise, state houses in red states are dominated by gun propo-nents such as the Texan governor, Greg Abbott, who in 2015 implored his fellow Texans to buy more guns: 'I'm EMBARRASSED. Texas #2 in nation for new gun purchases, behind CALIFORNIA. Let's pick up the pace Texans.' Since then, Texas has witnessed the Dallas police shooting, killing five officers; the Sutherland Springs church shooting, killing 26; the El Paso Walmart shooting, which killed 23; the Midland-Odessa shooting, which killed seven; the Uvalde school shooting, which killed 21; and the Allen mall shooting which killed eight.

The massacre in 2022 at the Robb Elementary School at Uvalde was a rarity, in that it was followed by a legislative response. Astonishingly, more than a dozen Senate Republicans supported legislation strengthening background checks for those aged between 18 and 21, restricting access to guns for those found guilty of domestic violence, and providing incentives for states to pass 'red flag' laws aimed at stopping guns ending up in the hands of people considered a threat to themselves or others.

The Bipartisan Safer Communities Act was the first significant piece of legislation in almost three decades. However, it fell a long way short of what the American people wanted. In the aftermath of Uvalde, polls suggested almost 90 per cent support for universal background checks, 80 per cent support for a ban on selling assault weapons to those aged under 21, and 70 per cent support for raising the minimum age for any firearm purchase to 21.[43]

Just months later, when the murder of those children in Uvalde was still so raw, the Supreme Court ruled in favour of a major expansion of gun rights, by striking down a New York gun law and asserting the right to carry firearms in public for self-defence. The conservative justices were also unmoved by the fact that New York state was reeling still from a racist gun attack in Buffalo, in which an 18-year-old white supremacist shot dead ten people at a supermarket in a mainly African-American community.

Even if Congress did succeed in passing tight gun controls, there are already 400 million guns in circulation. Even if with some magic wand America returned to the days when the Second Amendment was viewed as the lost amendment, the constitutions of 44 out of 50 states protect an individual right to gun ownership. Banning the AR-15 would not be a panacea. Almost two-thirds of mass shootings, and 90 per cent of gun homicides, are carried out with handguns.[44] Gun-control advocates are essentially trying to cram the biggest and most homicidal of genies back into the tiniest of bottles. Moreover, the love of guns, and the devotion to gun culture, has become even more of an ideological touchstone for American conservatism than strong national defence or even lower taxes.

Tragically for its victims, then, gun violence is where a multitude of American problems intersect. The failure of its legislature to reflect the will of the people. The failure of the Supreme Court to reflect the will of the people. The power of a well-organised minority in the Senate to thwart change. The overrepresentation of rural, gun-friendly states in the upper chamber. The menace of the gun lobby in intimidating moderates tempted to support reform. The ideological extremism of modern-day Republicans. The success of corporate America in evading oversight and regulation. The distorted view of the Constitution. The danger of manufactured myth.

Guns are yet another realm where America is a prisoner of its history, both real, invented and imagined. So those drills in American classrooms will continue. So, too, the mass shootings that make them such a fatal necessity.

8

Roe, Wade and the Supremes

To cross from America into Canada during the Trump years felt more like entering an adjacent universe than traversing neighbouring lands. The border served not just as a line of geographical demarcation, but also as an ideological boundary: the dividing line between Justin Trudeau's liberal Canada and Donald Trump's increasingly authoritarian America. By the time I visited, however, just before Trump's second Christmas in the White House, it was not the telegenic young Canadian prime minister who was the face of north-of-the-border resistance, but rather one of his septuagenarian compatriots, the novelist Margaret Atwood.

Presenting myself before passport control at Toronto airport with my journalist's visa at the ready, I was asked rather officiously by a young female border agent to declare the specific purpose of my visit. 'I have come to interview Margaret Atwood,' I boldly stated, wondering what would be the response. Instantly, a look of unblinking delight appeared on her face, an expression, it seemed, borne both of patriotism and sisterhood. Then I was whisked through the arrivals halls, as if I myself was the VIP.

The television adaptation of Atwood's masterwork, *The Handmaid's Tale*, had premiered three months into Trump's presidency, and became an allegory for the dystopian zeitgeist of the times. In her imagining of the near future, north-eastern America had become Gilead, a totalitarian theocracy in which a poisonous brew of misogyny and environmental degradation had created a society in which the few women capable of bearing children were enslaved by religious elders. The handmaids' distinctive bonnet caps and hooded cloaks became as much a symbol of the Trump years as the pink woolly pussy hat. Their robes were repurposed as a protest uniform.

Her novel had first been published in 1985, just as a re-elected Ronald Reagan was promising to vanquish what he had called the Soviet Union's 'evil empire'. 'America was viewed as the shining light,' Atwood told me, 'the home of the free.' So much so that her depiction of Gilead was met with scepticism. 'No shiver of recognition ensues,' wrote the novelist Mary McCarthy in an excoriating review for the *New York Times*, which rejected any similarities with the rise of the Moral Majority. 'I just can't see the intolerance of the far right, presently directed not only at abortion clinics and homosexuals but also at high school libraries and small-town schoolteachers, as leading to a super-biblical puritanism by which procreation will be insisted on and reading of any kind banned.'[1]

Yet Atwood's writing had been grounded in history, and specifically Puritan tenets and jurisprudence that held sway in 17th-century New England. Moreover, from the piety of the Pilgrim Fathers, through the series of religious revivals known as the 'Great Awakenings', to the rise of the modern-day Religious Right, a fundamentalist streak had provided a near-continuous throughline. 'They couldn't believe it because they didn't know much American history,' said Atwood of her early critics. 'They couldn't believe that would ever happen in the United States, though it already had, several times, in several ways.'

In conjuring up such a miserable future, Atwood believed she was merely jogging the American memory – reaching back to what she called the country's 'foundational platform of 17th-century theocratic totalitarianism'. In the 1980s there were also contemporary analogues. Among the dog-eared newspaper clippings Atwood used for research was an Associated Press report on a modern-day religious sect in New Jersey in which wives were labelled 'handmaidens'.

So was there a shiver of recognition in the present day? Was *The Handmaid's Tale* to the Trump age what Arthur Miller's *The Crucible* had been to the era of McCarthyism? Atwood thought Trump too clownish to appear as a character in her novel. 'He would have to pious up a lot,' she laughed. Mike Pence, an evangelical Christian who freely admitted that he never dined alone with any woman other than his wife, whom he called 'mother', was 'more like the real thing'. Direct comparisons between Gilead and Trumplandia, though, were overblown, she said: 'We're not there yet.'

On the question of *Roe v. Wade*, she was alarmed that Republican-controlled state legislatures were passing anti-abortion trigger laws that would come into effect if ever the 1973 ruling was overturned. Yet it was not time to break the emergency glass. When we met, Ruth Bader Ginsburg was still drawing breath, and Trump's first two Supreme Court appointees, Neil Gorsuch and Brett Kavanaugh, had stated under oath at their confirmation hearing that they respected precedent rulings, which was code for intimating that *Roe* was not in imminent danger.

Everything changed, however, on a Friday night in September 2020, just two months before the presidential election. The Supreme Court announced that Ruth Bader Ginsberg – 'RBG', as she was known to her adoring liberal fan base – had died. Roughly an hour later, acting in obscene haste, Mitch McConnell said he would move to fill the vacancy, something he had infamously refused to do in 2016, more than eight months out from the presidential election, when the death of Antonin Scalia presented Barack Obama with the opportunity to replace a conservative justice with a liberal, Merrick Garland.

Trump unveiled his third Supreme Court nominee the following weekend: Amy Coney Barrett, a midwestern law professor, staunch Catholic and mother of seven who, in an odd coincidence uncon-nected with Atwood's novel, had once held the title in a charismatic Christian group called People of Praise of 'handmaid'. The arithmetic of the Supreme Court had shifted radically. Trump had been able to achieve what Reagan and the two Bushes had failed to do: construct a majority in the Supreme Court that could overturn *Roe*.

That moment arrived on Friday, 24 June 2022, with a ruling in *Dobbs v. Jackson Women's Health Organization* that came with the shock of a gut punch, even though it had been heavily previewed the month before in an unprecedented leak to the website Politico. It was a male hand that penned the majority ruling. Justice Samuel Alito pronounced that *Roe*, and the subsequent rulings affirming it, were 'egregiously wrong' and amounted to 'an abuse of judicial authority'.

After Politico published its original scoop, Margaret Atwood penned an essay in *The Atlantic* that instantly went viral. 'I stopped writing [*The Handmaid's Tale*] several times, because I considered it too far-fetched,' she wrote. 'Silly me.'[2] Contemporary America was giving dystopian literature a run for its money. An anti-abortion campaign which had begun almost 50 years earlier had achieved its most triumphant victory yet. When it came to reproductive rights for women, America had returned to 1973.

Forty-eight hours into Richard Nixon's second term as president came two breaking news stories of such import that the *New York Times* took the unusual step of running competing banner headlines, stretching the entire width of its front page. The first, rendered in giant capital letters, read: 'LYNDON JOHNSON, 36th PRESIDENT, IS DEAD.' The second, in lower case, noted: 'High Court Rules Abortions Legal the First 3 Months.' The all-male Supreme Court had overruled all state laws that prohibited or restricted a woman's right to abortion in the first semester, a decision that invalidated anti-abortion laws in 31 states.[3]

In its coverage, the *Times* mentioned that an anonymous Texas woman identified as 'Jane Roe' had brought the case – her name was in fact Norma McCorvey, and she would eventually become an anti-abortion activist. But it omitted any mention of Henry Wade, the district attorney of Dallas County who had tried to deny her access to an abortion. Nor did the reporter cite the docket name for the Supreme Court case, a surprise omission given how, over the coming decades, *Roe v. Wade* would become three of the most explosive words in American national life.

Under the headline 'Cardinals shocked', the *Times* ran a perfunctory article on how reaction to the ruling 'fragmented yesterday along predictable lines'. Leaders of the Roman Catholic Church expressed alarm. Women's rights activists expressed delight. Absent from the coverage was any reaction from white protestant evangelicals or leading Republicans. This was not some journalistic lapse or editing error. Instead, it accurately reflected the politics of the time. Opposition to abortion had not yet become a Republican article of faith, or even a priority for evangelicals. Back then, they were more perturbed about court-ordered school desegregation and the threat it posed to whites-only educational institutions – so-called 'segregation academies' – than the rights of the unborn child.

In its 7–2 ruling, the Supreme Court did not break along partisan lines. Three out of four of Nixon's nominees voted to legalise abortion. The sole hold-out was the ultra-conservative William Rehnquist, the future chief justice. A Democratic appointee, Byron 'Whizzer' White, a former college football star who had served in the Kennedy Justice Department before being elevated by JFK to the court, was the only other dissenter. *Roe* had brought about a 'historic resolution of a fiercely controversial issue', reckoned the *New York Times*. The matter seemed settled. History had moved on.[4]

Unlike the *Brown* decision in the 1950s, *Roe* did not look like a potential nation breaker. There was no equivalent of the campaign of massive resistance. When, at the start of 1974, 20,000 protesters converged on Washington for the inaugural 'March for the Right to Life' protest against *Roe*, it was predominantly a Catholic throng. In the 1974 congressional midterms, the first electoral test of *Roe*, abortion was not an issue. That year, the Southern Baptist Convention, the body representing the largest evangelical denomination in the land, reaffirmed a resolution it had first passed prior to *Roe*, which called for the legalisation of abortion.[5] Many Baptists actively welcomed the ruling. 'Religious liberty, human equality and justice are advanced by the Supreme Court abortion decision,' noted Barry Garrett, the Washington bureau chief of the *Baptist Press.*[6]

Partisan divisions were more pronounced on hip-pocket issues such as taxation than values questions such as abortion. Although the GOP labelled George McGovern, the party's left-wing presidential nominee, the 'Triple-A candidate: acid, amnesty and abortion', Nixon's southern strategy focused on race rather than concerns about unborn foetuses, which aligned with evangelical thinking.

Throughout the 1970s, there were anti-*Roe* Democrats, many of them Catholics who represented socially conservative working-class constituencies, and pro-*Roe* Republicans, among them the new First Lady Betty Ford, who described *Roe* as 'a great great decision'. When the Hyde amendment first passed Congress in 1977, which placed restrictions on federal funding of abortion through Medicare, it enjoyed bipartisan support. Polls suggested that, if anything, Democrats were more anti-abortion than Republicans. Rather than the Bible Belt, opposition to *Roe* was strongest in the heavily Catholic Democratic north-east. Ted Kennedy, who later became an ardent pro-choice politician, started out as avowedly pro-life. 'Wanted or unwanted, I believe that human life, even at its earliest stages, has certain rights that must be recognized,' he wrote in 1971, 'the right to be born, the right to love, the right to grow old.'[7]

The politics of abortion changed ahead of the 1976 presidential election, when the Republican Party saw an opportunity to peel away Catholic voters from the Democrats, their traditional home. Meeting for their convention in Kansas City, the GOP adopted a platform calling for an anti-abortion constitutional amendment to 'restore protection of the right to life for unborn children'. Yet the party was hardly united on the issue. Fewer than 40 per cent of the delegates were thought to be 'pro-life'.

At the Kansas City convention, where Gerald Ford, the incumbent president, fought Ronald Reagan, his insurgent challenger, in the battle to lead the Republican ticket, abortion was more a political football than a matter of high principle. To bolster his appeal to the socially conservative wing of the party, Reagan repudiated his earlier support for the liberalisation of abortion laws in California, and endorsed a constitutional amendment curtailing reproductive rights. Determined to protect his right flank, Ford said he supported abortion only in limited cases, such as rape, incest or where the life of the mother was endangered.

Narrowly, the president managed to see off Reagan's challenge, but the party had shifted markedly to the right. In late 1975, partly because of the mounting influence of conservatives within the party, Vice President Nelson Rockefeller, a moderate who as New York governor had authored the most expansive abortion law in the land, announced he would not be Ford's running mate. His replacement on the ticket was Bob Dole, a then youthful senator from Kansas, who adopted a strong anti-abortion stance to impress hardliners.

The reverberations from Rockefeller's departure would be felt for decades. North-eastern GOP moderates, labelled 'Rockefeller Republicans', eventually became an endangered species. The locus of the party shifted from the boardrooms of Wall Street and country clubs of Connecticut to the mega-churches and gun ranges of the Bible Belt and Sun Belt. The party's stance on abortion became more extreme. So even though Jimmy Carter went on to win the 1976 election – a born-again southern Baptist who was the most prayerful of all the post-war presidents – the Republican Party became the spiritual home of religious social conservatives.

Still, however, *Roe* was not the paramount issue for southern evangelical Christians. Many continued to be motivated more by resistance to school desegregation, and the campaign by the Internal Revenue Service to remove tax-exempt status for 'segregation academies', such as the notorious Bob Jones University in South Carolina. Reagan understood this when, during the 1980 campaign, he delivered a landmark speech at a conference in Dallas that brought together a who's who of moral crusaders and TV evangelists – Pat Robertson, Oral Roberts, Phyllis Schlafly and Jerry Falwell. Addressing the 15,000-strong congregation, Reagan spoke of how, if ever he was stranded on a desert island, he would need only one book, the Bible; linked 'old-time religion' with the 'old-time Constitution'; lambasted the Internal Revenue Service for targeting church schools; conjured up his 'shining city upon a hill'; and delivered an opening pitch that consummated his relationship with the Christian right: 'I know this is non-partisan, so you can't endorse me, but I want you to know that I endorse you.' Tellingly, however, he did not mention abortion.[8]

It was only when evangelical groups such as the Moral Majority, which had been founded by Jerry Falwell in 1979, realised that defending the tax-exempt status of 'segregation academies' was becoming politically alienating that abortion became their signature issue. Championing the rights of the unborn child, and railing against *Roe*, became an effective means of galvanising their evangelical base, and fundraising from the right-wing faithful. For the Christian right, legal abortion also became more broadly emblematic: a symptom of unchecked feminism, secular liberalism and societal breakdown. A post-*Roe* spike in the number of abortions only fuelled their righteous rage.

The rhetoric of Reagan reflected this change. When in 1983 he addressed the National Association of Evangelicals, this time he devoted an entire section of his speech to the rights of the unborn child. 'Unless and until it can be proven that the unborn child is not a living entity,' he vowed, 'then its right to life, liberty, and the pursuit of happiness must be protected.' That year, in another indication of how the conservative movement was becoming more faith-based and moralistic, he published an essay on the question, *Abortion and the Conscience of the Nation*. In it, he likened abortion to the evil of enslavement. Abortion was no longer a policy issue. It was doctrinal.

For all that, Reagan was not quite all in, and his political handlers feared that aligning himself too closely with the evangelical right would ostracise mainstream voters. Rather than address the annual 'Right to Life' march in Washington in person, the Great Communicator did so by phone, a form of political ghosting (Donald Trump was the first Republican president to appear before the rally in the flesh).

Well into the '80s, partisan dividing lines on abortion also remained blurred. When in June 1983, a constitutional ban on abortion came before the Senate, which the National Abortion Rights Action League slammed as 'the most devastating attack yet on abortion rights', 15 Democrats voted for it, while 19 Republicans voted against. Serving on the Senate Judiciary Committee, Joe Biden, a devout Catholic, initially supported the constitutional ban – although he voted against when it came before the full Senate.[9] For lawmakers on both sides of the aisle, abortion was still a matter of conscience, rather than party identification. It was not until 1988 that polling from Gallup showed a clear partisan divide had opened up, with more Democrats than Republicans supporting reproductive rights.

Throughout this period, as they sought to overturn *Roe*, Republican pro-lifers pinned their faith on Congress passing a constitutional amendment banning abortion. The Human Life Amendment, it was called. But even though the Republicans controlled the Senate from 1981 to 1987, they still did not have sufficient numbers to win its enactment. This basic political arithmetic brought about a Damascene change of strategy. Rather than persist with the legislative route, the anti-abortion movement shifted its focus to the Supreme Court, in the belief that conservative jurists might one day kill off *Roe*. In the fight for abortion rights, the Supreme Court therefore became the battlefield.

The Founding Fathers would have been shocked at the modern-day sway of the Supreme Court, for the Constitution envisioned a comparatively limited role for the federal bench. 'The judiciary is beyond comparison the weakest of the three departments of power,' wrote Alexander Hamilton in *Federalist No. 78*, since it would not wield any influence 'over either the sword or the purse'. In a footnote, he underscored its relative powerlessness: 'The judiciary is next to nothing.'[10] When it came to separating the powers, the judiciary was very much the third party. For a time, the framers debated whether it should form, along with the executive, part of a 'council of revision' to review legislation passed by Congress. But that veto power ended up being vested solely in the presidency. As the legal historian Linda Greenhouse has put it: 'In the beginning, the prospect seemed distant that the Court would matter much at all.'[11]

Not considering the work of the Supreme Court a high priority, the framers left it to Congress to delineate its precise powers. The 1789 Judiciary Act set up a three-tiered federal judiciary – trial courts, appeals courts and a supreme court – and decided that six justices should sit on the highest court in the land (between 1807 and 1869, the number of justices changed five times, before eventually settling on the present-day nine). Because it was assumed that jurists would not fall prey to partisanship, nor be heavily involved in the most contentious issues of the day, judgeships were made lifetime positions.

Unlike Congress and the presidency, the Supreme Court did not even have a proper building, a state of homelessness which reflected its lowly status. It was only in 1932, after 150 years of peripatetic wandering, that the cornerstone was finally laid on its present home. The originalist theory of jurisprudence, embraced by present-day conservative justices – centred on the idea that the 18th-century intentions of the framers should determine 21st-century law – therefore falls at the first hurdle. Staying faithful to the original intent of the framers would mean relinquishing much of their judicial power and accepting a diminished role. As scholars have frequently pointed out, the Supreme Court was not meant to be supreme.[12]

It did not take long for the judiciary to become politicised, a process that began with John Adams, the country's second president. In his final hours in office in 1801, as he prepared to relinquish power to Jefferson, his great rival, he worked with a Federalist 'lame duck' congress to create a swathe of new judgeships and reduce the number of Supreme Court justices from six to five. With this flagrant act of court packing, Adams sought to turn the judiciary into a Federalist Party stronghold: an 'Adams court' which could advocate for a strong central government.

Among these so-called 'midnight' appointments, none was more significant than John Marshall, a 45-year-old former soldier, congressman and diplomat, who went from serving as secretary of state to chief justice of the Supreme Court, a position he occupied for a record-setting 34 years. Determined that the judiciary should enjoy greater parity with the other branches of government, Marshall sought to vastly expand its influence. This he achieved in what became the Supreme Court's most significant ruling. In *Marbury v. Madison*, a case which centred on Adams' flurry of 11th-hour appointments, the court struck down as unconstitutional a section of the 1789 Judiciary Act, and thus established its power of judicial review. In a move that totally transformed US constitutional law, the Supreme Court asserted its authority to declare an act of Congress void if it was deemed to violate the Constitution. As Marshall explained, 'It is emphatically the province and duty of the judicial department to say what the law is.' The Supreme Court thus became the arbiter of the constitutionality of legislation passed by Congress and signed into law by the president. By making itself the constitutional referee, the Supreme Court now had the power to dramatically alter the course of history, a prerogative it showed no hesitation in using.

Frequently in the following decades, rulings from the Supreme Court were of greater significance than bills passed by Congress. This was especially true of the notorious *Dred Scott* case in 1857, a 'constitutional bombshell' dropped on a deeply divided nation, which decreed that no-one of African descent could ever become a US citizen.[13] A court with a heavy bias toward slavery – five of the justices were from slaveholding families, and seven had been appointed by pro-slavery presidents – set the country on a path to civil war, by fuelling the outrage of northern abolitionists, invalidating the Missouri Compromise and essentially ruling out a political solution to the question of enslavement.

Throughout the 19th century, the Supreme Court became the most reactionary force in politics. In the aftermath of the Civil War, even a court dominated by justices appointed by the Republican Party, who might have been thought to have abolitionist sympathies, handed down ruling after ruling invalidating the reforms of the Reconstruction era and codifying what they deemed to be the racial inferiority of freed Blacks. In 1883, it struck down the Civil Rights

Act of 1875, which had banned racial discrimination in businesses and public accommodations. In *United States v. Harris* – which was also dubbed the Ku Klux Klan case – it ruled that the federal government had no authority to prosecute a group of white men who had lynched four Blacks. In 1896, it handed down the notorious *Plessy v. Ferguson* ruling, which endorsed state segregation laws by upholding the constitutionality of 'separate but equal' facilities based on race. In 1898, with *Williams v. Mississippi*, it unanimously ruled in favour of literacy tests. Jim Crow had few more supportive friends than the justices on the country's highest court.

During the Gilded Age of the late 19th century, when US capitalism ran rampant, the Supreme Court regularly intervened on the side of Big Business. In 1918, it ruled that Congress could not ban child labour in interstate commerce. It struck down laws limiting working hours, supported restrictions on the rights of union members to strike, and opposed moves to break up monopolies. In 1927, in *Buck v. Bell*, it upheld the right of states to forcibly sterilise people deemed unfit to have children of their own, a major victory for the eugenics movement. By the end of the 1920s, the Supreme Court had also accrued even greater prerogatives, after Congress enabled its jurists to decide which cases it considered.

In the 1930s, the Supreme Court used its power to thwart the New Deal, which prompted FDR to declare war on the third branch. In a fireside chat explaining his plan to expand the court, Roosevelt spoke of the need 'to save the Constitution from the Court, and the Court from itself' – although both the president and the court were guilty of overstepping the constitutional mark.

If, in those pre-war years, the Supreme Court acted as a bulwark against reform, in the post-war era it became a driver of social change. And whereas the federal judiciary had long been an ally of Jim Crow, now it came down firmly on the side of the civil rights movement. Under its new chief justice, Earl Warren, it became an active participant in the Second Reconstruction. The *Brown* decision in 1954 was the most significant ruling handed down in the 20th century, not only because it brought about the slow desegregation of southern schools but because it placed the court on a par with Congress and the presidency in shaping domestic policy. So began a phase of judicial activism during which the Constitution was regarded as a living document that needed to be interpreted in the context of the present day – the antithesis of originalism.

Up until *Brown*, the Senate rarely used its 'advise and consent' role mandated by the Constitution to block nominees to the Supreme Court. Frequently, new justices had been nominated and confirmed on the same day. It was not until 1916, with the appointment of Louis Brandeis, the first Jewish justice, that public hearings were held before the Senate Judiciary Committee. Between 1894 and 1968, the Senate rejected just one nominee. But the liberalism of the Warren court meant that the Senate approval process became more politicised.

When in 1967 Lyndon Johnson nominated Thurgood Marshall to become the first Black member of the court, segregationists subjected him to a grilling during his confirmation hearings that resembled the kind of literacy tests used to bar Blacks from voting. In this racist game of Trivial Pursuit, they even demanded that Marshall identify the individual committee members who had drafted the 14th Amendment.

Marshall made it through, but the following year controversy flared again after the retirement of Earl Warren, when Johnson nominated his friend and personal attorney from Texas, Abe Fortas, to become chief justice. Back then, senators still carried on the pretence that the ideology of a nominee should not bar them from the court, so they opposed Fortas on ethical grounds – he had received an unusually large fee of $15,000 for speaking at a university seminar. Yet it was primarily the fact that he was a member of the activist Warren court that raised hackles among conservatives.

Following a four-day filibuster by Republicans and southern Democrats, Johnson withdrew his friend's name, bemoaning the Senate's obstructionism as 'historically and constitutionally tragic'.[14] It was the first time since 1930 that a president's nominee had been blocked, and the start of a new era in the partisan politics of the Supreme Court. Thus, when Nixon became president, Democrats carried out a tit-for-tat reprisal, and blocked the first two of his appointments. No longer were nominations a fait accompli. After 1965, a quarter of nominations failed, mainly because they were rejected by the Senate or the nominations were withdrawn.

The Reagan years only intensified these battles, partly because his administration sought to advance its agenda through the federal courts in order to bypass Congress. There was also an upping of the ideological ante. The early '80s saw the rise of the Federalist Society, which was founded in 1982 by a group of conservative law students at Harvard, Yale and the University of Chicago to push back against the judicial activism of liberal judges and left-wing law professors. Its aim was to shift the federal judiciary rightward, and to embed originalism more firmly, an approach which achieved almost instant results. By the end of his eight years in office, Reagan had picked half of all the federal judges, and, as the historian Ari Berman has noted, his nominees were 95 per cent male, 94 per cent white and 95 per cent Republican.[15]

Despite his blatant politicisation of the judiciary, Reagan's first Supreme Court pick, Sandra Day O'Connor, was fairly benign. Even though this one-time Republican Arizona state senator was more conservative than the justice she replaced, few wanted to stand in the way of the first female judge shattering the legal glass ceiling.

Promoting William Rehnquist to chief justice, which was also subject to Senate confirmation, proved more contentious. Highlighting his appalling civil rights record, Democrats on the Senate Judiciary Committee, led by Joe Biden and Ted Kennedy, took Rehnquist to task for the support he had once expressed for *Plessy v. Ferguson*, for harassing voters in Arizona, and the restrictive covenants on two of his homes, which barred their sale to non-whites and people 'of the Hebrew race'. Even so, the battle still did not unfold along strict partisan lines. When Rehnquist's confirmation came before the full Senate, 16 Democrats voted for him, while two Republicans voted against.[16]

The furore surrounding Rehnquist's nomination explains one of the anomalies of Supreme Court politics: of how Antonin Scalia, who went on to become the darling of the Federalist Society, the high priest of originalism and a hero of Fox News, sailed so effortlessly through his Senate confirmation. As Democrats freely admitted at the time, it would have been impossible to fight simultaneously on two fronts. Besides, Rehnquist was more of a liberal bogeyman back then than Scalia, a Roman Catholic father of nine who became the first Italian-American to serve on the bench. During his confirmation hearings, Biden praised Scalia for his fair-mindedness. Ted Kennedy judged him 'clearly in the mainstream'. Just ten minutes after the roll call on Rehnquist's nomination, the Senate confirmed Scalia's appointment unanimously in a 98–0 vote.[17]

Nomination battles turned fissile when Reagan picked Robert Bork to fill the next vacancy. The solicitor general during the Nixon administration, Bork had agreed to execute the president's orders to fire the Watergate special prosecutor, Archibald Cox, on what became known as the 'Saturday Night Massacre', after his two seniors at the Justice Department, the attorney general, Elliot Richardson, and deputy attorney general, William Ruckelshaus, had resigned in protest. An outspoken social conservative and the foremost academic proponent of originalist jurisprudence, Bork had opposed the 1964 Civil Rights Act, argued there was no constitutional right to engage in homosexual conduct, and opposed *Griswold v. Connecticut*, the Supreme Court ruling in 1965 which overturned a state law criminal-ising the use of contraceptives by married couples.

The fear amongst liberals was that he would vote to overturn *Roe*, and reverse other civil rights. 'Robert Bork's America is a land in which women would be forced into back-alley abortions,' thun-dered Ted Kennedy on the Senate floor just hours after Reagan had announced his nominee, 'blacks would sit at segregated lunch count-ers, rogue police could break down citizens' doors in midnight raids.'

Washington was on a war footing. For the first time, a widely broadcast television attack ad was put to air opposing a Supreme Court nominee, which was narrated by Gregory Peck, the actor who had played Atticus Finch in *To Kill a Mockingbird*. 'He defended poll taxes and literacy tests which kept many Americans from voting,' intoned Peck, in the now-familiar prosecutorial style of negative attack ads. 'He opposed the civil rights law that ended "whites only" signs at lunch counters. He doesn't believe the Constitution protects your right to privacy.'[18] To highlight that last point, a reporter from the *Washington City Paper* managed to get hold of Bork's video-rental history. All it contained was mainstream titles rather than anything more salacious, but it illustrated how vicious and intrusive nominating battles had become.

Televised on C-SPAN, the Bork hearings quickly took on the feel of a show trial. Senators played to the cameras. Flashpoints made it onto the evening news. A nomination hearing became a national melodrama, a pass-the-popcorn spectacle rivalling the daytime soaps. Amidst Republican cries of character assassination, the Senate rejected his nomination. 'Borking' entered the political lexicon. His surname became a verb.

The nomination of Clarence Thomas four years later turned hearings before the Senate Judiciary Committee into a blockbuster franchise that would run and run for decades. Replacing the legendary civil rights crusader, Thurgood Marshall, with a right-wing Black justice was always going to be controversial. Thomas's arch-conservatism – by comparison, even Rehnquist looked almost like a snowflake – made George H. W. Bush's choice still more provocative. 'We're going to Bork him,' declared Flo Kennedy, a lawyer for the National Organization for Women, 'we need to kill him politically.'[19] When the University of Oklahoma law professor Anita Hill disclosed to the FBI that Thomas had allegedly sexually harassed her when he was her boss at the Equal Employment Opportunity Commission, the combination of sex, race, politics and pornography – at one point the testimony centred on an adult film star called 'Long Dong Silver' – held the nation spellbound.

As his reputation was shredded in front of millions watching on television, Thomas raged against the committee. 'This is a circus, it is a national disgrace,' he seethed, 'a high-tech lynching for uppity Blacks.'[20] Still, though, the Senate confirmed him, albeit narrowly in a 52–48 vote, after the Democrats decided against mounting a filibuster.

Again, the vote was not uniformly partisan. Two Republicans voted against, while 11 Democrats backed Thomas.

With a Black conservative taking the seat of a Black liberal, the ideological balance of power shifted to the right. This raised hopes amongst conservatives that *Roe* would finally be overturned. Yet the year after Thomas joined the bench, when the court took up another landmark abortion case, *Planned Parenthood of Southeastern Pennsylvania v. Casey*, six of the other Republican nominees ruled in favour of upholding reproductive rights. Two of Reagan's appointees, O'Connor and Anthony Kennedy, joined the majority. So, too, did, David Souter, a federal judge from New Hampshire appointed by George H. W. Bush, who was expected to be reliably conservative, but who ended up committing the apostasy of siding with the liberal wing.

The *Casey* ruling, which upheld *Roe* but paved the way for further restrictions on abortion access, felt like a centrist compromise. It aligned with the then President Bill Clinton's Third Way maxim that abortion should be 'safe, legal and rare'. But this weakening of *Roe* was nowhere near enough for anti-abortion activists, and the *Casey* ruling led to a rethink on the American right.

In their campaign for hearts and minds, conservative strategists realised they had to forego shrill anti-feminist rhetoric. The anti-abortion movement also needed to distance itself from the violent excesses of Operation Rescue, which had terrorised abortion clinics and their staff. The movement's new slogan, 'Love them both,' the mother and the child, signified a new compassionate approach.[21]

Pro-lifers, as they were now called, also believed the vetting of future Supreme Court justices would have to be more rigorous. No longer would a centrist such as Souter be allowed to slip through. Nor moderate conservatives, such as Kennedy and O'Connor. They would watch out for clues of potential 'ideological drift'. John Paul Stevens, for instance, had been appointed by Gerald Ford, but become one of the court's prominent liberals. The litmus test would be a prospective justice's stance on *Roe*.

This heightened vigilance became evident when in 2005 George W. Bush chose his friend and White House counsel Harriet Miers to replace O'Connor. Miers ended up withdrawing her name from consideration ostensibly because doubts were raised about her qualifications. Yet conservatives had been unwilling to battle on her behalf because she had once argued that 'self-determination' was important in abortion, which sounded dangerously liberal-minded.[22] As her replacement, Bush nominated Samuel Alito, a staunch conservative, card-carrying member of the Federalist Society, and the eventual author of the ruling overturning *Roe*.

By now, the Supreme Court had become entangled in the hoopla of Washington, its justices not just prominent legal figures but pivotal political players. Bill Clinton's impeachment trial in 1998, only the second in the country's history, placed Chief Justice Rehnquist in the spotlight, because the Constitution required that he preside over the proceedings. The Supreme Court's intervention in the disputed 2000 presidential election brought him notoriety, as well as fame. By essentially deciding the election in favour of George W. Bush, the Rehnquist court looked flagrantly biased.

Supreme Court justices were becoming improbable celebrities. In this more performative age of politics, Rehnquist had an eye for the theatrical. After watching a local production of Gilbert and Sullivan's comic opera *Iolanthe*, which featured a lord chancellor as its main protagonist, he decided to add four gold stripes to his black robes. Clinton's choice of Ruth Bader Ginsburg to replace Justice Harry Blackman, the author of the *Roe* majority opinion, brought a feminist trailblazer with star quality to the fore. Deliberately, she set out to write pithy dissenting opinions that had cut-through with the media. Like Rehnquist's golden stripes, her collars became a trademark and fashion statement – for dissenting opinions, she always wore a black bib rhinestone necklace. Just as 'RBG' rose to become a pop-culture icon for progressives, Antonin Scalia became a talismanic figure for conservatives. Though friends and fellow opera buffs, they personified an ever-more-polarised court.

An irony here is that Reagan's pick of Sandra Day O'Connor, who had previously served as the Republican majority leader in the Arizona state Senate, had ended the long tradition of appointing one-time politicians to the court. William Howard Taft, who in 1921 became chief justice, had also been president. Four of the justices who delivered the *Brown* ruling had been elected officials. In the 21st century, Supreme Court justices became more overtly political, even though no appointee had pursued a conventional political career.

Now that packing the federal courts with partisan picks had become the norm, the nominating process became even angrier. Senators in the majority moved swiftly to tilt the federal judiciary in their favour. Senators in the minority used their filibuster power to gum up the works. When George W. Bush came up against the obstructionism of Democrats, who blocked an unparalleled number of judicial nominees, the then Republican Senate Majority Leader Trent Lott threatened what he called 'the nuclear option', which would allow federal judges – though not Supreme Court nominees – to win approval with a simple majority of 51, rather than the super-majority of 60 needed to overcome a filibuster. When Republicans adopted the same blocking tactics against Barack Obama's nominees, the then Democratic Senate Majority Leader, Harry Reid, went atomic.

At the time, Mitch McConnell warned that the Democrats would regret changing the rules, and so it proved. With norms now cast aside, and the nominating process degenerating into a political free-for-all, McConnell barred Obama's choice to replace Scalia, Merrick Garland, from even getting a hearing before the Senate Judiciary Committee. Then, when Donald Trump selected his first Supreme Court pick, Neil Gorsuch, McConnell announced that the nuclear option would now be applied to nominees to the highest court. Under this rule change, Democrats were unable to filibuster, and Gorsuch was confirmed in a 54–45 vote.

Nastier still was the second Supreme Court battle of the Trump presidency, when his nominee, Brett Kavanaugh, a veteran of the Florida recount and a staffer in the George W. Bush White House, faced allegations of sexual assault. Christine Blasey Ford, a professor of psychology, accused him of attempting to rape her at a high-school party. Another woman, Deborah Ramirez, told the FBI he had thrust his naked penis towards her while they were students at Yale.

Once again, the country was riveted by explosive confirmation hearings, which saw Blasey Ford calmly and bravely recount her ordeal. In response, Kavanaugh delivered a 45-minute rant accusing his accusers of 'grotesque and obvious character assassination'. Never before had Capitol Hill witnessed such intemperate confirmation hearings, a low point of which came when, in answer to questioning about his adolescent drunkenness, Kavanaugh yelled like some inebriated frat boy, 'I like beer.'

In the lead-up to the nomination vote, hundreds of demonstrators, including the comedian Amy Schumer, had been arrested after trying to occupy a Senate office building. On the day of his actual confirmation, an even larger crowd converged on Capitol Hill, with protesters at one point surging towards the steps on the East Front. With surprisingly few police officers standing in their way, it looked for a time that the demonstrators could easily breach the doors, rampage through the corridors and take their protest to the floor of the Senate. Following in their wake, I was stunned that they encountered such little resistance. Had it not been for the self-restraint of protesters, who seemed to sense that there were democratic guardrails which barred them from entry, if not sufficiently strong security barriers, we may have spoken of October 6th, the day of Kavanaugh's confirmation, in the same breath as January 6th. If nothing else, the protest demonstrated how easily Congress could be besieged.

Trump's third appointment to the court came after the retirement of Anthony Kennedy, who had cast so many pivotal swing votes during his 30 years on the court that he was often referred to as 'the decider'. In his place, Trump selected the staunch conservative Amy Coney Barrett, whose nomination is best remembered for her maskless unveiling in the Rose Garden of the White House during the Coronavirus pandemic – what instantly became a superspreader gathering.

Conservatives now enjoyed a solid 6–3 majority. The decades-long campaign to replace liberal judicial activists had succeeded in putting conservative judicial activists in their place. The Supreme Court belonged to the Republican Party. *Roe*'s days were numbered.

So once again a federal courthouse had to be ring-fenced in steel, for immediately after the *Dobbs* ruling came down in the summer of 2022 protesters from both sides of the abortion battle squared off outside this supposed temple of American justice. Pro-life campaigners, who saw in the overturning of *Roe* a gift from God, first huddled in prayer and then raised their arms in rapture. 'The future is anti-abortion,' read their signs. '*Roe* is dead.' Pro-choice protesters held aloft placards that had just been rendered meaningless across large swathes of the country: 'My Body My Choice.'

The practical consequences of the ruling were instantaneous. Trigger laws depriving women of their reproductive rights, which would have been illegal just moments before, took immediate effect. That very day, receptionists at abortion clinics had to inform women who had booked the procedure that it was now prohibited. One clinic in Houston cancelled 35 appointments. A 25-year-old, who was driving to the clinic when she received a phone call informing her of the news, stopped at a traffic light and sobbed.[23] In West Virginia, the state's sole clinic cancelled all its appointments, fearful that a law dating back to the 1800s which criminalised the procedure could now be enforced.

In overturning *Roe*, the conservative court was flying in the face of public opinion. Going back years, polls have consistently shown that a solid 60 per cent of Americans believed abortion should remain legal, which partly reflected how common the procedure had become. By the age of 45, nearly one in four American women have terminated a pregnancy. In drafting the *Dobbs* decision, however, Samuel Alito rejected the unwritten principle that the court should align with the majority view of Americans on divisive issues. Quoting a well-known line from Rehnquist, he wrote, 'The Judicial branch delivers its legitimacy, not from following public opinion, but from deciding by its best lights.' Throughout the ruling, Alito adopted the same defiant and dismissive tone, and made no attempt to be conciliatory or empathetic, even though the ruling raised so many health concerns for women. It read like a middle-finger ruling.

Afterwards, the proportion of Americans who expressed no confidence in the court leapt to 43 per cent. Prior to the overturning of *Roe*, it had been 27 per cent. Pew Research found that the court's overall approval ratings were more negative, and more polarised, than at any time in three decades of polling. Less than 30 per cent of Democrats and Democrat-leaning independents viewed the court positively. By contrast, almost three-quarters of Republicans were satisfied.[24]

Glaring now was the court's unrepresentativeness, a process that had been in train since at least the start of the century. Since 2000, it had moved 'to the ideological right of roughly three-quarters of all Americans', according to a study in the Proceedings of the National Academy of Sciences.[25] Though America was becoming more secular, the Supreme Court had become more pious. Four of the five justices who overturned *Roe* were men. Four of the five judges had been confirmed by a Republican-controlled Senate, which represented a minority of American voters. The Democrats had won the popular vote in seven out of the last eight presidential elections, yet the court now had a solid 6–3 conservative majority with the potential to dominate US jurisprudence for decades. As the Harvard professor Maya Sen has noted, 'The court falls more squarely in line with the average Republican, not the average American.'[26] Most of the major decisions on the voting system, stretching back to *Bush v. Gore*, have benefited the Republicans. Majority opinions often read like GOP talking points and commentary from the Federalist Society.

For right-wing jurists, the court of public opinion no longer appears to matter. As if to underscore how untethered it had become from public opinion, just hours after overturning *Roe* the court handed down a ruling weakening gun controls in New York. 'If, over time, the court loses all connection with the public and with public sentiment,' bemoaned associate justice Elena Kagan, an Obama appointee, 'that is a dangerous thing for democracy.'[27]

Given the gridlock in Washington, and the need for the court to more regularly adjudicate between the legislative and executive branches, the Supreme Court has come to wield even more outsized influence. Supreme Court justices have become what the Democratic Senator Elizabeth Warren has called super-legislators. They have turned the Supreme Court into an unelected third legislative chamber. The most undemocratic branch of government has made a country with a democracy problem even less democratic.

Justices appointed to uphold the Constitution seem also now to consider themselves to be above the law. For years, Clarence Thomas has accepted high-value gifts from a super-rich GOP donor, Harlan Crow, including trips on his yacht and private plane, without disclosing them, as required by federal law (though he claims he was advised at the time by judicial colleagues that he did not have to report the hospitality). Thomas's wife, Ginni, is a prominent Trump supporter who attended the January 6th Stop the Steal rally, and joined in the attempt to overturn the 2020 election, even as her husband continued to hear cases on it. When the Senate Judiciary Committee asked Chief Justice John Roberts to testify in a hearing, amidst calls for the court to be bound by an ethics code as lower court justices are, he refused, citing the separation of powers. What his refusal to appear implied was that the court was not just supreme but untouchable.

Senior Republicans, such as Mitch McConnell, who have strategised for decades about how to populate the federal bench with hardline conservatives, have made no apology for fashioning a judiciary mirroring their thinking. 'The Supreme Court exists to protect unpopular views,' he said in 2022. 'Virtually everything in the Constitution is designed to defend the minority against the majority. It is not a majoritarian institution in the sense that it needs to follow public opinion. That's our job.'[28] On this point, McConnell's reading of the Constitution was historically sound.

What *is* blatantly ahistorical is the creed of originalism. First, it implies a unanimity of thought, a groupthink, among the Founding

Fathers that simply did not exist. Second, it skirts around how the Constitution, for the purposes of papering over regional divides and reaching ultimate agreement, was deliberately ambiguous. 'Throughout American history,' the one-time constitutional law professor Barack Obama reflected after his presidency, 'the most important cases have involved deciphering the meaning of phrases like "due process", "privileges and immunities", "equal protection", or "establishment of religion" – terms so vague that it's doubtful two Founding Fathers agreed on exactly what they meant.'[29] The phrase 'high crimes and misdemeanours', the grounds for impeachment, could also be added to that list. It shows how the Constitution has always been shrouded in interpretative fog. Lastly, judicial supremacy, of the kind the court wields today, was never the intention of those who created the Supreme Court.

Following its rightward lurch, the court has also become more deeply religious and thus handed down more faith-based rulings. Yet the Constitution, which didn't mention marriage or even women, was drafted during the most secular phase in American history when the framers were determined to separate church and state and produced a Constitution which omitted any mention of God.

Put simply, then, originalism is the enemy of originalism. However, 18th-century America nonetheless remains the touchstone for 21st-century jurisprudence, as women in need of abortions have discovered to their cost.

9

Toxic exceptionalism

Even by the standards of the Trump era, the day, in April 2022, that he was arraigned on 34 felony counts relating to hush payments to the one-time adult film star, Stormy Daniels, was a three-ringed circus, Barnum and Bailey in scale and outlandishness. If not the greatest show on earth, it was certainly one of the strangest. In full O. J. Simpson 'White Bronco' mode, the cable news channels followed Trump's every move, from his convoy leaving the gates of his rococo mansion at Mar-a-Lago, to the runway of Palm Beach airport, where his private jetliner was waiting; from the touchdown at LaGuardia Airport in Queens, the borough of his birth, to his arrival at the Manhattan Criminal Courthouse, where a Gotham-sized scrum of media awaited – and so, too, an official ready to take his fingerprints.

As news choppers circled over Lower Manhattan, their cameras were trained on a small outcrop of land that had witnessed such gargantuan history. Just a few streets away the Twin Towers had once stood. Close by was the New York Stock Exchange, the scene of the 1929 crash. Wall Street was also where George Washington had been inaugurated as America's first president. Now Donald Trump, the 45th occupant of that office, had become the first current or former president ever to be charged with a crime. Waving slowly from side to side a giant flag at a rally held in the square opposite, a Trump supporter drew a line between those two events. It read: '1776, 2024, Trump or Death.'

Noteworthy about the fight over Trump's arraignment was the repeated use, on both sides of the row, of the phrase 'banana republic' to describe the country's slide. Supporters of Trump complained the prosecution was politically motivated, and thus the sort of 'witch hunt' that only happened in failed states. Foes of Trump claimed that no-one should be beyond the reach of justice, and that America needed to show the watching world – and the world *was* watching – that it remained a 'nation of laws and not of men', as John Adams had once put it. Yet long before Trump's fingertips made contact with the ink pad – ahead of time, he apparently moistened them with hand lotion – many international observers had formed a view: that a country that liked to think of itself as a beacon of democracy was now a dumpster inferno.

At the heart of American exceptionalism lies a faith in the superiority of the US system and a belief, blending the messianic with the Manichean, in the promotion of democratic ideals overseas. During the Great War, Woodrow Wilson spoke of making the world 'safe for democracy'. In the fight against fascism, FDR positioned the country as an 'arsenal of democracy'. Just before he became president, in a speech at the Massachusetts State House, John F. Kennedy revived Winthrop's *Arbella* sermon: 'We must always consider that we shall be as a city upon a hill – the eyes of all people are upon us.' For Ronald Reagan, the city upon a hill became a leitmotif throughout his career. 'I've spoken of the city on a hill all of my political life,' he noted in his farewell address to the nation in January 1989. 'And she's still a beacon, still a magnet for all who must have freedom, for all the pilgrims from all the lost places who are hurtling through the darkness, toward home.' Always keen to twirl a phrase until it twinkled, Reagan also added the word 'shining' to 'city upon a hill'.

George W. Bush placed the promotion of democracy at the heart of the post-9/11 mission. 'It is the policy of the United States to seek and support the growth of democratic movements and nations in every nation and culture,' he noted in his second inaugural address. On the 50th anniversary of Bloody Sunday, Barack Obama described America as a 'beacon of opportunity' that served as a guiding light for people the world over. 'Young people behind the Iron Curtain would see Selma and eventually tear down that wall. Young people in Soweto would hear Bobby Kennedy talk about ripples of hope and eventually banish the scourge of apartheid.' Yet for all the high-blown rhetoric, and the oft-sung arias of exceptionalism, the United States was no longer such an attractive proposition. In 2021, the Economist Intelligence Unit decided to label the United States a 'flawed democracy'.[1] The democracy advocacy group Freedom House ranked it alongside Panama, Croatia and Romania.[2]

American exceptionalism has become almost an entirely negative construct. The phrase 'only in America' has become a term of derision, as opposed to a boast. Americanisation is something to be avoided, rather than emulated. The America of Kitty Hawk and Cape Canaveral has been supplanted in the global consciousness by the America of Columbine and Sandy Hook. The land of MLK had become associated with the strange world of another Georgian, MTG.

Marjorie Taylor Greene, the QAnon-supporting congresswoman who postulated that California's 2018 wildfires could have been ignited by space lasers controlled by a secretive cabal of prominent Jewish businessmen, has come to personify the loss of reason in modern-day US politics. Yet this prom queen of Trumplandia is hardly an isolated figure. Now that the fringe has become its centre, the GOP increasingly feels like a sect populated by the kind of people who as a student I recall seeing working the edges of Times Square, wearing sandwich boards bearing warnings that the end was nigh. Frequently now the Republican congressional caucus is compared with the Mos Eisley cantina, the dim-lit tavern in *Star Wars*, with its assortment of oddball characters.

It brought together chaos merchants such as Matt Gaetz, a Florida congressman who promotes himself on his website as 'Trump's Ultimate Defender', who just days after Trump had been indicted for conspiring to defraud the American government continued to state publicly that 'force' was the only way to bring about change in Washington. There is the cadre of gun-toting conservatives who pose each year with their families for annual Christmas-card photographs, cradling AR-15s like baby Jesus – an NRA nativity. Before his expulsion from Congress in 2023, it even included the serial fabulist George Santos, a Republican from Long Island, who completely concocted his life story with false claims that his grandparents had survived the Holocaust and that his mother was in the South Tower of the World Trade Center on September 11th, when she was living in Brazil at the time. All are representative of a new breed of nihilistic politician, preoccupied with performing political stunts, stoking the furnace of the right-wing media outrage machine, and ginning up the most extreme and conspiratorial members of the Republican base.

A striking feature of the Trump age is how once-respected figures have joined the circus. One-time Never Trumpers, such as Senator Lindsey Graham, who in 2015 described him as a 'race-baiting, xenophobic, religious bigot … unfit for office', have become sycophantic hangers-on. Once-imposing figures like Trump's Secretary of State, Mike Pompeo, a top-of-his-class student at West Point and Harvard Law School, have become figures of Trumpian ridicule – an unnamed former US ambassador told the *New Yorker* that the one-time tank commander was 'like a heat-seeking missile for Trump's ass'.[3] Rudy Giuliani has plummeted the furthest, from his valorisation as 'America's Mayor' after September 11th to his insurrectionism on January 6th, when he egged on the crowd by exclaiming, 'Let's have trial by combat.' Not only was he indicted as an alleged co-conspirator in the attempt to overturn the 2020 election, but also had to file for bankruptcy after being ordered to pay almost $150 million to two Georgian election workers he had defamed.

Witness the transformation of Dr Ronny Jackson, the US Navy rear admiral who served in the White House medical unit during three administrations and was given the sobriquet 'Physician to the President' by Barack Obama, because he was regarded as such a pillar of the West Wing. After entering Republican politics, Jackson instantly became one of the more maniacal Trumpistas. Not only did he attend the Stop the Steal rally on January 6th, but promoted the conspiracy theory that the Democrats had created a new strain of the Coronavirus ahead of the 2022 congressional elections in an attempt to hold onto the House and Senate – he called it MEV, the 'Midterm Election Variant'.

Consider the strange career of J. D. Vance, the Yale Law School graduate from Appalachia who penned *Hillbilly Elegy*, the insightful rumination on white-collar detachment and 'learned helplessness' in the hollowed-out heartland communities that provided the seed-bed for Trumpism. Back then, Vance helped contextualise the rise of Trump – he described him as 'cultural heroin' – and frequently took him to task. 'My God, what an idiot,' he tweeted in 2016. Then in 2022, when he needed the former president's backing to win the Ohio Senate race, he repurposed himself as a Trump impersonator. When they appeared together at an election rally in Youngstown, Trump now mercilessly mocked him: 'J. D. is kissing my ass.'[4]

As Vance's presence reminds us, the Senate has increasingly taken on the character of the House. Gone from its chamber and cloak-rooms are old lions like Daniel Patrick Moynihan, Richard Lugar, Ted Kennedy and John McCain, who commanded global respect. Now its mahogany desks are occupied by rabble-rousers such as Ted Cruz, who says his personal pronouns are 'kiss my ass' and Josh Hawley, who goaded the crowd on January 6th – Ivy League populists who discredit their elite alma maters and make a mockery of the boast that the Senate is the world's greatest deliberative body.

Promising young conservative politicians, who it was once hoped might help de-radicalise the conservative movement, have been tainted. Take Trump's first ambassador to the United Nations, Nikki Haley, who as governor of South Carolina was behind the bravest political act that I have witnessed in the past decade: the unfurling of the Confederate flag at the grounds of the State House. In better times, this profile in courage would have propelled her towards the White House. But when she announced her presidential bid in 2023, with a biographical video splicing together career highlights, footage from that momentous day in Columbia had been banished out of fear, presumably, of inflaming the Trump right. When asked what caused the Civil War during a campaign stop in New Hampshire, Haley, astonishingly, omitted slavery from her answer.

Conservatives not so long ago derided as extreme and dangerous now seem like paragons of moderation. George W. Bush has been repurposed as an elder statesman, not least because of his reaction to Trump's inaugural address: 'That was some weird shit.' His former vice president, Dick Cheney, who was once cast as the 'Dr Evil' of the Bush White House, has joined his daughter, Liz, in becoming one of Trump's most dogged right-wing foes.

America's political recession, of course, has been heavily previewed over the past 30 years. When, on the eve of the 1994 midterms, Newt Gingrich replaced as House Republican leader Bob Michel, an amiable WWII veteran celebrated for his spirit of patriotic bipartisanship. When, from the start of the Clinton presidency, the use of the filibuster as a partisan weapon became rife (of the 2,000 or so times it has been used since 1917, nearly half have been in the past 12 years).[5] When in 1998 the former professional wrestler Jesse Ventura won the governorship of Minnesota. When in 2008 John McCain picked as his running mate Sarah Palin. When in 2010 Republican primary voters selected as their candidate for the Senate seat in Delaware vacated by Joe Biden a Tea Party favourite, Christine O'Donnell, who had dabbled in witchcraft – a revelation unearthed not by a journalist but by the comedian Bill Maher, which speaks of how late-night funny men have become Menckens of our time.

To a watching world it now looks as if US political culture has absorbed the worst traits of American popular culture. The faux combat and pantomime-style chanting of trashy daytime television. The theatrics of professional wrestling. The venality and amorality of reality shows, such as *Survivor*, with its win-at-all-costs contestants (*Survivor*'s executive producer, Mark Burnett, came up with a corporate version of his hit show – *The Apprentice*, starring Donald Trump). The narcissism and attention-seeking of social media influencers. From the 1990s, when entertainment, politics and even journalism became ever more symbiotic, we have been watching the Jerry Springerisation of national life.

The talk-show host himself, a one-time liberal mayor of Cincinnati who had worked on Robert Kennedy's 1968 campaign, hated the direction of travel. 'Hillary belongs in the White House,' he tweeted after watching a presidential debate in 2016, 'Donald Trump belongs on my show.' But those Clinton/Trump debates felt like Springer had produced them; and never more so than when, after the *Access Hollywood* tape emerged, Trump arranged for some of Bill Clinton's female accusers, including Paula Jones and Juanita Broaddrick, to sit in the studio audience.

As those debates attested, set-piece events which should showcase the best of US democracy frequently end up displaying the worst. At the 2020 State of the Union, the House speaker Nancy Pelosi theatrically ripped up the printed copy of Trump's speech – beforehand, the president also appeared to snub her offer of a handshake. In 2023, Republicans repeatedly interrupted Joe Biden with a barrage of heckles. As recently as 2009, when the Republican congressman Joe Wilson shouted, 'You lie!', at Barack Obama during a speech before a joint session of Congress, there was shock and even bipartisan condemnation. Now that behaviour is standard fare. Congress feels like a rowdy studio audience. C-SPAN, the channel that airs the proceedings of Congress, has come to resemble tabloid TV.

What should be orderly democratic processes have more recently produced mayhem. January 6th, the day when the electoral votes are counted by Congress, used to be a small diary entry for the media, which passed uneventfully. The only time I remember cable news paying much attention was in 2000, when Vice President Al Gore experienced the awkward displeasure of presiding over his own defeat and turning down demands from a handful of mostly African-American Democrats to challenge the results.

Likewise, the election of the House Speaker is usually a happy formality – a coronation of sorts. In January 2023, however, it took 15 votes for Kevin McCarthy to finally capture the gavel, amidst scenes of bedlam and a near punch-up between Republican lawmakers themselves. Just seven months later, he became the first House Speaker in US history to be ousted in the middle of a congressional session, following a motion to vacate pushed by Matt Gaetz and his cannibalistic far-right cabal. The House Speakership remained vacant for weeks thereafter, as the Republicans' internecine conflict continued to rage. Even as the Middle East faced its most serious crisis in decades, after Hamas carried out the shock 7 October attacks on Israel, an entire branch of US government was taken offline.

Routine parliamentary business, such as raising the debt limit, has become riven by partisan posturing and bloody-minded brinksmanship, even though the consequences of failing to reach agreement are so financially catastrophic. Regular government shutdowns, a symptom of dysfunction, are a uniquely American phenomenon.

Finding the vocabulary to describe the downward slide has become problematic, so we have come to rely on hyphenated terminology. Hyper-partisanship. Extreme polarisation. Since the 1990s onwards, traditional phraseology has become obsolete. No longer can we talk of 'liberal Republicans'. Not many members of the GOP caucus could even be described as 'moderate' or 'traditional' Republicans.

Washington politics not only looks unhinged, it feels tired and exhausted. Every day in office, Joe Biden has set a new record as the oldest president to occupy the White House. Nancy Pelosi was aged 82 when she finally had to relinquish the gavel. Her then deputy, the House Majority Leader, Steny Hoyer, was a year older. Senator Dianne Feinstein, who died in September 2023, had recently celebrated her 90th birthday. The Republican senator Chuck Grassley was also born in the first year of FDR's presidency. Mitch McConnell is in his early 80s, and exhibiting signs of dementia. Though sprightly by comparison, the Senate Majority Leader, Chuck Schumer, is in his early 70s. It brings to mind Oscar Wilde's famous quote: 'The youth of America is their oldest tradition. It has been going on now for three hundred years.' Congress looks similarly geriatric.

If the criticism now is that America has become a gerontocracy, only a few years ago, in the aftermath of the *Citizens United* ruling, we were bemoaning how plutocratic it had become. America had the best democracy that money could buy. Before that, it was overly dynastic: a land where famous political families, such as the Kennedys, the Cuomos, the Bushes and Clintons, seemed to possess a divine right of kings. Always it has been excessively patriarchal, a men's club predominantly. Russian meddling in the 2016 election showed how vulnerable it had become to foreign interference.

Far from being a model democracy, America in recent times has been superspreading dysfunction. After the 2022 Brazilian presidential election, supporters of the defeated president Jair Bolsonaro, who rejoiced in his nickname 'the Trump of the tropics', mounted their own version of the January 6th insurrection, by storming Congress, the Supreme Court and presidential palace in Brasilia on 8 January. In Britain, Boris Johnson, a populist Old Etonian who his friend in the White House labelled 'Britain Trump' [sic], displayed disturbingly Trumpian traits. These included lying to parliament, breaking his government's own pandemic lockdown rules, violating international treaties, and attempting to cling onto power in the summer of 2022 when his Cabinet and parliamentary party made it clear that he should vacate 10 Downing Street.

In Australia, anti-lockdown protesters brandished Trump banners on the streets of Melbourne that we were more used to seeing in Mississippi or rural Michigan. Protesters paraded a gallows through the streets of the Victorian capital, upon which was hung an effigy of the Labor state premier, Daniel Andrews – or 'Dictator Dan', to use the moniker favoured by the local Murdoch tabloid, *The Herald Sun*, which had come to sound more like its News Corporation sibling Fox News. In what seemed like another admiring nod towards the insurrectionists of January 6th, unruly demonstrators even urinated on the temple-like Shrine of Remembrance, Melbourne's most sacred site.

The American hardline right, which frequently bemoaned the severity of the 'Fortress Australia' lockdowns, egged on their new antipodean friends. The right-wing talk-show host Candace Owens called for the deployment of US troops. 'When do we invade Australia,' she screamed, 'and free a suppressed people who are suffering under a totalitarian regime?' Ron DeSantis suggested breaking off diplomatic relations. Ted Cruz bemoaned the 'Covid tyranny' of a country he regarded as 'the Texas of the Pacific'. Tucker Carlson lamented that demonstrators were not allowed to carry guns, 'since Australians were completely disarmed by their government several years ago'. Donald

Trump Jr added his voice to this howl of protest. 'Don't Australia my America,' he tweeted in September 2021. But having just returned to live in Sydney, after my eight-year assignment in New York and Washington, I found myself thinking, 'Don't America my Australia.'

The creed of American exceptionalism owes more to the Pilgrim Fathers than the Founding Fathers. It was John Winthrop, remember, the English Puritan and founder of the Massachusetts Bay Colony, who spoke of 'a City upon a Hill' in a sermon on the deck of the *Arbella* as the ship approached the north-east coast in 1630. Winthrop was not suggesting that the new colonies would be inherently superior. Nor, obviously, did he have any conception of what would become the United States. Rather, he was delivering a spiritual pep talk, reminding his fellow travellers that they were Christian ambassadors and would be closely watched by the rest of the world.

Almost 150 years later, after winning the War of Independence, the Founding Fathers were surprisingly unmessianic in their thinking. Though the new republic would doubtless benefit from the vast landmass on its doorstep and its fast-expanding population, they did not universally subscribe to the belief that Americans could bank on the favouritism of the Almighty. Having deliberately detached church from state, they regarded this more as a leap of ungodly faith, rather than a divinely ordained sure bet. An experiment with the potential to fail. Spreading freedom around the planet was not on the agenda. George Washington warned against foreign entanglements.

Exceptionalism is sometimes traced back to an oft-quoted section of Alexis de Tocqueville's four-volume masterwork, *Democracy in America*, published between 1835 and 1840. 'The situation of the Americans is therefore entirely exceptional,' he noted, 'and it may be believed that no democratic people will ever be put in the same situation.' But the French aristocrat was not suggesting that America was intrinsically superior or that its national mission set it apart. Indeed, his comments on the United States being 'entirely exceptional' were prefaced with the statement: 'I cannot agree to separate America from Europe, despite the ocean that divides them.'[6]

By the middle of the 19th century, American expansionism had become the spur for a heightened sense of exceptionalism, which came to be articulated in the doctrine of 'manifest destiny'. The term was coined in 1839 by the journalist John O'Sullivan, who wrote of 'the fulfillment of our manifest destiny to overspread the continent allotted by Providence for the free development of our yearly multiplying millions'. Then he prophesied 'the boundless future will be the era of American greatness'. Still, though, the term American exceptionalism had not entered the lexicon, even if its central tenets had taken shape.

Seemingly, Joseph Stalin was the first person to conflate the words 'American' and 'exceptionalism'. Yet rather than alluding to its superiority, an ideological compliment no self-respecting communist would ever make, he was referring to the paradox of how a country of such capitalist excess had so obdurately resisted Bolshevism. When in 1929 the US communist leader, Jay Lovestone, explained to Stalin that the world revolution would not be Americanised, the Russian bemoaned this 'heresy of American exceptionalism'.[7] The roots of 'American exceptionalism', then, are not as deep as is commonly supposed.

Certainly, this galvanising idea, with its can-do sense of the possible, has contributed to America's remarkable achievements. The construction of its vertiginous cities. The creation of its powerhouse universities. Its singular triumph of putting a man on the moon. Its superpower status. But American exceptionalism has also been something of a curse. A self-aggrandising doctrine has regularly inflicted self-harm. Problems have been exacerbated because America has denied the possibility that other countries have better ways of doing things. The belief in the country's unique goodness has blinded it to the ways in which it is unusually bad.

Gun culture is rooted in exceptionalism, the mistaken belief that America has an unparalleled relationship with the gun. This ignores the experience of other frontier nations, such as Canada and Australia, which also relied heavily on firearms in their coloniser-settler days but which have nonetheless enacted commonsense gun laws.

For decades, universal healthcare has been derided as European-style 'socialised medicine', despite an overwhelming body of evidence showing it is far more cost effective and egalitarian than America's largely private system. These failings became glaringly apparent during the Coronavirus pandemic, when a country with just 4 per cent of the world's population suffered 20 per cent of the deaths. Here, though, an Americanism is deployed to fend off a Europeanism: the threat to personal freedom that public medicine supposedly represents.

Exceptionalism has launched America on self-destructive foreign policy adventures, as in Vietnam. The belief in American indispensability has been used to justify US unilateralism, even when it violated international law, as with the invasion of Iraq. With the belief that the country is blessed by God comes the temptation to act as if only higher laws apply. Exceptionalist thinking has also been a bar to understanding why rival nations, such as China, resent and reject the sine qua non of US foreign policy, that its pre-eminence is preordained and thus non-negotiable. It implies foreign countries do not themselves have much agency.

This doctrine has also obscured how national self-doubt is as integral to the American story as national self-confidence. At the turn of the 19th century, it remained questionable whether America could become a cohesive nation – and 60 years later, of course, it fractured in two. Manifest destiny, and the tensions over enslavement that westward expansion brought to the surface, contributed to its break-up. Out of the rampant urbanisation and rapid industrialisation in the second half of the 19th century arose fresh concerns that America was faltering. This national persecution complex provided the spur for the progressive movement of the early 20th century, which combined liberal ideas about social activism with illiberal theories of eugenics. The Great Depression brought into question whether capitalism and democracy would survive.

Even after asserting its dominance in World War II, a phase when it should have been smelling the flowers, America did not always feel superior. McCarthyism stemmed from a paranoia that communism posed an existential threat to the American way of life. The launch of Sputnik 1 in October 1957, a satellite the size of a large medicine ball, also fuelled fears that the Soviets enjoyed a technical edge and would win the space race. The turbulence of the 1960s. The failed war in Vietnam. Watergate. The sight of American diplomats being blindfolded and held hostage in Tehran. All brought on more doomsaying.

Yet despite this ambiguous history of exceptionalism, and intermittent bouts of uncertainty and despondency, expressions of doctrinal doubt have become as much a presidential taboo as publicly questioning the existence of God. In the late '70s, at the depth of what one historian called the 'Great Funk', Jimmy Carter was pilloried for delivering a downbeat 'malaise speech' – which did not include the word 'malaise' – because to critics he appeared to be referring to American greatness in the past tense.[8] Heresy was also the cry when in 2009, at celebrations held in Strasbourg marking the 60th anniversary of NATO, Obama publicly mused that American exceptionalism was no different from 'Greek exceptionalism' or 'British exceptionalism'. By the time he left office, Obama had actually used the term 'American exceptionalism' more than Reagan, the two Bushes and Clinton combined – although the title of his memoir, *A Promised Land* rather than *The Promised Land*, hinted at an ongoing ambivalence.[9]

Back in 1984, the then Governor of New York, Mario Cuomo, delivered a captivating challenge to exceptionalist rhetoric when at that year's Democratic convention he took on Reagan's use of Winthrop's language. 'This nation is more a tale of two cities than a shining city on a hill', Cuomo lyrically lamented. 'There is despair, Mr President, in the faces you don't see, in the places you don't visit in your shining city.' Tellingly, though, voters agreed with Reagan that it was 'morning again in America', and he won re-election with a whopping 49-state landslide.

Personally, I have always been inclined to look upon the United States as a force for good in foreign affairs. I have watched American medics deliver emergency assistance to Iranians injured in the 2003 Bam earthquake, using as their base the barracks of the Iranian Revolutionary Guard. I have sailed onboard a US Pacific carrier fleet as it steamed towards Burma in the aftermath of Cyclone Nargis in 2008, laden with aid for the victims – although the military junta spurned it. With my own eyes I have seen the nation-building once done in Afghanistan, although the US forces which constructed bridges, roads and girls' schools never described it as such for fear of infuriating the then Defense Secretary Donald Rumsfeld, who banned the phrase. At a polling station in Kabul, I watched women queue in their burkhas to vote for the first time in the 2005 Afghan presidential election.

For all that, the idea that the United States is especially virtuous is nonsensical, while the rhetoric of beacons and radiant cities upon a hill has always put American hypocrisy into harsher glare. From the atrocities of the Philippine-American war at the turn of the last century to the massacre at My Lai in Vietnam, from the waterboarding of terror suspects in CIA Black sites, the secret prisons operated in friendly countries, to the torture at Abu Ghraib, the conduct of foreign policy has regularly fallen way short of the values America professes to uphold. Indeed, during the war on terrorism, the watchtowers of Guantánamo Bay became as much a symbol of post-9/11 America as the Statue of Liberty.

So although it was grating to hear Donald Trump heap his customary praise on Vladimir Putin in an interview early in his presidency with the then Fox News presenter Bill O'Reilly, his response to the assertion that the Russian president was 'a killer' rang true: 'Well, you think our country is so innocent?'[10] In a statement widely interpreted as sounding the death knell of American exceptionalism, Trump neatly summarised foreign scepticism in a sullied creed.

———

A trip across the Pacific in the twilight years of the Obama presidency spoke of America's otherworldliness. To catch up on the overnight news, I had turned on the television in my Sydney hotel room, which showed a breaking story out of Adelaide, where an anguished young reporter stood in front of a school building which the graphic at the bottom of the screen indicated had gone into lockdown. The television was on mute. It was hard to tell precisely what was going on. Yet so habitualised had I become to school shootings after living for so long in America that naturally I feared the worst. Surely this could not be happening in Adelaide, of all places? Surely Australia had rid itself of this scourge after the Port Arthur massacre in Tasmania in 1996, when 35 people were killed? Australia had responded, just as Britain had done after the Dunblane massacre which happened the month before, by tightening its gun laws.

Hurriedly, I grabbed the remote and turned up the volume. Finally, I could hear what the reporter was saying. A burglary had been committed in a neighbouring street, and the school had shut its doors because the assailant had not yet been apprehended. Blood had not been shed. There was no sign of any firearms. It was morning in Australia, rather than morning in America.

Gun violence is obviously the source of much of the toxic exceptionalism. America is the only country in the world with more guns than citizens: 120.5 firearms for every 100 residents, more than double the next country, war-torn Yemen. A country with five per cent of the world's population possesses 46 per cent of the world's civilian-owned firearms.[11] The gun homicide rate is 26 times higher than in other high-income countries.[12] About 42 per cent of US adults live in a household that contains a firearm. Surely America is the only country where the largest supermarket chain, Walmart, is also the largest gun retailer.

Police killings are another point of difference. Between 2000 and 2016, British police officers killed 42 people. In March 2016 alone, American police forces killed 100.[13] The United States has become the world's sole carceral state, with the highest number of incarcerated individuals of any country. Each night, more than two million people are held under lock and key, around 2,500 of them on death row. Decades after its abolition in most other advanced nations, America still retains capital punishment – although of the more macabre indicators of its decline has been the failure in recent years to efficiently put to death those found guilty of capital crimes. The European Union, in a sign of global displeasure, instituted an export ban in 2011 which made it harder for US prisons to procure sodium thiopental, an anaesthetic used in lethal injections. This led to a spate of botched executions in which death-row prisoners experienced agonising pain.

At the apex of a malfunctioning criminal-justice system sits the Supreme Court, which brings into sharp relief another American abnormality: the politicisation of the judiciary and prosecutorial system. The United States is surely the only country in the world where citizens can name the justices on their highest court. Still to this day, an aspect of American life which I find jolting is the yard signs at election time, drumming up support for the district attorney, police chief or local judge.

Life expectancy in the United States is now lower than in Cuba and Lebanon.[14] No other country is experiencing an opioid crisis on anywhere near the same scale. In 2022 alone, it claimed 82,998 lives, tens of thousands more Americans than were killed over the 20 years of the Vietnam War. Even before the overturning of *Roe*, America's maternal mortality rate was twice that of most other high-income countries.

Ending the nationwide right to abortion drew an acid shower of international criticism. Justin Trudeau called the Supreme Court's ruling 'horrific'. Boris Johnson described it as a 'big step backwards'. Yet Samuel Alito, the author of the ruling, seemed to bask in his international notoriety. 'I had the honour this term of writing, I think, the *only* Supreme Court decision in the *history* of that institution that has been lambasted by a whole string of foreign leaders,' he boasted during a speech in Italy, in which he essentially embraced negative exceptionalism, and recast international opprobrium as a plus.

The religiosity of America, which drove the overturning of *Roe*, sets it apart. The mega-churches. The white protestant fundamentalism. The widespread belief in Creationism. The demonisation of Darwinism. The growth of sects, such as the Church of Scientology. The peculiarities of Mormonism, mocked so mercilessly in the international stage hit, *The Book of Mormon*. The excesses of TV evangelists, like Jim and Tammy Faye Bakker, the so-called 'Barbie and Ken' of Christian cable, and the central characters in the 'Pearlygate' scandal (the one-time that the cliched '-gate' suffix was worth redeploying). When I was young, Billy Graham could pack out my local football stadium, Villa Park in Birmingham. But no contemporary American evangelical has anywhere near that kind of pulling power overseas, which speaks both of the secularisation of my homeland and resistance to the gospel according to America. To a watching world, it often looks like the country is speaking in tongues.

At a time when the climate emergency has emerged as the planet's foremost issue, America's environmental record has undercut its claim to global leadership. With its addiction to multi-lane freeways, super-sized SUVs, home air-conditioning and urban growth in the Sun Belt, the region with both the hottest average temperatures and many of the fastest growing conurbations, the United States has become the biggest polluter in history.

The technology sector, polling suggests, is the area of American excellence which continues to command the greatest global respect.[15] But Silicon Valley has recently been in a reputational ditch. A string of scandals, from the prosecution of Elizabeth Holmes, the supposed biotechnological brain behind the blood-testing start-up Theranos, to the downfall of Sam Bankman-Fried, the founder of the crypto trading exchange, FTX, have exposed the fraudulence of the 'Fake it till you make it' ethos. Elon Musk, after the success of Tesla, has turned Twitter, or X as he insists on calling it, into a poison brand, and even more of a digitised Tower of Babel.

The idea of venturing into a 'metaverse' with Mark Zuckerberg feels like entering a lion's den, or even worse. The Facebook founder's mantra, 'Move fast and break things,' has been discredited, not least by revelations that the company knew its logarithms were so destructive, contributing both to the worsened political and mental health of the country. Big Tech has displayed the venality of Big Tobacco. Understandably, policymakers in other countries have sought to protect themselves from these American leviathans.

To international onlookers, Hollywood, America's great dream factory, has lost much of its La La Land allure. The serial rapist Harvey Weinstein, once the darling of the industry, brought international ignominy. The accidental killing of the cinematographer Halyna Hutchins, who was shot at close range with prop-gun fire by the actor Alec Baldwin while filming the Wild West movie *Rust*, weaved together a series of unattractive American traits. Gun culture. Litigation culture. The puerile, sophomoric nature of the culture wars. Immediately afterwards, Donald Trump Jr mocked the actor who had parodied his father on *Saturday Night Live*, and marketed t-shirts bearing the slogan, 'Guns Don't Kill People, Alec Baldwin Kills People.'

Increasingly, Hollywood awards ceremonies have become an arena in which American culture wars have played out on a global stage. Usually, there is some kind of diversity row. Then, when the lack of diversity is recognised, and atoned for, come complaints that affirmative action and 'wokeism' is at play. Moreover, the battles look set to intensify. Already, there is pressure for the Oscars to drop its best actor and best actress categories on the basis they are too gender normative. The Oscars have become a barometer of diversity, and thus a barometer of polarisation.

At the 2022 Oscars, Will Smith's assault on the comedian Chris Rock – which was inevitably dubbed 'the slap heard around the world' – turned the industry's global showcase into a quintessentially American hot mess. There was also something so very meta about how Chris Rock responded, quipping, 'That was the greatest night in the history of television.' He instantly recognised the viral value of Smith's moment of madness, and how mayhem was the ultimate clickbait.

After the success of dystopian dramas during the Trump years – such as *The Handmaid's Tale* and *The Plot Against America*, the adoption of Philip Roth's classic counter-factual novel which imagined Charles Lindbergh winning the 1940 presidential election as the flag-bearer of the America First movement – the US entertainment industry has found there are profits to be made from a genre that perhaps should be labelled 'decline dramas.' *The Dropout* told the story of Elizabeth Holmes. *WeCrashed* chronicled the meltdown of WeWork. *Madoff: The Monster of Wall Street* dramatised the illegal Ponzi scheme orchestrated by the Wall Street financier, Bernie Madoff. Netflix's *Silicon Valley*, which was centred on a start-up called Pied Piper, got a rise from the absurdities of Big Tech. *Dopesick*, starring Michael Keaton, highlighted the role of Big Pharma in the opioid crisis. The setting for *American Rust* was a hollowed-out Pennsylvanian steel town. *Mrs.*

America placed Cate Blanchett in the role of Phyllis Schlafly, one of the midwives of modern-day polarisation. *Succession*, the dark comedy which parodied a right-wing media empire spreading misinformation about the outcome of a disputed presidential election in the hope of monetising American mayhem, was art imitating life in real time. It is all a long way away from *The Waltons*, my childhood staple and a show that used to bring America together.

Dramas which present an idealised view of Washington politics have been pensioned off. *The West Wing* belongs in a bygone age. Gone are the days when Hollywood could get away with a mushy White House rom-com along the lines of *The American President*, starring Michael Douglas and Annette Bening; or a feel-good movie like *Dave*, where an idealistic presidential doppelgänger, played by Kevin Kline, takes charge while the villainous president is in a coma. Now we live in the world of *House of Cards*, and the amorality of its central character, President Frank Underwood, played by a scandalised actor, Kevin Spacey.

The feel-good movie with a happy American ending is not yet extinct. *Green Book*, based on the true story from the early 1960s of a racist bigot changing heart after serving as a bodyguard for the African-American pianist, Don Shirley, somehow won the Oscar for best picture in 2019. Yet instantly it was panned for promoting a white saviour narrative, and what the *New York Times* called a 'racial reconciliation fantasy'.[16]

The trend in movie-making has been for realism. *Nomadland*, which won the Oscar for best picture in 2021, was a tale of economic disruption, its main character a blue-collar worker made homeless after the sheetrock plant she worked at shuttered its doors during the Great Recession. *Spotlight*, which won for best picture in 2016, focused on the Boston Catholic Church scandal. *12 Years a Slave*, which lifted the best picture in 2013, previewed the modern-day awakening about the horrors of chattel slavery.

When, after a 36-year break, Tom Cruise returned to play the naval aviator Pete 'Maverick' Mitchell in a sequel to *Top Gun*, the movie reflected the mood change in Hollywood, from the triumphalism of the 1980s to the loss of American confidence. In *Top Gun,* the United States ruled the skies. In its sequel, *Top Gun: Maverick,* the Pentagon struggled to maintain its technological edge. The very fact that America's new Asian geopolitical rival went unnamed also spoke of Hollywood's fear of upsetting China. In the days of the Cold War, Corporate America displayed no such qualms about poking the Soviet bear.

The American music industry has been hit by a string of scandals, from the sickening secrets of Michael Jackson's Neverland ranch, which became a playpen for his paedophilia, to R. Kelly's sexual molestation of minors. The reputation of American sport has been damaged by the defenestration of some of its biggest global stars. Lance Armstrong and Tiger Woods have experienced dramatic falls – although the comeback mounted by the golfer shows how America remains a country of second chances.

Few US icons have self-destructed quite so publicly and spectacularly as Kanye West, who went, via a bizarre appearance with Donald Trump in the Oval Office, from being a megastar to a mouthpiece of the alt-right. But who was more representative of modern-day America? Barack Obama or Kanye West? Obviously, I want to say Obama, but the answer is no longer clearcut.

That the United States has become so polarised is itself a marker of toxic exceptionalism. US disunion is 'especially multi-faceted', according to the political scientists Thomas Carothers and Andrew O'Donohue, because it brings together 'a powerful alignment of ideology, race and religion'. As they astutely observed, 'It is hard to find another example of polarization in the world that fuses all three major types of identity divisions in a similar way.'[17]

The problem of historical overload distinguishes it still further. In most other advanced countries, fundamental organisational questions, such as the role of central government and the scope of the courts, have largely been settled. Likewise, in most other Western nations there is broad agreement on the rules of democracy, based on the consensus that the right to vote is sacrosanct and citizens should be encouraged to exercise it. January 6th brought all this together. Nobody anymore was proclaiming *nous sommes tous Américains*, as we had done after September 11th. Instead, it was a case of *quelle horreur*.

———

What a sea change. In the Britain of my youth, we usually welcomed Americanisation with open arms. I am embarrassed to admit the thrill I felt as a child when McDonald's opened its first branch in my hometown's colourless post-war shopping centre, and the joy at taking my first voluptuous gulps of a vanilla thickshake. Yet over the years we came to realise that Big Macs and fries tasted more like the representation of food, rather than the real thing. Besides, who wanted to be a *Fast Food Nation*, the title of the 2001 expose by the journalist Eric Schlosser that lifted the lid on the slaughterhouses, grim packing plants, meagre wages and manipulative marketing aimed at children, which fuelled America's obesity epidemic.

When the UK's Channel Four first launched in 1982, and brought gridiron into our homes, there was talk of how American football might one day supplant British football. Nowadays, however, anything that smacks of Americanisation is treated with caution. When, in 2021, 12 of Europe's top football clubs announced plans for a breakaway super league, much of the backlash from fans grew out of fears about the Americanisation of the world game. The plan was for a cartel-like closed competition, where no side would ever face relegation, as was the norm in American football, basketball and baseball. But it violated the European sense of competition and fair play. Nor did it help that two of the main drivers of the league, Liverpool and Manchester United, were American-owned, and that JPMorgan Chase, the Wall Street super bank, was underwriting the deal. On the football front, the TV character Ted Lasso was more to global liking, the hapless but humble coach who embraced Britishness rather than imposed Americanism. He was the antidote rather than the poison.

There was the same allergic reaction to the launch in 2021 of GB News, a right-wing cable news channel which was likened to

Fox News with an English accent. British viewers largely rejected hyper-partisan anchors, and US-style opinionated news. When a number of Conservative parliamentarians became hosts on the channel it was widely regarded as another hammer blow to standards in UK public life.

In so many spheres, the American model is now being rejected. When the British Labour Party proposed the abolition of the House of Lords, critics feared the introduction of a US-style Senate, with all the gridlock it would entail. Polling in Australia suggests that a major obstacle in the way of the republican movement is the fear that the British monarchy would be replaced by a US-style presidential system.

The flipside of American decline, however, is that it has reinforced its cultural hegemony. The simple fact that the country has so often become a bad meme has made it, in the social media age, the indispensable nation. It is precisely because of its dysfunction and negative exceptionalism that it remains the pre-eminent cultural trendsetter.

The #MeToo movement, sparked by a tweet from the American actress Alyssa Milano urging victims of sexual harassment or sexual assault to write 'Me Too' in their status profiles, brought about a comeuppance for Harvey Weinsteins the world over. Likewise, the murder of George Floyd turned the Black Lives Matter campaign into a global movement. Footballers in the English Premier League started mimicking American football players in the NFL, by taking a knee before kick-off. Black Lives Matter chapters sprung up all over the world. The demolition of statues across the American south brought about copycat monument removals in other countries. In Bristol, the city of my birth, protesters hauled down a statue of the slave-trader Edward Colston and hurled it into the nearby harbour, where his slave ships used to dock. In Sydney, a statue of the British explorer James Cook, whose explorations had led eventually to the invasion of Australia, was daubed with the word 'genocide'. Cancel culture became an American export.

Back in the 1990s, when the former Clinton administration official Joseph Nye coined the term 'soft power', he argued that the United States could 'shape the preferences' of other nations 'with intangible assets such as an attractive personality, culture, political values and institutions, and policies that are seen as legitimate or having moral authority'. Now it wields a more septic kind of soft power, maintaining a form of influence through the unattractiveness of its personality, culture, political values and institutions.

The problem with toxic exceptionalism, however, is that it undercuts that very thing that America's post-war alliance system was founded upon: the belief in shared values. In this Trumpian age, international leaders understandably question whether their countries still have that much in common with America. In 2023, after a summit with Xi Jinping in Beijing, the French President Emmanuel Macron called upon other EU nations to pursue a foreign policy more independent of America, which signalled a fracturing of the trans-Atlantic alliance. 'Strategic autonomy', it is called. Much of the commentary in Australia surrounding the AUKUS security pact, under which Washington agreed to share nuclear submarine technology with Canberra, has focused on the unreliability of United States as an ally, given that Trump, or a Trump-like president, could once again occupy the White House. Even the acronym AUKUS sounds like an affliction.

Again, to highlight the pitfalls of American exceptionalism is not to deny the country's mighty successes. Though I was lucky to attend ancient universities in Britain, it was my year as a visiting scholar at Massachusetts Institute of Technology when I felt that I was at the academic cutting edge. MIT, after all, had helped invent the American future, and some of the great innovations of the 20th century – radar; the forerunner of the worldwide web; the guidance computers that made possible the Apollo moon landings. New York still feels like the maximum city. Wall Street remains the fulcrum of global finance. The *New York Times* is the greatest newspaper in the world. This is the land of Toni Morrison, Cormac McCarthy, Philip Roth and Harper Lee. Few, if any, non-Americans can match the star power of Taylor Swift or Beyoncé.

NASA can still put on a show. In 2021, it safely landed the Perseverance rover on Mars, and then engineered an encore with the launch of its ingenious helicopter, Ingenuity. But it was also impossible to ignore that life on earth was more problematic, as the *Washington Post* found when it reported from communities in Houston close to the Johnson Space Center. Water coming out of the taps was 'as dark and dingy as the Martian landscape', the paper found, adding, 'America can put a rover on Mars, but it can't keep the lights on and water running in a city that birthed the modern space program.'[18]

That is why the rhetoric of exceptionalism, which so many presidents and wannabe presidents persist with, sounds so discordant to international ears. We get what is going on. We have been watching. We have been rubber-necking.

Plainly, the 'Trump effect' has contributed profoundly to this international image problem. In 2020, the Pew Research Center found that US favourability ratings in several countries, like Britain and Australia, had plummeted to their lowest level in the nearly two decades of polling. However, Trumpism is not solely to blame for the decline of America's foreign standing.

My sense is that one of the most crushing blows to American prestige came from the anticlimax of seeing a once-in-a-generation politician stymied by a poisonous political culture and failing in his mission to make America 'a more perfect union'. The Obama effect. If a leader as gifted, graceful, pragmatic and poetic could not repair the breach, then maybe America could not be saved. Watching him hand over power to Donald Trump was devastating for American esteem. A president widely deemed to embody the best of the country had also brought out the worst. American carnage.

All too real, then, is the risk that the 21st century could become what the public intellectual Zachary Karabell has called the 'anti-American century'.[19] That to me sounds too strong, not least because a world in which authoritarian China becomes dominant is so deeply unattractive. But given how many countries are now trying to inoculate themselves, not just against Trumpism but Americanism more broadly, it is easy to imagine this becoming a century of anti-Americanisation.

10

The Two Americas

Even by the first anniversary of the January 6th insurrection, it was clear that Joe Biden's national reunification project had failed. Since taking office, he had tended to avoid talking directly about the assault on democracy, but on this 'day of remembrance', as he called it, in a speech on Capitol Hill, he used his strongest language yet to condemn his predecessor – although, Voldemort-like, he still refused to mention Donald Trump by name. This 'defeated former president', as the victorious present president called him, was guilty of holding 'a dagger to the throat of America'.

The setting for his speech symbolised the country's unceasing conflict: National Statuary Hall, a chamber adjacent to the House of Representatives with a mausoleum-like collection of statues. In 2013, Congress had added Rosa Parks, making her the only African-American to be memorialised with a full-length statue within the precincts of the Capitol. Heavily outnumbering her, however, were white supremacists chiselled in white marble. At least a dozen of the 35 historical figures on display honoured Confederates, including Jefferson Davis, his vice-presidential deputy, Alexander Stephens, and John C. Calhoun.[1] Even after the monument toppling of the George Floyd summer, the ghosts of the Confederacy still had not been banished from the halls of government.

As Biden himself emphasised, this was a sanctum rich in history. It was where the House of Representatives had met for 50 years in the lead-up to the Civil War. Peering down on them was a statue of Clio, 'the muse of history'. Fittingly, then, his speech became something of a heritage tour, taking in Lexington, Concord, Gettysburg, Seneca Falls, Pearl Harbor, Omaha Beach and Selma. From the brutality of Bloody Sunday had come historic voting-rights legislation, he noted: 'So, now let us step up, write the next chapter in American history where January 6th marks not the end of democracy but the beginning of a renaissance of liberty.'[2]

When Woodrow Wilson had delivered a speech marking the 50th anniversary of Gettysburg, he did not mention slavery, the cause of the Civil War. Yet Biden clearly thought it would be preposterous to mark this 'day of remembrance' without addressing what was being remembered, even if it meant heightening partisan tensions. Sure enough, the headlines came not from his defence of democracy but from his attack on Donald Trump and the GOP, which he claimed was no longer the party of Lincoln, Eisenhower, Reagan or the Bushes.

Even more fiercely partisan was a speech delivered by Biden the following week in Atlanta, Georgia. Again, his script was freighted with history, incorporating the 'murdered four little Black girls' from the Birmingham church bombing, Selma, Bloody Sunday and the Voting Rights Act. Then he turned to what he called 'Jim Crow 2.0': voter suppression and election subversion. Urging lawmakers to back the proposed Freedom to Vote Act currently stalled in Congress, he posed what he knew was an incendiary question, 'I ask every elected official in America … Do you want to be on the side of Dr King or George Wallace? Do you want to be on the side of John Lewis or Bull Connor? Do you want to be on the side of Abraham Lincoln or Jefferson Davis?'[3]

The last in this trilogy of speeches came in another epic setting, Independence Hall in Philadelphia, whose facade was bathed in red, white and blue floodlights, and whose entrance was flanked by two US Marines dressed in ceremonial regalia, who looked like sentinels of democracy. Biden refrained from equating Trumpism with 'semi-fascism', as he had done in remarks the previous week. Nonetheless, his primetime speech sounded like a wartime address, targeting an enemy within. 'Donald Trump and the MAGA Republicans represent an extremism that threatens the very foundations of our republic,' he warned. 'They live not in the light of truth but in the shadow of lies.'[4] This birthplace of the Constitution had again become a place of angry contestation.

Much of the coverage afterwards focused on the optics of the speech. Though in person, the red floodlighting of Independence Hall looked spectacular, on television it resembled congealed blood. One of the country's most beloved landmarks looked vampiric, a Halloween house of horrors, more Transylvania than Pennsylvania. On Fox News, Tucker Carlson described it as a 'blood-red Nazi background'.

There was also a howl of conservative protest about Biden's stridently divisive tone. J. D. Vance complained that Biden had spoken of his fellow citizens as if they were 'sewer rats'. Mike Huckabee, the Fox News host and former governor of Arkansas, called it 'a hate speech'.[5] The *Wall Street Journal* likened the Philadelphia event to a Trump rally, and attacked the president for deliberately stoking division. 'His strategy is to out-Trump Trump by polarizing the electorate around the former President because he thinks a majority will come his way,' the paper editorialised. 'Mr. Biden had become his foe's polarizing mirror image. It is exactly what he promised as a candidate he wouldn't do.'[6]

Coming at the outset of an election year, there was an obvious motive in mounting a partisan attack: Trump remained the Democrats' most useful foil. Perhaps the rhetoric was too factional. But this series of speeches also revealed a new American dilemma. No longer was it possible for a US president to defend democracy without being castigated for being overly political. Upholding the simple principle that everyone should abide by the results of a free and fair election had become a partisan issue.

A presidential peacemaker no more, the question now was not whether Biden could bring the country back together. It was more urgent and existential: was it possible to prevent the cold Civil War from turning hot? Biden himself had long been worried. On the Sunday before Election Day in 2020, he had ruminated on the question with the Democrat congressman Hakeem Jeffries. 'I certainly hope this [my presidency] works out,' he said. 'If it doesn't I'm not sure we're going to have a country.'[7]

The advice I used to impart to young correspondents pitching up at the BBC's bureau in Washington was to remember that America had fought a civil war in the mid-19th century and was still arguing over the terms of a fractious peace. Much like the modern-day phrase 'sorry but not sorry', which is used sarcastically to indicate a lack of remorse, the brief ceremony at Appomattox Court House, which brought the armed fighting to an end, was a surrender but not a surrender. More than 150 years on, there is an extent to which we continue to live in the post-bellum era.

Yet we continue to live in the antebellum era as well, because so many of the issues that led to the break-up of the union have never fully been resolved. That is why I would now amend my advice. The existence of two Americas long predates the battle of Fort Sumter. Division has always been the default setting. Victory at the Battle of Yorktown brought American independence, but did not mean American nationhood was a given.

'Exhibit A' is the Declaration of Independence itself, which became 'A Unanimous Declaration of the Thirteen United States of America', rather than just 'the United States'. The use of the plural 'States' rather than the singular 'State' was indicative.[8] So, too, the tendency of early Americans to say the 'United States are a republic', rather than the 'United States is a republic'. Maybe even the fact that the new country felt the need to describe itself as 'United' was symptomatic. Perhaps it was too try-hard, and hinted immediately at the new nation's predisposition towards disunion.

The interim Articles of Confederation, the agreement in 1777 between those 13 colonies which is sometimes called the first founding, read in parts like a treatise opposing nationhood. 'Each state retains its sovereignty, freedom and independence,' its preamble noted, 'and every power, jurisdiction and right which is not by this confederation expressly delegated to the United States in Congress assembled.' The Annapolis convention in 1786, convened to remedy the shortcomings of the Articles of Confederation, was only attended by delegates from five states, and ended in failure.

For a period between the end of the war in 1783 and the start of the Philadelphia convention in 1786, it seemed like the states might enter into two or three confederations, rather than a singular nation. 'No morn ever dawned more favourable than ours did,' wrote a melancholic George Washington, as he surveyed his splintered country, 'and no day was ever more clouded than the present.'9 Washington was determined to see the emergence of a stronger nation, and, vitally, became a driving force behind the constitutional convention in Philadelphia. Still, success was by no means certain.

Most of the great battles which have recurred in different forms ever since received an airing in Philadelphia. State sovereignty versus federal sovereignty. Hamiltonian strong government against the Jeffersonian aversion to the centralisation of power. Abolitionists against slaveholders. How much power should be granted to the American people. How much power should be allotted to the executive and legislature (the judiciary, as already observed, was not looked upon as an equal partner). The constitutional convention did not resolve these issues. Nowhere near. In some ways, the Constitution was a written agreement to keep disagreeing. Madison regarded it as a triumph that no-one had argued 'in favour of a partition of the Empire into two or more confederacies'.10

After the contentiousness of the constitutional convention, the ratification process became a close-run thing. This was especially true in the three most influential states, Virginia, Massachusetts and New York, which only gave its blessing by a slim majority of 30–27. America continued to feel like a confederation of states, rather than a country. Though it was hardly a forced union, neither could it be described as an entirely happy marriage.

Old allegiances died hard. Jefferson continued to look upon himself as a Virginian more so than an American. So did James Madison. Notions of Virginian exceptionalism predated any sense of American exceptionalism. Massachusetts, another of the early colonies, had the same superior air. Loyalty to state was more powerful than loyalty to country. Tellingly, the word 'nation' did not appear in the US Constitution.

When the first Congress convened in New York in 1789, the body's 22 senators and 59 members of the House were hardly in any rush to get the new country up and running. Washington's inauguration in March that year was attended by less than a third of lawmakers. It took another month before enough members of Congress assembled in New York to reach a quorum.

In the running of the new country, states continued to act as if they were autonomous entities, erecting customs barriers and taxing each other's goods. New York imposed taxes on ships that passed through its waters to conduct trade with New Jersey and Connecticut.[11] Polycentrism was baked in from the start. Philadelphia, New York and Boston remained vital centres of power. Federalism was based on devolution, rather than the concentration of power at the centre. A state-nation rather than a nation-state is how we should think of the new America, according to the historian David Armitage, 'which arises when the state is formed before the development of any sense of national consciousness'.[12] Because of the land gains achieved through the Louisiana Purchase, America arguably became an empire before it became a fully-fledged nation – Jefferson's 'empire of liberty'.

The new capital, the District of Columbia, itself became a landmark of division, its location on the banks of the Potomac the product of the famous compromise between Hamilton and Jefferson over the federal assumption of state debts, which significantly strengthened the national government. For much of the year, it did not feel like a capital at all. Congress was only in session from November to March. The Supreme Court convened for a few months each year. In 1802, the federal government had only 9,000 employees, and most of them were employed in defence or customs and mail.[13]

Despite the warning against partisanship in George Washington's farewell address – 'the baneful effects of the spirit of party', he called it, in an oration which was itself partisan because it was penned by Alexander Hamilton and thus a Federalist text – a party system quickly emerged. In the 1800 election, Adams was the candidate of the Federalists and Jefferson was the candidate of Democratic-Republicans. Jefferson's words proved prophetic when he predicted 'the president of the United States will only be the president of a party'.[14]

The 1800 election almost broke the fledgling country because the contest was so partisan and the aftermath so confused. During the campaign, Jefferson argued that four more years of Adams would create an oppressive national government that would emasculate the states. Afterwards, tensions rose still further, when the Electoral College produced the absurdity of a tie between Jefferson and his vice-presidential running mate, Aaron Burr (the 12th Amendment, ratified three years later, rectified this flaw in the Constitution whereby electors originally made no distinction in casting their votes between the presidency and vice presidency). With the election thrown into the House of Representatives, it required 36 votes to determine the winner, a fraught process which briefly raised the spectre of armed conflict if Jefferson was denied the presidency.

Ultimately, 1800 became the first US presidential election which resulted in a transfer of power from one political party, the Federalists, to another, the Democratic-Republicans. Yet in an expression of his disgust, Adams rode out of town on the eve of the inauguration, a history dusted off when Donald Trump boycotted Joe Biden's swearing in.

In these early decades, finding commonality, a sense of national spirit, was far from straightforward. One thing that many of the new Americans shared was a British heritage, but as is often pointed out, that was hardly something to shout from the rooftops after sending the Red Coats packing at Yorktown. One of the few areas of agreement was on the fragility of the American experiment, and the potential for it to blow up.

The War of 1812, and the torching of the Capitol and the President's House – it was renamed the 'White House' after it was rebuilt and repainted – forged a greater strength of comity. But only up to a point. When the country's sixth President, the Federalist John Quincy Adams, proposed a bout of nation building in the 1820s, which included the creation of a national university, a proper US navy, and common weights and measures, he was met with a wall of resistance in Congress where his program was seen as a federal power grab.

Not until its 50th birthday did the notion of American nationhood firmly take hold – a golden jubilee marked, by strange coincidence, by the deaths of both Jefferson and Adams. When in 1831 James Monroe became the third of the five Founding-Father presidents to draw his last breath on July 4th, many interpreted this concurrence of death as proof that their glorious creation, the United States, had the imprimatur of God. As the Massachusetts Congressman Daniel Webster waxed lyrical in his eulogy, 'As their lives themselves were the gifts of Providence, who is not willing to recognise in their happy termination, as well as in their long continuance, proofs that our country and its benefactors are objects of His care?'[15]

For all that, the July 4th celebrations also brought to the fore America's ongoing racial divide. So used were they to being set upon by white mobs when they tried to celebrate this national holiday, many Blacks held commemorations on July 5th instead. It was at an Independence Day celebration held on 5 July 1852 that Frederick Douglass delivered his most memorable address, an oration in which he asked, 'What to the slave is the Fourth of July?' 'This Fourth of July is yours not mine,' he said. 'You may rejoice, I must mourn.'

The founders always knew that the issue of slavery had the potential to tear the country apart, which is why they made so many accommodations in the Constitution. 'I know it is high treason to express a doubt of the perpetual duration of our vast American empire,' Adams wrote to Jefferson in 1819, as the Missouri question reared its head, but divisions over slavery threatened to produce 'as many Nations in North America as there are in Europe.'[16]

Enslavement also acted as a bar on nation building, and especially the centralisation of power. 'Tell me if Congress can establish banks, make roads and canals,' noted the prominent Virginian, Nathaniel Macon, 'whether they cannot free all the Slaves in the United States.'[17] From the outset, the bondage of African-Americans was a ticking time bomb. Less than a hundred years after its creation, America exploded, leading to a full-blown civil war. Modern-day American disunity is, in many aspects, a reversion to type.

A trip to the southern border at the midpoint of the Trump presidency brought home the sharp lines along which America continues to be divided. The president had travelled to McAllen, Texas, to dramatise how illegal crossings from Mexico underscored the need to build a giant border wall – a vanity project intended as the great megalith, or 'MAGAlith', of his presidency.

Crowds had gathered to greet the president, in what had now become a ritualised form of polarisation. On one side of the street, lined up almost in battle formation along the kerb, was a boisterous throng of supporters. Facing them on the other side, ranked like an opposing battalion, was an equally vociferous mass of protesters. Patrolled by local law enforcement, the road between these groups served as a buffer zone. Red America was facing off against blue America. Just a short drive from the actual US border, the white lines that marked the middle of the road served temporarily as an internal US border. McAllen looked that day like an interface in America's cold civil war.

The signs of separatism are everywhere. State lines have become partitionist divides: boundaries between two distinct Americas with two distinct sets of laws, especially on polarising issues such as abortion, guns, transgender rights, and even what books children can read at school. Red state governments have sought to reverse many of the gains of the 'Rights Revolution', such as voting and reproductive rights, and focused instead on protecting liberties, like unfettered access to guns. Blue state governments have done the opposite. The 'great divergence' is how the political scientist Ron Brownstein has described this schism, 'a dramatic erosion of common national rights'.[18] The separation of the states is not just de facto, but increasingly de jure.

California instituted a 'sanctions regime' against 17 states deemed to discriminate against LGBTQIA+ citizens on the basis of their gender identity or sexual orientation. Red states have retaliated with a wave of so-called 'anti-woke' laws. In 2022, 17 conservative states passed 44 bills penalising companies which have taken stances on issues such as transgender rights, gun control and climate change. To fend off threats of economic boycotts from liberal states, the prominent conservative law professor Jonathan Turley has urged red states to form a NATO-like alliance, based on the defence pact's famed Article Five: 'An attack on one is an attack on all.'[19]

On wedge issues, such as immigration, performative politicians have engaged in performative polarisation: stunts choreographed to heighten tensions between red-dominated and blue-dominated states. The Texas governor, Greg Abbott, hired a fleet of buses to dump on the streets of New York City immigrants who had crossed over the southern border. The Florida governor, Ron DeSantis, chartered a private jet to fly immigrants to Martha's Vineyard, the exclusive redoubt of the East Coast elites. California's Democratic governor, Gavin Newsom, has baited Texas and Florida in television advertisements aired in those states. 'I urge all of you living in Florida to join the fight or join us in California,' Newsom told the people of the Sunshine State. 'Freedom of speech, freedom to choose, freedom from hate and freedom to love.' When in the spring of 2023 he conducted a tour of Deep South states, which included visits to a series of old civil-rights battlefields like Montgomery, Alabama, Politico described it as a mission 'behind political enemy lines'.[20]

Some of the most populous states, such as Texas and Florida, where Republicans control the governorship and legislature, are increasingly acting like self-governing sovereign entities. In June 2022, DeSantis announced plans for the creation of a 'Florida State

Guard', distinct from the Florida National Guard and outside the usual Pentagon chain of command. In 2015, when the US military conducted a training exercise in the Lone Star State, Greg Abbott ordered the Texas State Guard to closely monitor what was going on. Conspiracy theorists claimed that 'Jade Helm 15', the codeword for the exercise, was an attempt by the federal government to confiscate guns. So Abbott used the state militia to police the US Army, acting like a Lone Star commander-in-chief.[21]

The Coronavirus only exacerbated the sense of separatism. Democratic states favoured stricter and longer lockdowns. Republican states were more averse to economic shutdowns. Early in the pandemic, when New York became its epicentre, President Trump raised the possibility of sequestering the Empire State, which its then Governor Andrew Cuomo described as 'a civil war kind of discussion'. Federally imposed lockdowns of individual states, Cuomo added, would constitute 'a federal declaration of war'.[22]

Though America still operates a single economic market, ever wider are the discrepancies between the states in the regulation of business and commerce. From 2035, the sale of petrol-powered cars will be banned in California. West Virginia, by contrast, has announced a boycott of five major banks which have criticised Big Coal.[23]

The Civil War era doctrine of nullification has been repurposed, with recalcitrant states passing bills aimed at making federal law null and void. This kind of state resistance became a hallmark of the crusade to overturn *Roe v. Wade*. When Texas enacted a law banning abortion after about six weeks of pregnancy, a flagrant subversion of *Roe*, the Supreme Court justice Sonia Sotomayor called it 'a brazen challenge to our federal structure. It echoes the philosophy of John C. Calhoun, that virulent defender of the slaveholding South who insisted that States had the right to "veto" or "nullify" any federal law with which they disagreed.'

To resist any federal attempt to infringe upon gun rights, 11 red-dominated states have dubbed themselves 'Second Amendment Sanctuaries'. In Missouri, the GOP-controlled legislature has even passed a 'Second Amendment Preservation Act' based on the constitutionally dubious premise that state firearms laws 'exceed' federal laws when it comes to regulating and registering guns.[24] In 2015, Mitch McConnell urged states to mount an aggressive resistance campaign against what he called the Obama administration's 'war on coal' by blocking new regulations limiting carbon emissions.[25]

For their part, Democratic governors, during the Trump years especially, reworked the reactionary creed of states rights and turned it into a liberal doctrine. 'Progressive federalism', it has been called. When Trump withdrew from the Paris climate-change agreement, Democratic states pledged they would continue to abide by the international treaty. Since 2012, 21 liberal-minded states have legalised marijuana, despite it being federally illegal.

Major liberal metropolises have also acted like city states. In response to the Trump administration's hardline immigration policies, Boston, Chicago and New York declared themselves sanctuary cities, and limited their cooperation with federal agencies. Red states, such as Alabama, Florida and South Carolina, responded by passing laws prohibiting the creation of these kinds of civic havens. The widening divide between liberal cities in conservative states has created yet another fissure. Arizona, for instance, has made it illegal for municipalities to ban gifts in McDonald's Happy Meals. Oklahoma has prohibited the regulation of e-cigarettes. Mississippi has granted similar legal protections to sugary drinks, to stop liberal do-gooders in the state's few progressive enclaves from banning them.[26]

Modern-day secessionism is on the rise. Conservatives in Texas have raised the possibility of 'Texit', which would make the Lone Star State an independent republic. 'Cal-exit', backed by west coast liberals, would do the same for California.[27] In the run-up to the 2020 presidential election, a Hofstra University poll found nearly 41 per cent of Democrats favoured their state leaving the union if Joe Biden lost the presidential election, and that 44 per cent of Republicans thought the same if Trump failed to win four more years.[28]

Some red states are considering redrawing their maps to absorb the conservative regions of neighbouring liberal states. The Greater Idaho movement seeks to incorporate red parts of blue Oregon. More than two dozen rural counties in Illinois have explored the possibility of divorcing their own state, because of the influence of blue Chicago.

The trend since the turn of the century has been for Americans of antagonistic views to deliberately live more distantly apart, overlaying ideological separation with physical separation. As Bill Bishop identified in his 2009 book *The Big Sort: Why the Clustering of Like-Minded America Is Tearing Us Apart*, people have come to reside in partisan bubbles alongside people with the same political viewpoints and cultural mores. As a result, the rural counties have become more red, while the cities have become more blue.

In yet another indication of extreme polarisation, there are more trifecta states than ever before, in which the governorship and both houses of the state legislature are held by a single party. In 2010, around half of the states were controlled by one party. In 2022, that figure had risen to 39 – 22 Republican, 17 Democrat.[29]

Presidential elections now witness a record number of mini-landslides in counties where Republicans heavily outnumber Democrats, and vice versa. In 1976, only a quarter of American voters lived in counties where Jimmy Carter or Gerald Ford won by 20 per cent or more of the vote. By 2016, when Trump beat Hillary Clinton, that figure had leapt to 62 per cent (it declined slightly in 2020 to 58 per cent).[30] In hardly any rural counties are presidential elections competitive, which makes sense of one of Donald Trump's favourite maps, which he hung in the West Wing, that depicted the continental land mass largely coloured red – a work of political pornography.[31] Conversely, Democrats dominate the cities. Population density has become a partisan marker. The closer that people live together, the more likely they are to vote Democrat.

Gone are the days when presidential elections produce landslides. It is hard to foresee any modern-day candidate winning 44 states, as Lyndon Johnson did in 1964; or 49 as Nixon and Reagan managed in 1972 and 1984; or even the 40 racked up by George Herbert Walker Bush in 1988. Contemporary America is simply too divided, and too evenly split, to produce these kinds of one-sided results. In 2020, 25 states voted for Biden and 25 for Trump.

National holidays have ceased to be truly national. Nowadays, a journalistic staple in the run-up to Thanksgiving is for news organisations to run stories on how families can no longer gather around the same table because of political antagonism. Yuletide brings that hoary canard, 'the war on Christmas'. The 4th of July has never been quite the same since Donald Trump militarised the Lincoln Memorial in 2019. Holidaying the year after on Fire Island off the coast of Long Island became a tale of two communities. In one town, heavily populated by cops, firemen and construction workers, virtually every house displayed either a Stars and Stripes, a Trump banner or both. In the neighbouring village, a preppy enclave where the dress code was loafers and Ralph Lauren, it felt more like the 4th of June. There were few outward signs of celebration.

Likewise, red-letter days in the national calendar no longer have the same convening power, that capacity to bring the country together. The Super Bowl has become as much a cultural event as a sporting fixture, with all the politicisation that implies. In 2023, controversy flared over the singing of the Black national anthem, 'Lift Every Voice and Sing', before 'The Star Spangled Banner'. The previous year, conservatives complained about the appearance of Dr Dre, who in 1988 had released a protest song entitled 'Fuck tha Police'. In 2021, even the Major League Baseball All-Star Game became a flashpoint, after it was moved away from Atlanta in protest at Georgia's new restrictive voting law. It is hard to think of a unifying cultural event. 'The safety of a republic depends essentially on the energy of a common national sentiment; on a uniformity of principle and habits,' Hamilton once reflected.[32] In modern-day America, that spirit no longer exists.

New faultlines are also opening up. The most noticeable political realignment over the past decade has centred on education, with the college-educated gravitating towards the Democrats and those without degrees leaning Republican. What's been labelled the 'diploma divide' is becoming as much a marker of political identity as income and class, which raises the spectre of further mass defections of working-class voters to the GOP, and also offers an explanation why Trump has performed unexpectedly well among the very racial groups, Blacks and Hispanics, that he has so frequently maligned. This educational divide is particularly divisive, because of the risk that politics gets framed as a contest between an enlightened elite and an irrational horde, the haughty versus the hoi polloi.

A welter of polling data already points to the mutual seething of Americans. A YouGov poll suggested that 60 per cent of Democrats saw the Republicans as 'a serious threat to the United States'.[33] Seventy per cent of Republicans thought the same of Democrats. Research presented in 2019 by Nathan P. Kalmoe and Lilliana Mason, on what they ominously labelled 'Lethal Mass Partisanship', suggested that 42 per cent of Democrats and Republicans looked upon the other side as 'downright evil'. One in five agreed that their partisan opponents 'lack the traits to be considered fully human – they behave like animals'.[34] This dehumanisation of fellow compatriots is a particularly perturbing trend.

Both sides feel profoundly aggrieved. Conservatives begrudge liberals for wielding so much cultural power and imposing their 'wokeism' on debates over gender equality, same-sex marriage and transgender sports. Progressives complain that conservatives benefit from a constitutional system that disproportionately empowers the Republican Party in Congress and reactionaries on the Supreme Court.

These two Americas are producing two very different versions of American life. Gross domestic product per capita is 25 per cent greater in blue America, the states where Democrats control the governorship and state legislature, than the red, according to research by Michael Podhorzer of the Analyst Institute. Life expectancy is 80.1 compared to 77.4. Covid vaccination rates were 20 per cent higher in blue America, while Covid deaths were 20 per cent higher in red America.[35] In California, the liberal state with the strictest gun laws, there are nine gun deaths per 100,000 people. In Arkansas, the conservative state where gun rights are most unfettered, it is 23.[36] Even more so than race, educational status has become an augur of how long Americans will live.

It is possible to visit these two Americas from the comfort of your sofa by flicking between the main cable channels, MSNBC, CNN and Fox News. For along with identity politics has come identity journalism. Often, the consumption of news is less about finding out what is going on and more about confirming one's biases. The information silos, filter bubbles and echo chambers of social media have only added to the country's mental dismemberment.

Some of the most profitable media organisations and social media companies – notably Fox News and Meta, the owners of Facebook – have become propagators of misinformation. As the Dominion Voting Systems defamation case proved, Fox News continued to spread lies about the 2020 presidential election, which even hardline presenters such as Tucker Carlson described as 'shockingly reckless' and 'absurd', because it feared haemorrhaging viewers to its far-right rivals, Newsmax and One America News.[37] As CNN showed again in 2023, when it gifted a town-hall platform to Donald Trump, along with an auditorium packed with boisterous MAGA devotees, lies are a surefire ratings winner. What that Trump town hall also demonstrated, as the host, Kaitlan Collins battled to correct in real-time his mistruths about the election, is that facts are not the antidote to falsehoods. Trying to hold him to account only heightened the sense of combat, and made his supporters barrack for him more wildly.

This mainstreaming of misinformation is especially worrying. When Trump first started spreading his birther lies, for example, he was not just a regular guest on Fox News, but invited to air his conspiracy theory on CNN, NBC's *Today* show, and ABC's *The View*. When Obama finally, and reluctantly, felt the need to hold a press conference to release his birth certificate, it was carried, unusually, by the major networks, which demonstrated the appetite for the false story. 'We're better than this. Remember that,' Obama concluded that press conference by saying. But that was now up for debate.

Disinformation experts talk of pre-bunking rather than debunking: of trying to combat falsehoods before they become entrenched. It follows the medical model that prevention is better than cure. The problem, alas, is that we face an infodemic, and it is hard to nurture healthier information diets when the plague is out of control.

Just as no longer are there shared facts, there is no longer a shared vocabulary. The gender-neutral neologism 'LatinX' is deemed on the left to be inclusive and progressive. To use the term 'Latino' now carries the risk of being accused of racial insensitivity, or worse. Yet only one in four American Hispanics had heard of the phrase by the summer of 2020, and 3 per cent used it.[38] The 'New Left' language of safe spaces and micro-aggressions which emerged on American campuses in the 2010s is an alien tongue not just to middle America but large swathes of moderate America. Conversely, conservatives apply the catch-all 'woke' to anything they find even mildly upsetting, and often to what are now mainstream viewpoints, such as same-sex marriage. There is an absolutism on the left, and even more so on the right, that often drowns out voices of moderation.

The absence of an agreed-upon set of baseline facts and truths held universally to be self-evident has created a reality-based America and a reality-averse realm pockmarked with various rabbit holes. 'Alt-America' is how the author David Neiwert has described the part of the country which believes that paedophile rings are run by senior politicians, and operated out of the basements of pizza restaurants that do not actually have basements. This is the fantasyland which still hangs on the prophecies from 'Q', even though his – or her – soothsaying has proven so spectacularly delusory.[39] 'Truth isn't truth,' Rudy Giuliani declared in 2018 on *Meet the Press*. But ridiculous as Giuliani sounded, he had inadvertently come up with an epigram for the large swathes of modern-day America where facts no longer determine beliefs, and beliefs increasingly determine 'truth'.

This is not solely a Trumpian phenomenon. Back in 2005, the comedian Stephen Colbert coined the term 'truthiness', partly to describe how the then president, George W. Bush, relied more on his gut than hard evidence. But clearly the problem has grown exponentially worse. Longtime Washington observer Mark Leibovich has described it as 'trickle-down idiocy', which is precisely the kind of contemptuous jibe that further widens the breach.[40]

In this topsy-turvy world, in which it is harder, as Obama once put it, to distinguish between what is true and what is felt, a federal indictment for mishandling secret national security documents, backed by a mass of incriminating evidence, becomes a politically motivated witch-hunt. Likewise, the storming of the Capitol, which we all watched with our own eyes, becomes 'a normal tourist visit'. All of which brings to mind Voltaire's famous warning: 'Those who can make you believe absurdities can make you commit atrocities.'

Modern-day US politics not only mirrors these divisions, the political business model is based on rupturing them still further. Since the turn of the century, the strategy of both major parties has been to maximise turn-out amongst their own bases, rather than appeal to the dwindling number of swing voters in the middle. As political identity has become more of an expression of racial, religious and ethnic identity, the focus has been on emotional issues, such as abortion and transgender rights, rather than traditional hip-pocket issues, such as taxation. Politics has become a battle of warring tribes, with all the reflexive contrarianism that involves. Negative partisanship has become a driver of electoral politics, based on heightening hatred towards the other side, with all the tit-for-tit reprisals that entails.

Increasingly, the playbook has relied on top-down polarisation, where political strategists deliberately divide the electorate by manufacturing 'us versus them' controversies – the phony 'war on Christmas' is a prime example. Both parties routinely conduct market testing to discover which lines of attack resonate most strongly. Claiming it amounted to a 'government takeover' was found to be the most effective riposte to Obamacare. Transgender inclusion in sports evidently elicits a more powerful emotional response than transgender bathrooms. Another example of polarisation imposed from above is the form of manipulated populism known as astroturfing: grassroots activism funded by plutocrats, such as the right-wing Koch brothers.

This is not new. During the Nixon era, the southern strategy was based on precisely this calculus. Pat Buchanan once wrote to Nixon advising, 'If we tear the country in half, we can pick up the bigger half.' Nixon's attorney general, John Mitchell, spoke of 'positive polarisation'. But from the end of the Cold War onwards, it has become more intense. 'Polarisation is addictive,' observed the cultural critic Robert Hughes in the 1990s. 'It is the crack cocaine of politics – a short intense rush that the system craves again and again, until it begins to collapse.'[41]

Since the early 1990s, politics has also become more competitive, which has both heightened and hardened polarisation. In the 40-year period between 1955 and 1995, the Democrats essentially owned the Speaker's chair in the House of Representatives, which meant that the only way for the Republicans to influence the legislative process was to work in a bipartisan manner. Since House elections were a foregone conclusion, much of the heat was taken out of electoral politics. The 1994 Republican Revolution marked the shift, and since the turn of the century, the Speaker's chair has switched parties four times. In recent years, partisan parity has become even more marked. The Democrats' traditional advantage in party identification – in America, voters tend to indicate their affiliation when they register – is now the smallest it has been in 70 years, further ramping up tensions.[42]

Given the closeness of elections, there is no longer such an incentive for the losing party to change policies following a defeat. Instead, the focus has been on getting more of their supporters to the polls and, on the Republican side, trying to suppress the vote. It was telling in 2020 that the Republican defeat did not result in the kind of post-mortem that followed Mitt Romney's loss in 2012, which concluded the GOP needed to broaden its racial appeal. Partly this was because Trump refused to admit defeat. But party officials also believed they merely needed to redouble their efforts at blocking minorities from voting. Rather than changing policies, they have sought to change the rules of elections.

Not just polarisation, but 'calcification' is the result, according to the political scientists John Sides, Chris Tausanovitch and Lynn

Vavreck. 'When control of government is always within reach, there is less need for the losing party to adapt and recalibrate,' they have argued. 'And if it stays on the same path, voters have little reason to revise their political loyalties.' The partisan divide therefore becomes harder and self-reinforcing, all of which creates a 'rigidity in politics'.[43]

Compounding all these problems is the emergence of a new generation of politicians who are fluent only in the language of cultural combat, and illiterate in more vital areas of governance, such as economics, health policy and foreign affairs. Often, phony polarisation is their only political trick.

Certainly, the parties have become more extreme. Under Trump, the Republicans have lurched to the hard right, vacating the middle ground. The Democrats, rather than claiming the centre, have moved further to the left. Biden has conducted a more progressive presidency than Obama. It was not until 2012, remember, that Obama came out publicly in favour of same-sex marriage. And imagine how his celebrated 2008 race speech would be received today, especially the passage in which he maligned Jeremiah Wright for expressing 'a profoundly distorted view of this country'. Rather than being garlanded, Obama might have been cancelled.

On both sides, the politics of compromise, and the policies they have produced, are frowned upon. For the Democrats, the Third Way centrism of the Clinton years has been discredited, partly because it worsened more problems than it solved. The welfare bill created more child poverty. The repeal of the Glass-Steagall Act from the New Deal era, which reflected the Democrats' new deregulatory impulses, led directly to the sub-prime crisis and Great Recession. The zero-tolerance approach to crime, of which Senator Joe Biden was also a key legislative architect, led to mass incarceration. The aversion to regulating the digital economy, an ideological and political concession to Reaganism, meant that Clinton's much-vaunted bridge to the 21st century looked more like a bypass in the post-industrial towns of the Rust Belt.

Anything that even hints at centrism is now anathema to the Republican right. Such was the ideological antipathy towards George W. Bush's 'big government conservatism' in response to the financial meltdown in 2008 that it spawned the Tea Party movement. As for his 'compassionate conservatism', it would be laughed out of school.

There are structural reasons why politics has become so angry, not least the unrepresentative nature of the American democratic model. Understandably, Democrats in the most populous states feel aggrieved that half of the population is represented by just 18 senators, while the other half gets 82. Moreover, 41 senators representing just 10 per cent of the population can block legislation, because of the vagaries of the filibuster rule. The irony here is that conservatives have cast themselves as an oppressed minority, even though the Republican Party has come to wield such disproportionate minoritarian power, especially in the Senate and on the Supreme Court. A further problem with this counter-majoritarian model is that the Republicans do not need to adopt majority positions, especially on polarising questions such as gun control and abortion.

There are further systemic deficiencies. Because of the biennial electoral cycle, congressional politics has become a permanent campaign, with all the partisan warmongering and time-consuming fundraising it entails. Gerrymandering heightens polarisation, because so many congressional seats are uncompetitive. The winner-takes-all rules of the Electoral College have always raised the political stakes. If states had mechanisms to split their electoral votes, as Nebraska and Maine do, disputes such as the Florida recount in 2000 might not have been such a fight to the death. It would also reduce the sway of the small handful of swing states, such as Pennsylvania, Wisconsin and Michigan, that tend to decide presidential elections, and make them a truly nationwide vote.

A trench warfare-like stalemate is so often the end result, partly because power in these disunited states resides in different places. Again, it begs the question, will this cold war turn hot?

'This is the final battle', yelled Donald Trump at a rally in Georgia in June 2023, his first public appearance after federal prosecutors charged him with 37 felony counts of mishandling top-secret documents in a case docketed '*United States of America v. Donald J. Trump*'. 'We have now reached a war phase,' tweeted the Republican congressman Andy Biggs. 'Eye for an eye.' 'If you want to get to President Trump,' declared Kari Lake, the one-time TV anchor turned Republican firebrand, 'you are going to have to get through me, and you are going to have to go through 75 million Americans just like me. And I'm going to tell you, most of us are card-carrying members of the NRA.' On rightwing talkback radio, there were calls for US marines to storm the White House and remove Joe Biden, and also to assassinate the Pentagon high command.[44] 'January 6th is gonna look like a playground,' one of Trump's supporters told FreedomNews.TV, as he headed to the Miami federal courthouse where Trump was due to appear. 'All we need is an order, we are ready.'

This kind of civil-war rhetoric has now become almost an everyday feature of political discourse. 'Folks keep talking about another civil war,' read the meme posted on Facebook in March 2019, by Iowa Congressman Steve King, a Republican who keeps miniature Confederate and Gadsden flags on the desk of his office on Capitol Hill. 'One side has about eight trillion bullets, while the other side doesn't know which bathroom to use.' Earlier, in 2018, King had tweeted, 'America is heading in the direction of another Harpers Ferry. After that comes Fort Sumter.'

In this age of potentially catastrophic polarisation, the question of whether the United States is headed towards Civil War 2.0 no longer feels hyperbolic. Moreover, the country's long-established expedient to ease separatist tensions – the denial of basic civil rights to Black Americans, which was used in brokering the Constitution and again for almost 90 years after the end of Reconstruction – is no longer available.

The polling on this question is horrible. In 2021, 46 per cent of Americans thought civil war was likely, according to Zogby.[45] A YouGov poll in 2022 found that two out of five Americans thought the country was likely to be in a state of civil war within the decade. At least half of those surveyed by the Violence Prevention Research

Program at the University of California Davis said they expected the country to descend into civil war even sooner, within four years.

In her timely 2022 book, *How Civil Wars Start: And How to Stop Them*, Barbara Walter suggested two highly predictive risk factors. First, civil wars tend to erupt in countries inhabiting a grey zone between democracy and autocracy – an anocracy is the term. Second, countries where the major parties become almost exclusively organised around ethnic, religious or racial identity are more prone to armed conflict. When Trump was in the White House, America came dangerously close to satisfying both criteria.

In raising the spectre of armed conflict, Walter was not predicting a 21st-century version of the 19th-century conflagration, with armies facing off on the modern-day equivalents of Antietam or Gettysburg. 'If a second civil war breaks out in the US,' she suggested, 'it will be a guerrilla war fought by multiple small militias spread around the country.' Following the advice laid out in *The Turner Diaries*, they would avoid direct confrontation with the US military. Instead, their targets would include minority groups, federal employees, opposition leaders, judges, Black churches and synagogues.[46] Even if not a mass conflict, it would nonetheless be bloody.

Some have used the analogy of 'The Troubles' in Northern Ireland, which saw sporadic bomb attacks and political assassinations over a 30-year period – although it is hard to imagine troops patrolling the streets of major cities, as they did in Belfast and Londonderry, or setting up forward operating bases in hostile territory, as in County Armagh, the IRA's notorious 'Bandit Country'. Still, it requires no great leap of the imagination to see sporadic militia violence becoming a permanent feature of American life, especially around flashpoints such as elections and polarising court cases.

Even if the fissile state of politics feels more like the 1860s than the 1960s – the last time the country was such a powder keg – there are obvious differences to the lead-up to Fort Sumter. There is not the same north-south geographic divide. Though racism in myriad forms persists, it does not have the same explosive power as enslavement. It is not just a single issue that divides the country, but a whole swathe of issues, another point of difference with 1861. There's a strobe effect to American division, rather than a laser.

Within the states themselves are gaping political divides. Texan Republicans like to think of the Lone Star State as a red citadel, but at the 2020 election Joe Biden won 46 per cent of the vote. Three out of four of Texas's biggest cities, Houston, Dallas and Austin, have Democratic mayors. The fourth, San Antonio, is run by an independent. Florida, the state where woke supposedly goes to die, is similarly split. Biden won almost 48 per cent of the vote.

Following January 6th, fears of further domestic terror attacks causing mass bloodshed have not yet eventuated. Securing the convictions of more than 600 rioters and insurrectionists appears to have had the same dampening effect on militia activity as the crackdown in the aftermath of Oklahoma City. Seeing prominent militia figures, such as the Proud Boys' former leader Enrique Tarrio and the Oath Keepers' commandant Stewart Rhodes, convicted of seditious conspiracy had a deterrent effect. Just as importantly, it showed that the rule of law remained strong, and juries were prepared to imprison insurrectionists. Even if politics has entered a post-truth twilight zone, America still has a largely fact-based and evidential criminal justice system.

The midterm elections in 2022 were largely encouraging. Aside from the attack on the home of Nancy Pelosi, and the assault on her husband, they were not marred by widespread political violence. The most extreme Big Lie true believers were defeated. Voters spurned election deniers who tried at the state level to get their hands on the machinery of democracy. Nor was there any election-related violence afterwards. Overall, the results suggested that there was a sensible majority who believed in democracy and the rule of law.

Similarly, Trump's multiple arraignments in the spring and summer of 2023 did not produce the 'death and destruction' he predicted and seemingly hoped for. The response from his supporters was muted. When he called for a MAGA multitude to converge on the federal courthouse in Miami ahead of his second arraignment in the classified documents case, only a hundred or so turned up. The police were prepared for 50,000. Maybe they are lying low, and waiting for their moment to amass and strike. But many of the militias are populated by cosplay warriors, men who like dressing up as soldiers and brandishing their weapons, but who don't have the stomach for armed conflict.

Democracy has not yet ended in darkness, to borrow from the masthead slogan adopted during the Trump presidency by the *Washington Post*. But where are there shards of light? Extreme though polarisation unquestionably is, areas of consensus, and possible compromise, tend to get overlooked. Polls routinely show a sizeable majority support stronger gun controls. Support for abortion is the same. Only in eight states is there a majority in favour of making the procedure illegal in most instances.[47] Even in conservative bastions such as Kansas, voters rejected an amendment to the state constitution which would have kept abortion illegal.

Since the early 1990s, the political parties have become more polarised than the people they represent. Though areas of conflict inevitably receive more attention, Joe Biden has signed into law some major bipartisan legislation, such as a much-needed infrastructure program, a major Covid-19 relief act, the first gun-control legislation in decades, the 2023 debt-ceiling deal, and the 2022 CHIPS and Science Act, aimed at boosting America's domestic semiconductor manufacturing capacity. Responding to the threat from China has been a fruitful area for cross-party cooperation.

Often it is said that the country has survived phases of comparably chronic division, such as the racial and social turmoil of the 1960s, and the war in Vietnam. Yet a key difference between then and now was the workability of Washington politics. Decent-minded Republicans and decent-minded Democrats often set aside their differences at times of national crisis, most notably to pass the great civil-rights reforms of the 1960s, all of which required bipartisan support for their enactment. Even the impeachment process launched after Watergate, which forced the resignation of Richard Nixon, ended up being surprisingly bipartisan. That spirit of cooperation no longer exists. But bipartisanship has not completely broken down, as the votes on China attest.

In recent elections, the Republicans have made inroads with the Hispanic vote, while between 2016 and 2020 Black male support for Donald Trump went from 13 per cent to 18 per cent.[48] These gains might act as a brake on its path to becoming a white nationalist party. Polarising though residential sorting has become, it could be argued that it also acts as a safety mechanism. The lack of face-to-face contact makes people shout more loudly, but maybe it stops them from rubbing up against each other on a daily basis. Besides, for many partisans, politics has become like road rage: angry confrontation from a safe distance. A telling illustration often comes at Trump rallies. The MAGA mosh pit would barrack the press when there were security barriers separating them, but be courteous when, beforehand or afterwards, we came face to face. Even on the fringes of a Trump rally, polarisation can be unexpectedly polite.

Same-sex marriage and interracial marriage are areas that point to the possibility of progress. Once illegal, now they are widely accepted. But this is a rare coming together, driven in part by so many Americans knowing a friend or family member who is homosexual, at a time when the country is falling apart. The same-sex marriage debate also illustrates how progress in one area can become the precursor of conflict in another. After the Supreme Court delivered its *Obergefell v. Hodges* ruling in 2015, which guaranteed the right to have a same-sex marriage, LGBTQIA+ lobby groups looked for a new issue to champion, partly to maintain their donor base, and started pushing for transgender rights. This, in turn, provoked a Republican backlash. Some conservatives had heartfelt moral concerns. Some conservatives simply eyed the chance to create a new wedge issue.

In the absence of outright victory, conflicts ordinarily come to an end when it becomes clear that no side will win, and the warring parties become exhausted of fighting. That is a problem with America's forever war. Its combatants still want to engage in battle. Overturning *Roe* was never intended as the end game for anti-abortion activists. The holy grail of the pro-life movement is a nationwide ban on abortions. Hardline conservatives eye other prizes such as making certain forms of contraception, like the coil, illegal, and clamping down on in-vitro fertilisation (IVF), because embryos are often frozen or discarded.

The culture wars are so unending because the battlefields are so limitless. The 'bathroom battles' over transgender toilets only began a decade ago. Five years ago, few outside of academia had heard of Critical Race Theory. Recently, the state of Tennessee tried to ban drag shows, sparking a wave of copycat bills in conservative states.[49] North Dakota passed a law allowing teachers to ignore their students' preferred pronouns. Bud Light lost its place as America's bestselling beer after a transgender influencer, Dylan Mulvaney, was paid by the company to promote it on social media, and conservatives mounted a boycott. What Republicans deride as 'The Great Awokening' has opened up countless new lines of attack.

If America has been so perennially dysfunctional, how has it achieved such national success and global domination? Size, population and geography are three banal explanations. Were California to suddenly declare independence, it would become the world's fifth biggest economy. Texas and New York would also be in the top ten. Its military muscle is another decisive factor. In 2022, the United States accounted for 39 per cent of global defence spending, compared with China's 13 per cent and Russia's 3.9 per cent. The oceans that line its eastern and western shorelines have been critical for its national security, and meant that America did not suffer the same devastation as Europe and Asia during the first and second world wars. No country has ever developed such a web of foreign alliances and network of far-flung military bases.

The politics of America has not always been so self-destructive. Some of the country's biggest leaps have come during periods of commonsense bipartisanship, as in the 1950s and the first half of the 1960s. Phases of one-party dominance, most notably during Roosevelt's New Deal and Lyndon Johnson's Great Society, became periods of rapid reform.

Even if their provenance is historically dubious, national precepts such as the American Dream have provided animating oomph by creating a sense of the possible and nurturing a spirit of innovation and enterprise. America also illustrates how a country can achieve success while simultaneously being beset by division. Indeed, some of the factors which have created tension and exposed fissures have also provided the spur for national greatness.

Immigration is an obvious example. Throughout American history, it has heightened ethnic and sectarian rivalries but also been the great driver of economic growth. Into America have come some of the country's great entrepreneurs and innovators, such as Andrew Carnegie, Levi Strauss, Sergey Brin of Google, Steve Jobs and Elon Musk. Nearly half of the Fortune 500 companies in 2017 were founded by immigrants or their children.[50] Successive waves of immigrants have long been the source of the country's great energy and ambition.

The struggle for Black equality, another source and symptom of division, has always challenged America to be better. As the Black academic Nikole Hannah-Jones wrote in her introductory essay to the 1619 Project, 'More than any group in this country's history, we have served, generation after generation, in an overlooked but vital role: It is we who have been the perfecters of this democracy.'[51] As for the broader economic and cultural contribution of African-Americans, the rapper Jay-Z put it well in his song 'Dead Presidents II': 'We don't just shine we illuminate the whole show.'

Over the centuries, America has also grown used to coping with its divisiveness, just as a tropical country becomes proficient at dealing with extreme heat. It has learnt to adapt. It has accumulated a lot of muscle memory. As the Irish writer Fintan O'Toole has observed, 'Arguably, the real problem for the US is not that it can be torn apart by political violence, but that it has learned to live with it.'[52]

What will it take to bring the country together? January 6th did not change the Republican Party. Rather than being redemptive, it radicalised the GOP even further. Each time that Trump was arraigned – in New York, Miami, Washington and Atlanta, he racked up a grand slam of indictments, and all in the same calendar year – his stranglehold on the party got tighter. A crisis of the magnitude of the Coronavirus did not bring the country closer together but rather magnified its differences. The murder of George Floyd did not dramatically alter race relations. Likewise, the election of the country's first Black president made the country more racialised. A war with China might bring about a renewed sense of patriotic bipartisanship, especially if the homeland came under attack. But that is by no means certain. America's proxy war with Russia in Ukraine, rather than bringing about any consensus, has exposed the divisions over foreign entanglements. Even the attacks of 9/11 produced only a fleeting period of national unity. Divisions over what came to be known as the 'forever wars' in Iraq and Afghanistan highlighted the forever war at home.

In the immediate term, Donald Trump continues to pose a more imminent threat to America than China. If he contests and loses the 2024 election, he would dispute the result and attempt once more to mobilise his personal army of supporters. However, he would not have executive powers at his disposal to sow the same seeds of chaos as he did on January 6th, and there is a real chance, given the body of evidence in three of the criminal cases against him, that he would have to mount his challenge from behind bars. His imprisonment, of course, could become another flashpoint, but the post-January 6th prosecutions have weakened the militia groups which idolise him, and, again, pro-Trump protests have thus far been piecemeal and rather pathetic.

The greater danger, obviously, is if he makes a triumphant return to the federal mansion on Pennsylvania Avenue rather than being imprisoned in a federal penitentiary. Trump has signalled already he would pack his administration with loyalists unlikely to constrain him, while his joke on the eve of election year in 2024 that he would only become a dictator on 'day one' is chillingly unfunny because of his tendency to semaphore his rule-breaking. A Trump restoration would raise the spectre of regular showdowns with Democratic states, such as California and New York, and frequent stand-offs with protesters in the streets. The chief fear in these situations is not so much the prospect of violence from demonstrators but of a brutal crackdown by the state. Yet even then, a full-blown civil war would be by no means inevitable, partly because liberal Americans, so law-abiding by nature, are more likely to seek redress through the courts rather than armed resistance.

There is also the possibility, of course, that Trump could win the election while at the same time losing the criminal cases against him, in which case the president could plausibly end up a prisoner. And what if a re-elected Trump sought in 2028 to defy the Constitution by seeking a third term? A stress test could feasibly become a breaking point, which underscores why the American future is so dangerously unpredictable. Nothing can be ruled out.

Perverse though it sounds, the dysfunction of the US system serves as its own safety valve, not least the undemocratic features of its democracy. Imagine, for instance, if presidents were elected by popular vote, which would have given the Democrats a virtual lock on the White House for the past 30 years. Imagine the mood of insurrection in rural states awash with firearms if the Senate was not so malapportioned. Grievance politics has been dangerous enough at times when the Republicans have wielded an outsized amount of power in the White House, Congress and the Supreme Court, which was the case for the first two years of the Trump presidency. Stronger would be the chance of the country descending into open violent conflict if the Republicans were shut out of government, which could be the effect of a constitutional overhaul.

So the simple fact that the Constitution makes it so hard to alter the Constitution – the constitutional catch 22 – is actually a safeguard against the country spiralling out of control. Power sharing has long been a tool of conflict resolution – an accommodation between British unionists and Irish nationalists is what helped bring Northern Ireland's Troubles to an end. If not conflict resolution, power sharing in America is a means of conflict avoidance.

To make this point is not the same as applauding the perspicacity of the Founding Fathers, and celebrating the genius of their checks and balances. The design of their democratic architecture was intended to encourage compromise, rather than to produce deadlock. Instead, it is a case of pointing out that the impasses that the US constitutional structure so regularly produce have their uses in an ever more polarised politics. A broken system is preventing the United States from breaking apart. An antique Constitution has become a modern-day coping mechanism. What better illustration is there for how America is presently stuck? The country can't live with the Constitution as presently framed, and can't live without it.

Overall, my sense is that the conditions do not yet exist for all-out armed conflict, a second civil war, but nor do the conditions exist for reconciliation and rapprochement, which again speaks of this national stasis. The country occupies this strange betwixt and between: abyss adjacent, but a step or two back from the edge. Going to hell, as the wit Andy Rooney once observed, without ever getting there. Another way of thinking about America is as a patient suffering from a genetic condition so far without a cure, which is debilitating, and sometimes paralysing, but not terminal.

Richard Hofstadter, as ever, put it well in the book he edited in 1970 on American violence: 'The nation seems to slouch onwards into its uncertain future like some huge inarticulate beast, too much attained by wounds and ailments to be robust, but too strong and resourceful to succumb.'[53] Still more resonant is the concluding warning that came in 1969 from the US National Commission on the Causes and Prevention of Violence, that 'we have yet to understand fully how civil peace is created and maintained.'[54] That rings true today. Even if America does not descend into civil war, it is hard to envision it ever reaching a state of civil peace.

AFTERWORD

Goodbye America

Still I can pinpoint the precise moment I first cast eyes on the skyline of New York City. It was the late 1980s. Ronald Reagan was in the last summer of his presidency. An hour or so earlier, I had touched down at John F. Kennedy International Airport – which would probably still be known as Idlewild, had it not been for Dallas – with a student work visa in my passport and a plan to traverse as much of the continent as possible.

It was twilight. Our bus was stuck in traffic on the Van Wyck Expressway. Rush-hour tempers were beginning to fray. Yet as we edged stutteringly forward, the hiss of the pneumatic brakes punctuating our slow progress, there came a moment of rapture. Manhattan was now in view, a cityscape so beautiful that it looked as if some godly hand had scattered diamonds on the horizon.

Now, on this our final morning in America, I looked at that skyline anew. Our apartment packed up, our belongings enclosed in a shipping container that would soon be steaming towards Sydney, we had checked into a hotel on the banks of the East River with a panoramic view of the city. From the rooftop we could gaze across New York harbour to the Statue of Liberty, look over the river to Wall Street, and peer through the lattice suspension cables of the Brooklyn Bridge to the towers of midtown and beyond. A spectacle that had filled me as a young man with the thrill of new horizons now brought on more complicated feelings, of love and loss, of fading magic and melancholy.

Gone, obviously, were the Twin Towers, a reminder not just of the horrors of September 11th but the self-inflicted wounds committed thereafter. Though the skyline of Lower Manhattan had been repaired, and a new tower measuring 1776 feet had risen in its place, One World Trade Center lacked the braggadocio of the old World Trade Center. Less dominant now were the Empire State and Chrysler buildings, obscured by the muddle of midtown towers rising up like untamed weeds. The Brooklyn Bridge, which at its opening in 1883 had symbolised America's emergent global might, was now associated, in my mind at least, with protest. Over the course of the George Floyd summer I had watched thousands march beneath its stone arches, chanting, 'Black Lives Matter.' When our third child, Honor, was born in the midst of the protests, in our apartment overlooking the bridge as an NYPD helicopter, with its spotlight on, hovered overhead, she inhaled her first lungfuls of breath as demonstrators shouted, 'I can't breathe.'

The Statue of Liberty had lost much of its lustre, its pull no longer so magnetic. During the Trump years, Lady Liberty had become the muse for cartoonists, who had depicted the former president sexually molesting her, standing beside her with a sign reading 'Go Home,' and even, on the controversial cover of *Der Spiegel* magazine, decapitating her. On the morning after his shock victory in 2016, a British tabloid, the *Daily Mirror*, published on its front page an illustration of her with head in hands, accompanied by the headline: 'What have they done?'[1]

Writing at the beginning of the '70s, when the national mood had dipped, the author Joan Didion spoke of how the sight of the Hoover Dam now conveyed 'that sense of being a monument to a faith displaced'. That was how I felt now about the skyline of New York City. My faith had been displaced.

It was not just New York, America's great gateway. The family that had launched my America fascination, the Kennedy dynasty, had also lost much of its allure. In 2020, Joseph Kennedy III became the first family member to taste defeat in a political race in Massachusetts, when he lost the Democratic primary for the US Senate. His uncle, Robert Kennedy Jr, first challenged Joe Biden for the Democratic nomination, then announced he would run as an independent, but was viewed now as a fringe conspiratorialist who claimed that Covid had been manufactured in a way that spared Jewish and Chinese people.

The late-president's son, John F. Kennedy Jr, who had been killed when his plane crashed into the Atlantic Ocean off Martha's Vineyard in the summer of 1999, was now part of the far-right conspiracy mill. A theory popular amongst QAnon followers was that Hillary Clinton had ordered his 'assassination'. Some even believed that JFK Jr was 'Q' himself, and had faked his own death. In November 2021, on the 58th anniversary of JFK's assassination, QAnon diehards gathered in Dealey Plaza in Dallas, fully expecting John Jr to dramatically reappear. In that miraculous moment, Donald Trump would be reinstated as president, and JFK Jr would become his deputy. So certain were conspiracy theorists of this prophecy that some turned up on the grassy knoll wearing 'Trump-Kennedy 2024' t-shirts.

Another of my childhood enchantments, Disney's Magic Kingdom, had also been tainted by the madness of modern-day politics. So captive was Ron DeSantis to cultural conflict that he had declared war on Mickey Mouse. Los Angeles, a city since my first visit that I had associated with American abundance, was now saddled with a homelessness crisis, its sidewalks carpeted with cardboard mattresses.

Chronicling America, a job that I loved and had wanted to do for most of my adult life, no longer filled me with such wonder or delight. In fact, I knew that night on the train home to New York after Joe Biden's inauguration that it was time to open a new chapter. Virtually every story that I covered – the 2020 election, the violence of January 6th, the often-hapless response to the Coronavirus pandemic – followed the same declinist script.

My last field report for the BBC, which came on the anniversary of George Floyd's death, drove home the point. Mid-morning, as flowers were being laid at the spot in Minneapolis where he was murdered, everyone had to scatter in panic as gunfire erupted in an adjacent street. Naturally, we feared the commemorations were being targeted by a racist gunman, that the story we would soon be telling was one of mass murder. But quickly it emerged that the shooting had been connected with a well-known crack-house, and the area returned to normal at breakneck speed. Shootings in this part of Minneapolis had been folded into the rhythms of everyday life. Later on that day, when that young woman of colour shouted into a microphone that white people could not be anything other than racist, it felt like another sign that America would always be stuck in the same historical rut.

The news cycle is the historical cycle in microcosm. We keep on revisiting the same arguments. We keep on going over the same ground. We keep on confronting the same unresolved problems. 'We cannot escape our history.' The words of Abraham Lincoln, contained in his message to Congress in December 1862, were just as resonant now as they were at the time of the Civil War.

History has become such a touchstone because so many conservatives and militia members are battling against the American future: the onset of a more secular country with a majority non-white population; a nation in which they would feel even more marginalised and threatened. Indeed, whereas people of colour look upon themselves as casualties of the American past, many Trump-supporting whites look upon themselves as victims of the American future. Back in the 1960s, William F. Buckley defined a conservative as 'someone who stands athwart history yelling "Stop!" at a time when no one is inclined to do so'. Now that epigram sounds even more like a mission statement of the right.

When as a student I started to study America more seriously, one of the finest and most formative books I read on modern US history was E. J. Dionne's *Why Americans Hate Politics*. The fact that it was published while I was studying for my doctorate in the very building, a 16th-century Oxford manor house, where the author had also lived as a postgraduate, added a personal connection. Among its many insights was that for America to find a new centre, the country had to make peace with the 1960s. More than 30 years on, it remains a persuasive argument, but only as far as it goes. Alas, the challenge is more daunting. The United States has to make peace with the 200 years which preceded the '60s, and also the turbulent decades which have since unfolded. Right now, it cannot even reach agreement on what happened on January 6th. So what chance the tumble of events since 1776?

The United States is buckling under the weight and contradictions of its history for the simple reason that so much of that history is unresolved. But it was ever thus. America has rarely had a sense of oneness, so why should we expect it today? Joe Biden will continue to 'fight for the soul of America', a staple of his presidential speeches. But as the Swedish sociologist Gunnar Myrdal remarked when he published his seminal 1944 study, *An American Dilemma: the Negro Problem and American Democracy*: 'America is continuously fighting for its soul.'[2]

In his 1993 inaugural address, Bill Clinton memorably proclaimed, 'There is nothing wrong with America that cannot be cured by what is right with America.' But attractive as that proposition sounds, the national story is full of instances where wrongs have been righted only for justice to be reversed. For much of the past 250 years, moreover, what is historically wrong with America has frequently outweighed what is historically right, enslavement and segregation being the most glaring examples. Most modern-day conservatives, however, are unwilling to make that intellectual concession, while most modern-day progressives, people of colour especially, are unwilling to cohabit some whitewashed historical halfway house crowded with so many myths and untruths. The result, again, is deadlock, a battlefield in the history wars with unmovable trenches.

My love affair with the United States has not ended. Far from it. We only had to drop in on our next-door neighbours in New York to be reminded of the opportunities that still exist there. A mixed-race couple, who had prospered in the dot.com boom through hard work and innovation, they embodied various American Dreams. Their daughter, who we had watched grow up, was making a name for herself as an actress in Hollywood. Their eldest son was studying marine biology at one of those powerhouse universities in southern California. They were warm-hearted, altruistic and unwilling to give up on a country that had brought them abundance and success.

Still, leaving America was less emotionally complicated than I imagined. Our kids had reached the age where they realised why they were crouching under their desks, the moment that my wife and I had always said would signal it was time to leave. Though our youngest daughter was a US citizen, we decided it was better to shield her from the land of her birth. We did not see a great future for her, or us, in a country that had become so hostage to its history: a country where being stuck in the past also meant it was stuck in the present.

During the Trump years especially, it felt like I had already said goodbye to the America I had fallen in love with as a teenager. But perhaps the country that so beguiled me had always been a kingdom of my mind, a mythic city upon a hill. Perhaps I was saying goodbye to something that never truly existed.

On that final morning, our journey out of the city took my family along the same highways I had travelled as a student. The New York skyline rose up behind us. But on the Van Wyck Expressway, as we headed for 'JFK', not one of us glanced over our shoulders. Not one of us looked back.

ACKNOWLEDGEMENTS

The first book I have written since jumping off the hamster wheel of day-to-day news, *The Forever War* has inevitably ended up being a more solitary undertaking than previous titles. Much of it was written in the seclusion of my study rather than newsrooms, television edit suites, airport departure lounges and the quiet cars of the Amtrak Acela express train as it crawled between New York and Washington. Still, though, I owe an enormous debt to my former BBC colleagues, especially the team in New York, which included Nada Tawfik, Ashley Semler and Andrew Herbert, and my boss in Washington, Paul Danahar, who always had my back. Though I am no longer a part of the BBC, the BBC is still very much a part of me.

I need also to thank the scholars, historians and journalists who have helped guide my thinking, a long list that includes Ari Berman, Ron Brownstein, Joseph Ellis, Jill Lepore, Pamela Haag, Jon Meacham, Ta-Nehisi Coates, Michael Waldman, Steven Levitsky, Daniel Ziblatt, Arthur M. Schlesinger Jr and David Reynolds. I was especially pleased to cite the work of Anthony Badger, my PhD examiner from 30 years ago, who has since become a dear and trusted friend.

Nobody has been of more help or inspiration than Professor Adam Smith, the director of the Rothermere American Institute at Oxford. It was listening to the backlist of Adam's exceptional podcast, *The Last Best Hope?*, during a summer spent in the English countryside after leaving America that convinced me to embark upon this project. Adam was also kind enough to read the manuscript and offer invaluable suggestions and morale-boosting praise.

It has been the usual pleasure to work with the team at Penguin Random House in Sydney, headed up by my publisher, the indefatigable Nikki Christer, trusted editor Patrick Mangan, and publicist Jessica Malpass.

My thanks to the team at Bloomsbury in London and New York. My publisher Tomasz Hoskins was hugely encouraging from the start. My UK-based editor, Matthew Taylor, was as forensic as ever. Sarah Jones, Sarah Head and Jessica Gray have been a delight. I am grateful to James Watson for designing such a jolting cover.

None of my books would have made it into print without the support of my agents, Pippa Masson in Sydney and Gordon Wise in London. It is always a privilege to work alongside two people with such a passion for the written word.

Friends in New York, such as Carley Roney, David Liu, Cameron Smith and Jeff Edwards, always reminded me of America's best self. For their help in making so happy our re-entry into Australia, I would especially like to thank Kat and Rob Laurie, Anna Funder and Craig Allchin, Nick Glozier, Angus Paull, Chris Reason and Michael O'Dwyer.

The single biggest upside of leaving the BBC has been to spend more time with my beloved family, and to be, for the first time in my career, an ever present at home. It is the greatest joy of my life to watch Bill, Wren and Honor grow and mature, and to see in them the influence of their years spent living in New York. Every time I hear our three-year-old, Honor, sing 'This Land Is Your Land', which has become something of a signature tune, it makes me miss the country that I fell in love with as a child.

My wife and best friend, Fleur Wood, continues to be my comfort and strength. Hopefully since returning to live in Sydney, I have been able to offer her the kind of support and back-up that she uncomplainingly offered to me during the mania of the Trump years. To Fleur and our beautiful children, I dedicate this book.

NOTES

PROLOGUE: 'DEMOCRACY HAS PREVAILED'

1   *Washington Post*, 24 January 2021.

INTRODUCTION: ESCAPING CAMELOT

1   *New York Times*, 9 November 1960.
2   William Manchester, *The Death of a President*, World Books, London, 1968, p. 287–8.
3   Jon Meacham, *The Soul of America: The Battle for our Better Angels*, p. 214.
4   *American Heritage*, October 1970.
5   *New Yorker*, 20 April 1968.
6   Nick Bryant, *The Bystander: John F. Kennedy and the Struggle for Black Equality*, Basic Books, New York, 2006, pp. 7–10.
7   Richard Hofstadter, 'The Paranoid Style in American Politics', *Harper's Magazine*, November 1964.
8   *Life*, 6 December 1963.

1: THE STRANGE CAREER OF AMERICAN DEMOCRACY

1   Joseph Ellis, *American Creation: Triumphs and Tragedies in the Founding of the Republic*, Vintage Books, New York, 2007, p. 241.
2   Letter from Thomas Jefferson to John Adams, 30 August 1787, National Archives.
3   Letter from Jefferson to Adams, 28 October 1813, National Archives.
4   Jill Lepore, *These Truths: A History of the United States*, W. W. Norton & Company, New York, 2018, p. 113.
5   Thomas Jefferson, *Notes on the State of Virginia*, Prichard and Hall, Philadelphia, 1785, p. 126.
6   Daniel Bullen, *Daniel Shays's Honorable Rebellion: An American Story*, Westholme Publishing, Yardley, Pennsylvania, 2021.
7   Letter from George Washington to James Madison, 5 November 1786, National Archives.
8   Letter from John Adams to John Taylor, 17 December 1814, National Archives.
9   Letter from John Adams to Thomas Jefferson, 6 December 1787, National Archives.
10 Lepore, *These Truths*, p. 121.
11 James Madison, *Federalist No. 62*.
12 Alexander Hamilton, *Federalist No. 68*.

281

13   Donathan L. Brown and Michael L. Clemons, *Voting Rights under Fire: The Continuing Struggle for People of Color*, Bloomsbury, London, 2015, p. 7.

14   Letter from John Adams to Abigail Adams, 14 April 1776.

15   David Reynolds, *America, Empire of Liberty: A New History of the United States*, Basic Books, New York, 2009, p. 62.

16   Lepore, *These Truths*, p. 163.

17   Alexis de Tocqueville, *Democracy in America*, p. 112.

18   Lepore, *These Truths*, p. 121.

19   Letter from Thomas Jefferson to Spencer Roane, 6 September 1819, National Archives.

20   Reynolds, *America, Empire of Liberty*, p. 95.

21   Eric Foner, 'South Carolina's Forgotten Black Political Revolution', *Slate*, 31 January 2018.

22   Lepore, *These Truths*, p. 457.

23   Anthony J. Badger, *Why White Liberals Fail: Race and Southern Politics from FDR to Trump*, Harvard University Press, Cambridge, 2022, pp. 75–80.

24   US Commission on Civil Rights Commission, 'The Mississippi Delta Report', February 2001.

25   Ari Berman, *Give Us the Ballot: The Modern Struggle for Voting Rights in America*, Farrar, Straus and Giroux, New York, 2015, p. 45.

26   Berman, *Give Us the Ballot*, pp. 47–8.

27   Ibid., p. 86.

28   Badger, *Why White Liberals Fail*, p. 137.

29   Ian Millhiser, 'Chief Justice Roberts's lifelong crusade against voting rights, explained', *Vox*, 18 September 2020.

30   *New York Times*, 30 June 1982.

31   Berman, *Give Us the Ballot*, p. 166.

32   Ibid., p. 206.

33   *New York Times*, 11 November 1994.

34   Charles L. Zelden, *Bush v. Gore: Exposing the Hidden Crisis in American Democracy*, University of Kansas Press, Lawrence, Kansas, 2008, p. 237.

35   Steven Levitsky and Daniel Ziblatt, *How Democracies Die*, p. 184.

36   *New York Times*, 12 April 2007; Berman, *Give Us the Ballot*, p. 229.

37   Alex Tausanovitch, 'The Impact of Partisan Gerrymandering', Center for American Progress, 1 October 2019.

38   Wendy Weiser, 'The State of Voting in 2014', Brennan Center for Justice, 17 June 2014.

39   *Shelby County v. Holder*, 570 US 529. Berman, *Give Us the Ballot*, p. 278.

40   Michael Waldman, *The Fight to Vote*, Simon & Schuster, New York, 2022, p. xiii.

41   '50 years later, Voting Rights Act under unprecedented assault', Brennan Center for Justice, 2 August 2015.

42   Speech by Barack Obama at the 50th anniversary of Selma to Montgomery marches, 7 March 2015.

43   Politico, 12 January 2018.

44   Final report of the January 6th Committee, 22 December 2022.

45 Louis Menand, 'American Democracy Was Never Designed to Be Democratic', *New Yorker*, 15 August 2022.

46 Waldman, *The Fight to Vote*, p. xiii.

47 *Washington Post*, 23 December 2022.

2: FROM JULY 4TH TO JANUARY 6TH

1   Ibid., 15 January 2021.

2   *New York Times*, 6 May 2022.

3   *Los Angeles Times*, 6 January 2020.

4   Letter from Thomas Jefferson to James Madison, 30 January 1787, National Archives.

5   Letter from Thomas Jefferson to Abigail Adams, 22 February 1787, National Archives.

6   Letter from Thomas Jefferson to William Stephens Smith, 13 November 1787, National Archives.

7   Christopher Hitchens, *Thomas Jefferson: Author of America*, HarperCollins, New York, 2005, p. 69.

8   *Law and Crime*, 20 October 2022.

9   *New York Times*, 3 June 1997.

10 Olivia Li, 'When Jefferson and Madison banned guns on campus', *The Atlantic*, 6 May 2016.

11 Letter from Jefferson to Madison, 30 January 1787. National Archives.

12 Wayne LaPierre, *Guns, Crime and Freedom*, Regnery, Washington DC, 1994, p. 7.

13 James Rankin, 'The Second Amendment gives no comfort to insurrectionists', *New York Times*, 27 September 2022.

14 Ben Winograd, SCOTUSblog, 26 June 2008.

15 Aziz Huq, 'On the Origins of Republican Violence', Brennan Center for Justice, June 2021; Mary B. McCord, 'Dispelling the Myth of the Second Amendment', Brennan Center for Justice, 29 June 2021.

16 *The Atlantic*, 7 March 2023.

17 *New York Times*, 5 April 2021.

18 Ibid., 31 July 2021.

19 *Vox*, 26 January 2021.

20 *Washington Post*, 11 October 2021.

21 Laura Jedeed, 'The Cult of the January 6th Martyrs', *New Republic*, 7 March 2023.

22 Bonnie Kristian, 'How the Founding Fathers Encourage Political Violence', *The Week*, 28 January 2021.

23 Kellie Carter Jackson, 'The Story of Violence in America', *Daedalus*, 1 January 2022.

24 Tim Madigan, *The Burning: Massacre, Destruction, and the Tulsa Race Riot of 1921*, Thomas Dunne Books, New York, 2001, p. xiii.

25 *Los Angeles Times*, 19 June 2020.

26 *Guardian*, 8 November 2019.

27 Benjamin Justice, 'Historical Fiction to Historical Fact: Gangs of New York and the Whitewashing of History', *Social Education*, 67, 2003.

28 Ta-Nehisi Coates, *We Were Eight Years in Power: An American Tragedy*, One World, New York, 2018, p. 245.

29 Meacham, *The Soul of America*, p. 111.

30 *Washington Post*, 9 December 2018.

31 Michael Wallace, 'The Uses of Violence in American History', *The American Scholar*, Winter 1970–1971.

32 Lorraine Boissoneault, 'The Attempted Assassination of Andrew Jackson', *Smithsonian Magazine*, 14 March 2017.

33 *The Charlotte Democrat*, 3 June 1856.

34 Joanne B. Freeman, *The Field of Blood: Violence in Congress and the Road to Civil War*, Farrar, Straus and Giroux, 2018, New York, pp. 5–6.

35 Report of the US National Commission on the Causes and Prevention of Violence, 1969; *New York Times*, 5 June 1969.

36 Richard Hofstadter and Michael Williams, *American Violence: A Documentary History*, Alfred A. Knopf, New York, 1970, pp. 3–4.

37 *Smithsonian Magazine*, 8 July 2015.

38 Kathleen Belew, *Bring the War Home: The White Power Movement and Paramilitary America*, Harvard University Press, Cambridge, 2018, p. 3.

39 *New York Times*, 12 January 2021.

40 Gavin Esler, *The United States of Anger*, Michael Joseph, London, 1997.

41 Catrina Doxsee, 'Examining Extremism: The Militia Movement', Center for Strategic and International Studies, 12 August 2021.

42 *Vox*, 29 September 2014.

43 Carol Leonnig, *Zero Fail: The Rise and Fall of the Secret Service*, Random House, New York, 2021, p. 295.

44 NPR, 9 January 2011.

45 *New York Magazine*, 21 September 2018.

46 Evan Osnos, 'The Fearful and Frustrated', *New Yorker*, 24 August 2015.

47 David Neiwert, *Alt-America: The Rise of the Radical Right in the Age of Trump*, Verso, New York, 2017, p. 321.

48 *The Atlantic*, 21 November 2016.

49 *Axios*, 18 October 2018.

50 *Vox*, 9 January 2021.

51 *NBC News*, 8 August 2019.

52 *New York Times*, 9 February 2022.

53 Ibid.

54 Cynthia Miller-Idriss, 'From 9/11 to 1/6', *Foreign Affairs*, 24 August 2021.

55 *The Economist*, 13 August 2022.

56 *New York Times*, 9 January 2021.

57 *The Economist*, 13 August 2022.

58 *The Conversation*, 12 January 2021.

59 'American Face of Insurrection', Chicago Project on Security and Threats, 5 January 2020.

60 NPR, 5 January 2022.

61 Politico, 4 May 2023.
62 *NBC News*, 15 October 2021.
63 CNN, 2 March 2023.
64 Rachel Kleinfeld, 'The Rise of Political Violence in the United States', *Journal of Democracy*, October 2021.
65 *Washington Post*, 1 January 2022.
66 *The Economist*, 13 August 2022.
67 *Commentary*, October 1956.
68 Ibid., August 1961.
69 Erick Trickey, 'Long before QAnon, Ronald Reagan and the GOP purged John Birch Extremists from the Party', *Washington Post*, 15 January 2021.
70 *New York Times*, 24 September 2023.

3: THE DEMAGOGIC STYLE IN AMERICAN POLITICS

1   Ellis, *American Creation*, p. 6.
2   Letter from George Washington to Lafayette, 6 June 1787, National Archives.
3   Alexander Hamilton, *Federalist No. 1*.
4   James Madison, *Federalist No. 10*.
5   'Election of 1828' by Robert V. Remini, in Arthur M. Schlesinger eds., *The Coming to Power: Critical Presidential Elections in American History*, Chelsea House, New York, 1972, pp. 67–90.
6   *Washington Post*, 15 March 2017.
7   *New York Times*, 11 July 1896.
8   David Michaelis, *Eleanor*, Simon & Schuster, New York, 2020, p. 506.
9   Meacham, *The Soul of America*, p. 219.
10 Dan T. Carter, *The Politics of Rage: George Wallace, the Origins of New Conservatism and the Transformation of American Politics*, University of Louisiana Press, Baton Rouge, 1996, pp. 415–50.
11 *The Atlantic*, February 1996.
12 Walter Isaacson, *Elon Musk*, Simon & Schuster, New York, 2023, p. 354.
13 Carter, *The Politics of Rage*, p. 424.
14 Meacham, *The Soul of America*, p. 195.
15 *New York Times*, 11 July 1982.
16 *Washington Post*, 27 March 1994.
17 *Time*, 16 April 2015.

4: AMERICAN AUTHORITARIANISM

1   Susan Glasser and Peter Baker, *The Divider: Trump in the White House, 2017–2023*, Penguin Random House, New York, 2022, p. 125.
2   Meacham, *The Soul of America*, p. 249.
3   Glasser and Baker, *The Divider*, p. 81.
4   *New York Times*, 1 October 2019.
5   John Bolton, *The Room Where It Happened: A White House Memoir*, Simon & Schuster, New York, 2020, p. 433.

6   Interview with Mark Esper on NPR, 9 March 2022.
7   *New York Times,* 11 June 2018.
8   Levitsky and Ziblatt, *How Democracies Die*, pp. 21–2.
9   Ruth Ben-Ghiat, *Strongmen: How They Rise, Why They Succeed, How They Fail*, Profile Books, London, 2020, p. 73.
10   Garry Wills, *Cincinnatus: George Washington and the Enlightenment*, Doubleday, New York, 1984, p. 23.
11   Letter from George Washington to Henry Knox, 1 April 1789, National Archives.
12   Eric Nelson, *The Royalist Revolution: Monarchy and the American Founding*, Harvard University Press, Cambridge, 2014, pp. 1–2.
13   Reynolds, *America, Empire of Liberty*, p. 64; *Washington Post*, 29 April 1989.
14   Levitsky and Ziblatt, *How Democracies Die*, p. 129.
15   Ibid., p. 100.
16   Ellis, *American Creation*, p. 225.
17   *Washington Post*, 8 September 2018.
18   Ellis, *American Creation*, p. 224.
19   John Yo, 'Jefferson and Executive Power', *Boston University Law Review*, Volume 88, 2008.
20   Nancy Isenberg and Andrew Burstin, 'The Democratic Autocrat'. *Democracy: A Journal of Ideas*, Fall 2017.
21   Daniel Feller, 'Andrew Jackson: Impact and Legacy', University of Virginia Miller Center.
22   Noah Feldman, *The Broken Constitution: Lincoln, Slavery and the Founding of America*, Farrar, Straus and Giroux, New York, 2021, p. 6.
23   Letter from Abraham Lincoln to Erastus Corning and others, June 1863, Library of Congress.
24   *Smithsonian Magazine*, 17 April 2017.
25   Adam Hochschild, *American Midnight: The Great War, a Violent Peace and Democracy's Forgotten Crisis*, Mariner Books, Boston, 2022, p. 2.
26   Howard Zinn, *A People's History of the United States*, HarperPerennial, New York, 2003, p. 392.
27   Franklin Delano Roosevelt, inaugural address, 4 March 1933.
28   Levitsky and Ziblatt, *How Democracies Die*, p. 132.
29   H. L. Mencken, *The American Mercury*, Volume 41.
30   Meacham, *The Soul of America*, p. 150.
31   Ibid., p. 166.
32   Arthur M. Schlesinger Jr, *The Imperial Presidency*, Houghton Mifflin, Boston, 1973, p. x.
33   Levitsky and Ziblatt, *How Democracies Die*, p. 164.
34   Politico, 4 August 2022.
35   Meacham, *The Soul of America*, p. 138.
36   *New York Herald Tribune*, 5 March 1933.
37   Lepore, *These Truths*, p. 434.
38   G. H. Bennett, *The American Presidency*, p. 98.
39   Jimmy Carter, *Keeping Faith: Memoirs of a President*, University of Arkansas Press, Fayetteville, 1995, p. 29.

40 Daniel Feller, 'Andrew Jackson's Shifting Legacy', Gilder Lehrman Institute of American History.
41 *New York Times*, 29 November 2016.
42 Ibid.
43 Politico, 17 January 2016.
44 *Axios*, 12 September 2022.
45 BBC Complaints Unit, 6 August 2020.

5: 1776 AND ALL THAT . . .

1   Executive Order 13958 establishing the President's Advisory 1776 Commission, 2 November 2020.
2   *New York Times*, 14 August 2019.
3   Reuters, 15 February 2022.
4   UCLA School of Law Critical Race Studies Program tracker.
5   *Guardian*, 27 February 2023.
6   Jacqueline Jones, 'Historians and their Publics, Then and Now', Presidential address of the American Historical Association, 5 January 2022.
7   James H. Sweet, 'Is History History?', *Perspectives on History*, 17 August 2022.
8   *Final Report of the January 6th Committee*, 22 December 2022.
9   Benson Lossing, *A Primary History of the United States for Schools and Families*, p. 6.
10 George Bancroft, *History of the United States, from the Discovery of the American Continent*, pp. 1–4.
11 Bancroft, *History of the United States, from the Discovery of the American Continent 1882 edition*, D. Appleton and Company, New York, 1855–60, p. 3.
12 William Wirt Henry, Address to the American Historical Association, 29 December 1891.
13 Sean Wilentz, 'Don't Know Much About History', *New York Times*, 30 November 1997.
14 Richard Hofstadter, *The American Political Tradition*, Vintage Books, New York, 1984, p. 25.
15 Robert Hughes, *Culture of Complaint: The Fraying of America*, Warner Books, New York, 1984, p. 125.
16 Zinn, *A People's History of the United States*, Harper Perennial, New York, 2015 edition, p. xviii.
17 *Wall Street Journal*, 20 October 1994.
18 David W. Blight, 'The Fog of the History Wars', *New Yorker*, 9 June 2021.
19 Reynolds, *America, Empire of Liberty*, p. 15 & p. 19.
20 Ibid., p. 8.
21 Lepore, *These Truths*, p. 55.
22 Ibid., p. 102 & p. 94.
23 Ellis, *American Creation*, pp. 8–9 & p. 11.
24 Tara Zahra, *The Great Departure: Mass Migration from Eastern Europe and the Making of the Free World*, W. W. Norton, New York, 2017.

25 J. A. Thompson, 'Woodrow Wilson and World War I: A Reappraisal', *Journal of American Studies*, December 1985.
26 Jeffrey G. Williamson and Peter Lindert, 'Unequal Gains: American Growth and Inequality Since 1700', Centre for Economic Policy Research, 16 June 2016.
27 Sarah Churchwell, *Behold America: A History of America First and the American Dream*, Bloomsbury, London, 2018, p. 170 & p. 7.
28 Meacham, *The Soul of America*, p. 160.
29 Robert A. Goldberg, *Enemies Within: The Culture of Conspiracy in Modern America*, Yale University Press, New Haven, 2001, p. 2.
30 Kurt Andersen, *Fantasyland: How America Went Haywire, a 500 Year History*, Simon & Schuster, New York, 2020, p. 11.
31 Meacham, *The Soul of America*, p. 53.
32 Women's Media Centre, 21 September 2022.
33 Question and answer with Anne-Marie Slaughter, 7 September 2021, Princeton University Press.
34 Hughes, *Culture of Complaint*, p. 125.
35 *Axios*, 4 May 2023.
36 Glasser and Baker, *The Divider*, pp. 5–7.
37 *New Yorker*, 9 June 2021.
38 *New York Times*, 20 February 2023.

6: AMERICA'S CONSTANT CURSE

1 Reynolds, *America, Empire of Liberty*, p. 31.
2 Edmund Morgan, 'Slavery and Freedom: The American Paradox', *The Journal of American History*, June 1972.
3 Letter from Thomas Jefferson to John Holmes, 22 April 1820, National Archives.
4 Franklin Pierce, inaugural address, 4 March 1853.
5 Arthur M. Schlesinger Jr, *The Disuniting of America: Reflections on a Multicultural Society*, W. W. Norton, New York, 1998, pp. 18–19.
6 Bryant, *The Bystander*, p. 43.
7 Coates, *We Were Eight Years in Power*, p. 275.
8 Lepore, *These Truths*, p. 147.
9 Ibid., p. 120.
10 Ibid., p. 147.
11 David O. Stewart, 'George Washington Struggles with Slavery', *American Heritage*, June 2021.
12 Jefferson, *Notes on the State of Virginia*, pp. 149–52.
13 Henry Wiencek, 'The Dark Side of Thomas Jefferson', *Smithsonian Magazine*, October 2012.
14 Letter from Abraham Lincoln to Horace Greeley, 22 August 1862. Library of Congress.
15 *NPR*, 11 October 2010.
16 Henry Louis Gates Jr, *Lincoln on Race and Slavery*, Princeton University Press, Princeton, 2009, p. xx.
17 Gates, *Lincoln on Race and Slavery*, p. xxiv.

18   Badger, *Why White Liberals Fail*, p. 39.
19   Meacham, *The Soul of America*, p. 162.
20   Badger, *Why White Liberals Fail*, p. 42.
21   Michelle Alexander, *The New Jim Crow: Mass Incarceration in the Age of Colorblindness*, The New Press, New York, 2012, p. 47.
22   Dean J. Kotlowski, *Nixon's Civil Rights: Politics, Principle and Policy*, Harvard University Press, Cambridge, 2002, p. 1.
23   Jonathan Alter, *His Very Best: Jimmy Carter, A Life*, Simon & Schuster, New York, 2020, pp. 167–8 & p. 356.
24   Tim Naftali, 'Ronald Reagan's Long-Hidden Racist Conversation with Richard Nixon', *The Atlantic*, 30 July 2019.
25   *The Nation*, 11 February 2011.
26   Barack Obama, *A Promised Land*, p. 122.
27   Ibid., p. 167.
28   Quoted in Ta-Nehisi Coates, 'Fear of a Black President', *The Atlantic*, 15 September 2012.
29   Obama, *A Promised Land*, p. 116.
30   *New York Times*, 20 June 2009.
31   Obama, *A Promised Land*, p. 116.
32   Coates, *We Were Eight Years in Power*, p. 131.
33   Alexander, *The New Jim Crow*, pp. 2–4.
34   Coates, 'Fear of a Black President', *The Atlantic*, 15 September 2012.
35   Coates, *We Were Eight Years in Power*, p. 147.
36   Keeanga-Yamahtta Taylor, 'From Color-Blind to Black Lives Matter' in Julian E. Zelizer eds., *The Presidency of Donald J. Trump: A First Historical Assessment*, Princeton University Press, Princeton, 2022, p. 212.
37   Politico, 23 May 2021.
38   Michael Cohen, *Disloyal: A Memoir*, Skyhorse Publishing, New York, 2020, pp. 106–10.
39   John Blake, 'There Was No Racial Reckoning for George Floyd', CNN, 18 April 2021.

7: IN GUNS WE TRUST

1   Reuters, 23 August 2023.
2   *Washington Post*, 11 June 2023.
3   CNN, 20 January 2023.
4   *New York Times*, 24 November 2022.
5   Associated Press, 8 May 2023.
6   *Federalist No. 29*.
7   *New York Review of Books*, 21 September 1995.
8   Carl Bogus, 'The History and Politics of Second Amendment Scholarship: A Primer', *Chicago-Kent Law Review*, October 2000.
9   Michael Waldman, *The Second Amendment: A Biography*, Simon & Schuster, New York, 2014, pp. 32–3.
10   *Salon*, 16 December 2017.

11   Jill Lepore, 'Battleground America', *New Yorker,* 16 April 2012.
12   *Daily Beast,* 6 August 2019.
13   Richard Hofstadter, 'America as a Gun Culture', *American Heritage,* October 1970.
14   Pamela Haag, *The Gunning of America: Business and the Making of American Gun Culture,* Basic Books, New York, 2016, pp. 187–93.
15   Bill Bryson, *Made in America: An Informal History of the English Language in the United States,* William Morrow, New York, 2001, p. 155.
16   Haag, *The Gunning of America,* p. xv.
17   'A Brief History of the NRA', National Rifle Association.
18   *Salon,* 14 January 2013.
19   *New Yorker,* 20 April 1968.
20   Jennifer Tucker, 'How the NRA Hijacked History', *Washington Post,* 9 September 2019.
21   *Medium,* 18 November 2021.
22   *New Yorker,* 20 April 1968.
23   *American Heritage,* October 1970.
24   *Washington Post,* 29 May 2018.
25   Richard Harris, 'If You Love Your Guns', *New Yorker,* 20 April 1968.
26   Michael Waldman, 'How the NRA Rewrote the Second Amendment', Politico, 19 May 2014.
27   Patti Davis, 'How Gun Violence Changed My Father, Ronald Reagan, and My Family', *New York Times,* 5 July 2022.
28   *Newsweek,* 27 April 2017.
29   *This Week,* 4 December 2015.
30   Ronald Reagan, 'Why I'm for the Brady Bill', *New York Times,* 29 March 1991.
31   *PBS MacNeil/Lehrer NewsHour,* 16 December 1991.
32   Waldman, *The Second Amendment,* p. 93.
33   Michael J. Klein, 'Did the Assault Weapons Ban of 1994 Bring Down Mass Shootings?' *The Conversation,* 9 June 2000.
34   Politico, 19 May 2014.
35   *Washington Post,* 12 January 2013.
36   *New York Times,* 7 August 2000.
37   Ibid., 8 May 2002.
38   *Washington Post,* 27 March 2023.
39   *New York Magazine,* 27 January 2023.
40   *New York Times,* 10 January 2009.
41   *Gallup,* 24 April 2014.
42   Matthew J. Lacombe, *Firepower: How the NRA Turned Gun Owners into a Political Force,* Princeton University Press, Princeton, 2021, p. 7.
43   *The Conversation,* 7 July 2022.
44   *Financial Times,* 26 February 2023.

8: ROE, WADE AND THE SUPREMES

1   *New York Times,* 9 February 1986.
2   *The Atlantic,* 13 May 2022.

3   *New York Times*, 23 January 1973.
4   Ibid.
5   Randall Balmer, 'The Religious Right and the Abortion Myth', Politico, 10 May 2022.
6   Randall Balmer, 'The Real Origins of the Religious Right', Politico, 27 May 2014.
7   Ted Kennedy letter to Tom Dennelly, 3 August 1971. Catholic League.
8   Ronald Reagan, speech in Dallas, 22 August 1980.
9   *New York Times*, 29 March 2019.
10   Alexander Hamilton, *Federalist No. 78*.
11   Linda Greenhouse, *The U.S. Supreme Court: A Very Short Introduction*, p. 7.
12   *Wall Street Journal*, 14 September 2018.
13   Michael Stokes Paulsen, 'Lincoln and Judicial Authority', *Notre Dame Law Review*, Volume 83, 2008.
14   David Greenberg, 'How Supreme Court Nominations Lost Their Apolitical Pretense', Politico, 30 June 2018.
15   Berman, *Give Us the Ballot*, p. 180.
16   *New York Times*, 18 September 1986.
17   Ibid.
18   Berman, *Give Us the Ballot*, p. 179.
19   Associated Press, 6 July 1991.
20   *New York Times*, 20 September 2018.
21   *Washington Post*, 7 May 2022.
22   *New Yorker*, 22 August 2022.
23   *New York Times*, 25 June 2022; BBC online, 25 June 2022; *Washington Post*, 24 June 2022.
24   Pew Research, 1 September 2022.
25   *New Yorker*, 28 August 2022.
26   *Washington Post*, 24 June 2022.
27   Reuters, 22 July 2022.
28   *New York Times*, 27 June 2022.
29   Obama, *A Promised Land*, pp. 387–8.

9: TOXIC EXCEPTIONALISM

1   *The Economist*, 2 February 2021.
2   'From Crisis to Reform: A Call to Strengthen America's Battered Democracy', Freedom House, March 2021.
3   *New Yorker*, 18 August 2019.
4   CNN, 19 September 2022.
5   *ABC News*, 12 January 2022.
6   De Tocqueville, *Democracy in America*, p. 768.
7   Terrence McCoy, 'How Joseph Stalin Invented "American Exceptionalism"', *The Atlantic*, 15 March 2012.
8   Alter, *His Very Best*, pp. 467–9.
9   Obama, *A Promised Land*, p. xvi.
10   *Washington Post*, 4 February 2017.

11 'US Gun Policy: Global Comparisons', US Council on Foreign Relations, 10 June 2022.
12 BBC News, 11 October 2022.
13 Alex S. Vitale, *The End of Policing*, Verso, New York, 2018, p. 25.
14 NPR, 25 March 2023.
15 Pew Research Centre, 1 November 2021.
16 *New York Times*, 23 January 2019.
17 *Foreign Affairs*, 29 September 2019.
18 *Washington Post*, 13 March 2021.
19 *Foreign Policy*, 13 July 2020.

10: THE TWO AMERICAS

1 Associated Press, 13 June 2020.
2 Remarks by President Joe Biden, 6 January 2022.
3 Speech by Joe Biden, Atlanta University, 11 January 2022.
4 Speech by Joe Biden, Independence Hall, Philadelphia, 1 September 2022.
5 *New Yorker*, 2 September 2022.
6 *Wall Street Journal*, 2 September 2022.
7 Jonathan Martin and Alexander Burns, *This Will Not Pass: Trump, Biden, and the Battle for America's Future*, Simon & Schuster, New York, 2022, p. 19.
8 Jill Lepore, *This America: The Case for the Nation*, Liveright Publishing Corporation, New York, 2019, pp. 29–30.
9 Letter from George Washington to James Madison, 5 November 1786.
10 Ellis, *American Creation*, p. 111.
11 Hugh Brogan, *The Penguin History of the United States*, Penguin, London, 1985, p. 199.
12 *Foreign Affairs*, 5 February 2019.
13 Reynolds, *America, Empire of Liberty*, p. 71.
14 Ellis, *American Creation*, p. 205.
15 Constitution Daily, blog of the National Constitution Center, 4 July 2021.
16 Letter from John Adams to Thomas Jefferson, 21 December 1819. National Archives.
17 Ellis, *American Creation*, p. 175.
18 Ronald Brownstein, 'The Republican Axis Reversing the Rights Revolution', *The Atlantic*, 24 December 2021.
19 *The Hill*, 6 August 2022.
20 Politico, 7 April 2023.
21 Associated Press, 1 May 2015.
22 CNN, 28 March 2020.
23 *The Economist,* 3 September 2020.
24 *New York Times*, 9 September 2021.
25 Ibid., 19 March 2015.
26 David A. Graham, 'Red State, Blue City', *The Atlantic*, March 2017.
27 Michael J. Lee, 'Secession Is Here', *The Conversation*, 20 March 2023.
28 Brookings Institution, 13 December 2021.

29 FiveThirtyEight, 9 February 2023.
30 Bill Bishop, 'For Most Americans, the Local Presidential Election Was a Landslide', *Daily Yonder*, 17 December 2020.
31 *Washington Post*, 3 February 2021.
32 Alexander Hamilton, *The Examination Number VIII*, 12 January 1802.
33 *New Yorker*, 27 December 2021.
34 Nathan P. Kalmoe and Lilliana Mason, 'Lethal Mass Partisanship: Prevalence, Correlates and Electoral Contingencies', January 2019.
35 Ron Brownstein, 'America Is Growing Apart, Possibly for Good', *The Atlantic*, 24 June 2022.
36 Giffords Law Center, Annual Gun Law Scorecard.
37 *New York Times*, 7 March 2023.
38 Pew Research Center, 11 August 2020.
39 Neiwert, *Alt-America*, pp. 33–4.
40 *The Atlantic*, 22 September 2022.
41 Hughes, *Culture of Complaint*, p. 28 & p. 45.
42 *Washington Post*, 16 September 2022.
43 Ibid.
44 *New York Times*, 10 June 2023.
45 Zogby Analytics, 4 February 2021.
46 Barbara Walter, 'How Civil Wars Start: And How to Stop Them', *Observer*, 6 November 2022.
47 *New York Times*, 4 May 2022.
48 *Medium*, 13 November 2020.
49 *Guardian*, 10 March 2023.
50 *Medium*, 8 August 2018.
51 Nikole Hannah-Jones, 1619 Project, *New York Times*, 14 August 2019.
52 Fintan O'Toole, 'Beware Prophecies of Civil War', *The Atlantic*, 16 December 2021.
53 Hofstadter and Wallace, *American Violence*, p. 43.
54 *New York Times*, 5 June 1969.

AFTERWORD: GOODBYE AMERICA

1 *Daily Mirror*, 9 November 2016.
2 *Time*, 7 February 1944.

INDEX

NOTE ON THE AUTHOR

Nick Bryant was one of the BBC's most senior foreign correspondents, with postings in Washington DC, New York, South Asia and Australia. He left the BBC in 2021 and now lives in Sydney with his wife and children. Nick studied history at Cambridge and has a doctorate in American history from Oxford. He is the author of *When America Stopped Being Great: A History of the Present*, *The Bystander: John F. Kennedy and the Struggle for Black Equality*, *Confessions from Correspondentland* and *The Rise and Fall of Australia: How a Great Nation Lost its Way*. The *Washington Post* has noted: 'Bryant is a genuine rarity. A Brit who understands America.'

NOTE ON THE TYPE

The text of this book is set in Minion, a digital typeface designed by Robert Slimbach in 1990 for Adobe Systems. The name comes from the traditional naming system for type sizes, in which minion is between nonpareil and brevier. It is inspired by late Renaissance-era type.